Democratic Party Madness

A SAPIENT Being's Guide to the Progressivism Madness of Democratic Party Policies & Agenda

By

Corey Lee Wilson

Democratic Party Madness

Democratic Party Madness

Fratire Publishing books can be purchased in bulk with exclusive discounts for educational purposes, association gifts, sales promotions, and special editions can be created to specifications. All inquiries for such can be made below.

FRATIRE PUBLISHING LLC
4533 Temescal Canyon Rd. # 308
Corona, CA 92883 USA
www.FratirePublishing.com
FratirePublishing@att.net
1+ (951) 638-5502

Fratire Publishing is all about common sense and relevant books for sapient beings. If this sounds like you and you can never have enough common sense, wisdom, and relevancy, then visit us and learn more about the 40 *MADNESS* series of book titles at www.fratirepublishing.com/madnessbooks.

Printed paperback and eBook ePUB by Ingram Spark in La Vergne, Tennessee, USA
Copyright © 2022: First Edition August 2022
ISBN 978-0-9994017-9-8 (Paperback)
ISBN 978-1-953319-48-7 (eBook)
Democratic Party Madness-01-PDF (pdf)
LCCN 2022914832

Special thanks for the cover design by Jenny Barroso, J20Graphics, j20graphics@gmail.com and ebook conversion by Redeemer SoftTech, redeemer.softtech@gmail.com.

Contents

Acknowledgements

I owe a debt of gratitude to the following for "heavily" borrowing at times pieces of their and/or outright sections. I do this unashamedly to use the sapient phrase, "if it ain't broke—don't try to fix it." Most of the borrowed works and research cannot be improved upon—so why try? It's better to assemble these meaningful parts, profound messages, and eloquent arguments into a cohesive whole, told with high school and college students in mind, and that's what I've done and where my talent lies.

Below in alphabetical order are the major contributors to The SAPIENT Being that I borrowed verbatim, quoted, and conceptualized much of their content from a little to a lot. Wherever this happened, I did my best to acknowledge my source. If I didn't at times within the 15 chapters, I did so intentionally because doing so would have distracted from their message. Nonetheless, they are more than acknowledged in the References and Index sections of this textbook.

Epoch Times, The: Is America's fastest-growing independent news media, founded in 2000, and their mission is to bring readers a truthful view of the world free from the influence of any government, corporation, or political party. Contrary to other fake news organizations undue criticism of *The Epoch Times*, their aim is to tell readers what they see, not how to think; and they strive to deliver a factual picture of reality that lets readers form their own opinions—and their articles are consistently used throughout this textbook.

National Review: Is an American semi-monthly conservative editorial magazine, focusing on news and commentary pieces on political, social, and cultural affairs and contributed a significant number of articles to this textbook. The magazine was founded by the author William F. Buckley Jr. in 1955 and its editor-in-chief is Rich Lowry, and the magazine has played a significant role in the development of conservatism in the United States, and is a leading voice on the American right.

Newsweek: Is an American weekly news magazine and digital news founded in 1933, and was widely distributed through the 20th century, with many notable editors-in-chief. It was relaunched (print and digital) in 2014 under the ownership of IBT Media, which also owns the *International Business Times*, until it was spun off a few years later, and their news content has contributed many articles to this textbook.

Teixeira, Ruy: Is an American political scientist and commentator now with AEI who has written several books on various topics in political science and political strategy. He is most noted for his work on political demography, and particularly for *The Emerging Democratic Majority* (2002), which he co-wrote with John Judis, a book arguing that Democrats in the United States are demographically destined to become a majority party in the early 21st century.

The Heritage Foundation: Has provided the lion's share of book content for most every chapter of *Democratic Party Madness*. For the third year in a row, they ranked as the No. 1 think tank in the world for "Significant Impact on Public Policy," according to the latest edition of the University of Pennsylvania's annual report on think tanks. Heritage also ranked first again in the "Best Use of the Internet" category, the think tank's second consecutive year at the top of that category.

The Hill: Is an American newspaper and digital media company based in Washington, D.C. that focuses on politics, policy, business and international relations and their coverage includes the U.S. Congress, the presidency and executive branch, election campaigns., and the inner workings of government. Because they the nexus and leader of political analysis in America, many of their articles were used in this textbook .

Some readers of *Democratic Party Madness* will accuse me, without knowing the facts of course, of being a closet Republican and Trump supporter. The first claim is false and the second is misstated. For the record, I'm an independent and centrist voter who has never registered for a political party and abstained from voting for the most "sapient" presidential candidate in the 2016 and 2020 elections on ethical principles as being the Founder and CEO of the SAPIENT Being.

However, prior to that, I have voted for five presidential Democratic Party candidates and four Republican Party candidates in my lifetime as follows: D-Carter in 1976, R-Reagan in 1980 and 1984, no vote in 1988 (as I had a hot date that election night), D-Clinton in 1992 and 1996, R-Bush in 2000 and 2004, and finally D-Obama in 2008 and 2012.

A SAPIENT Being's Preface

Ruy Teixeira, a lifelong man of the Left, author of the 2002 *The Emerging Democratic Majority*, Senior Fellow at the Center for American Progress and fixture of Democratic Party politics for more than 30 years who very much wants the Democratic Party to succeed, reports—the Democrats and the Democratic brand are in deep trouble:

"That should have been obvious" he states "when Democrats underperformed in the 2020 election, turning what they and most observers expected to be a blue wave into more of a ripple. They lost House seats and performed poorly in state legislative elections. And their support among non-white voters, especially Hispanics, declined substantially."

Still they did win the Presidency, which led many to miss the clear market signals this underperformance was sending to Democrats. That tendency was strengthened by the Democrats' improbable victories in the two Georgia Senate runoffs, which gave them full control of the federal government, albeit by the very narrowest of margins.

Nonetheless, today's Democratic Party seems deranged and unpredictable—insisting men are actually women if they think they are, claiming Biden's multi-trillion-dollar spending programs and wild currency creation will "reduce inflation," engineering a full-scale invasion of the American homeland by millions of illegal aliens so Democrats can stay in power forever, and so on.

The Democratic Party was once the political home of farmers, blue-collar workers, and lower-middle-class, and mostly Catholic "white ethnic" voters. Today, it's the party of affluent urban and suburban professionals, and also, in no small part, the party of the genuinely rich, from Silicon Valley to Wall Street and from Greenwich to Aspen.

Per Joe Lieberman, "Democrats are in trouble because they have strayed from the pledge President Biden made to the American people during the 2020 campaign, and articulated so hopefully in his inaugural address, to establish a stable, moderate, bipartisan government in Washington…" and the polls reflect this.

Quinnipiac University is a major polling outlet not known for a bias has per their latest poll, Biden's overall job approval has plummeted down to 38 percent from highs in the mid-50s earlier in his presidency. Things look even worse for Biden when you look at the complete collapse of his support from political independents, who now disapprove of him by a 60 percent-to-32 percent margin.

How did this happen? Why did it happen? And what's next? Keep reading to find out and be forewarned: For some of you this *MADNESS* textbook will be a revelation, an epiphany, a sapient being moment. For others, it will be a triggering event, denial of truth, and a painful intervention.

Are you interested in learning about how far left, socialist, and progressive regressive the Democratic Party has turned in the 21st century and how close it is to destroying our republic? If yes, please read on and if you also believe in the message of this textbook and willing to fight for it—please considering joining or participating in one of the three SAPIENT Being programs below.

Sapient Conservative Textbooks (SCT) Program is a relevant and current events textbooks program (published by Fratire Publishing LLC) to help return conservative values, viewpoint diversity, and sapience to high school and college campuses—and enlighten them on the many blessings to humankind that are the direct result of Western European culture, American exceptionalism, and Judeo-Christian values.

Conservative Campus Advisor (CCA) Program helps fill and expand faculty or staff positions, throughout America's predominantly liberally staffed college campuses, that can serve as much needed conservative club advisors. Typically, conservative students across the country are facing difficulty when they attempt to start a right-leaning student organization on campus due to a lack of faculty members willing to serve as their advisor.

Make Free Speech Again On Campus (MFSAOC) Program is an interactive opportunity and nexus for high school and college students to start SAPIENT Being campus clubs, chapters, and alliances where independent, liberal, and conservative minded students can meet, discuss, and debate important issues by utilizing the sapient principles of viewpoint diversity, freedom of speech, and intellectual humility—and develop sapience in the process.

Are You a Sapient Being or Want to Be One?

Sapience, also known as wisdom, is the ability to think and act using knowledge, experience, understanding, common sense and insight. Sapience is associated with attributes such as intelligence, enlightenment, unbiased judgment, compassion, experiential self-knowledge, self-actualization, and virtues such as ethics and benevolence.

Being a sapient being is not about identity politics, it's about doing what is right and borrows many of the essential qualities of Centrism that supports strength, tradition, open mindedness, and policy based on evidence not ideology.

Sapient beings are independent minded thinkers that achieve common sense solutions that appropriately address America's and the world's most pressing issues. They gauge situations based on context and reason, consideration, and probability. They are open minded and exercise conviction and willing to fight for it on the intellectual battlefield. Sapient beings don't blindly and recklessly follow their feelings or emotions.

Their unifying ideology is based on the truth, reason, logic, scientific method, and pragmatism—and not necessarily defined by compromise, moderation, or any particular faith—but is considerate of them.

Most importantly, per a letter written by Princeton professor Robert George in 2017 and endorsed by 28 professors from three Ivy League universities for incoming freshmen, "Think for yourself!"

George's letter continues:

Thinking for yourself means questioning dominant ideas even when others insist on their being treated as unquestionable. It means deciding what one believes not by conforming to fashionable opinions, but by taking the trouble to learn and honestly consider the strongest arguments to be advanced on both or all sides of questions—including arguments for positions that others revile and want to stigmatize and against positions others seek to immunize from critical scrutiny.

The love of truth and the desire to attain it should motivate you to think for yourself. The crucial point of a college education is to seek truth and to learn the skills and acquire the virtues necessary to be a lifelong truth-seeker. Open-mindedness, critical thinking, and debate are essential to discovering the truth. Moreover, they are our best antidotes to bigotry.

Merriam-Webster's first definition of the word "bigot" is a person "who is obstinately or intolerantly devoted to his or her own opinions and prejudices." The only people who need fear open-minded inquiry and robust debate are the actual bigots, including those on campuses or in the broader society who seek to protect the hegemony of their opinions by claiming that to question those opinions is itself bigotry.

So, don't be tyrannized by public opinion. Don't get trapped in an echo chamber. Whether you in the end reject or embrace a view, make sure you decide where you stand by critically assessing the arguments for the competing positions. Think for yourself. Good luck to you in college!

Now, that might sound easy. But you will find—as you may have discovered already in high school—that thinking for yourself can be a challenge. It always demands self-discipline, and these days can require courage.

In today's climate, it's all-too-easy to allow your views and outlook to be shaped by dominant opinion on your campus or in the broader academic culture. The danger any student—or faculty member—faces today is falling into the vice of conformism, yielding to groupthink, the orthodoxy.

At many colleges and universities what John Stuart Mill called "the tyranny of public opinion" does more than merely discourage students from dissenting from prevailing views on moral, political, and other types of questions. It leads them to suppose that dominant views are so obviously correct that only a bigot or a crank could question them.

Since no one wants to be, or be thought of as, a bigot or a crank, the easy, lazy way to proceed is simply by falling into line with campus orthodoxies. Don't do it!

To be sure, our overly-politicized culture has a tough time viewing any "verbal cacophony" as a sign of strength and vibrancy. And perhaps nowhere is this truer than on many college campuses where political correctness is rampant, groupthink is common, and social media "mobs" arise in a flash to intimidate anyone who openly strays from the prevailing orthodoxy.

At the SAPIENT Being we're not intimidated—and our primary purpose is to seek the truth by enhancing viewpoint diversity, promoting intellectual humility, protecting freedom of speech and expression while developing sapience in the process—no matter what the cost on the intellectual battlefield, campus classroom, and marketplace of ideas. This is our ethos! Is it yours?

Best regards and sapiently yours,

Corey Lee Wilson

S.A.P.I.E.N.T. Being

1 – Today's Democratic Party Deficiencies: Culture, Economics, Patriotism & Much More

Credit: Dave Murray.

The future of the Democratic Party looks a lot like Alexandria Ocasio-Cortez as reported by David A. Graham in *The Atlantic* November 2018 article "How Far Have the Democrats Moved to the Left?"

Per Graham: Once it was the party of patrician liberals like Franklin Roosevelt; now women, people of color, and voters in big cities are the demographics at the heart of the party.

The question is whether the future of the Democratic Party votes like Ocasio-Cortez, a self-described Democratic socialist. Her June 2018 victory over incumbent Joe Crowley in a Democratic primary for a U.S. House seat in New York City was perhaps the most heralded example of what has been described as a burgeoning leftist shift in the Democratic Party.

For progressive activists, it's a boon decades in the making; for moderate Democrats, it's a political headache; and for Republicans, including President Trump, it's both a worrying sign of creeping socialism and an effective bogeyman for rallying supporters.

According to Pew data, 46 percent of Democrats and Democratic-leaning voters now identify as liberal—up from 28 percent 10 years ago. Meanwhile, the percentage who say they're moderates has dropped from 44 to 37. The number of conservatives continues to drop, too. But these changes most likely reflect the exodus of right-leaning Democrats as both parties become more ideologically homogeneous. It doesn't necessarily mean that there's been huge growth on the party's left wing.

How to Fix the Democratic Brand

Ruy Teixeira, a lifelong man of the Left, author of the 2002 *The Emerging Democratic Majority*, Senior Fellow at the Center for American Progress and fixture of Democratic Party politics for more than 30 years who very much wants the Democratic Party to succeed, reports on "How to Fix the Democratic Brand" in April 2022:

The Democrats and the Democratic brand are in deep trouble. That should have been obvious when Democrats underperformed in the 2020 election, turning what they and most observers expected to be a Democratic wave into more of a ripple. They lost House seats and performed poorly in state legislative elections. And their support among nonwhite voters, especially Hispanics, declined substantially.

Still they did win the Presidency, which led many to miss the clear market signals this underperformance was sending to Democrats. That tendency was strengthened by the Democrats' improbable victories in the two Georgia Senate runoffs, which gave them full control of the federal government, albeit by the very narrowest of margins.

At the same time, Trump's bizarre behavior around refusing to concede the outcome of the election—which probably contributed to the GOP defeats in the Georgia runoffs—and his encouragement of rioters who stormed the Capitol on January 6 led many Democrats to assume that the Republican brand would be so damaged by association that the Democratic brand would shine by comparison. And yet…here we are a year or so later and the Democrats are in brutal shape.

Biden's approval rating is in the low 40's, only a little above where Trump's was at the same point in his Presidential term which of course was the precursor to the GOP's drubbing in the 2018 election. Biden has been doing especially poorly among working class and Hispanic voters.

Biden's approval ratings on specific issues tend to be lower, in the high 30's on the economy and in the low 30's on hot button issues like immigration and crime. Off year and special elections since 2020 have indicated a strongly pro-Republican electoral environment and Democrats currently trail Republicans in the generic Congressional ballot for 2022. It now seems likely that Democrats will, at minimum, lose control of the House this November and quite possibly suffer a wave election up and down the ballot.

Most Democrats would prefer to believe that the current dismal situation merely reflects some bad luck. The Delta wave of the coronavirus undercut Biden's plans for returning the country to normal and interacted with supply chain difficulties to produce an inflation spike that angered consumers. There is some truth to this, but it is not the whole picture. The reality is that Democrats have failed to develop a party brand capable of unifying a dominant majority of Americans behind their political project.

Indeed, the current Democratic brand suffers from multiple deficiencies that make it somewhere between uncompelling and toxic to wide swathes of American voters who might potentially be their allies. I locate these deficiencies in three key areas: culture; economics; and patriotism.

8

Culture

The cultural left has managed to associate the Democratic party with a series of views on crime, immigration, policing, free speech and of course race and gender that are quite far from those of the median voter. That's a success for the cultural left but the hard reality is that it's an electoral liability for the Democratic party.

From time to time—the latest effort was in this month's State of the Union address--Democratic politicians like Biden try to dissociate themselves from super-unpopular ideas like defunding the police but the voices of the cultural left within the party are still more deferred to than opposed.

These voices are further amplified by Democratic-leaning media and nonprofits, as well as within the Democratic party infrastructure itself, all of which are thoroughly dominated by the cultural left. In an era when a party's national brand increasingly defines state and even local electoral contests, Democratic candidates have a very hard time shaking these cultural left associations.

How did this unfortunate state of affairs arise? To understand this, we must understand the trajectory of the American left in the 21st century. The culture of the left has evolved and not in a good way. It is now thoroughly out of touch with its working class roots and completely dominated by college-educated professionals, typically in big metropolitan areas and university towns and typically younger. These are the people that fill the ranks of the media, nonprofits, advocacy groups, foundations and the infrastructure of the Democratic party. They speak their own language and highlight the issues that most animate their commitments to 'social justice."

These commitments are increasingly driven by what is now referred to as identity politics. This form of politics originated in the 1960s movements that sought to eliminate discrimination against and establish equal treatment and access for women and for racial and sexual minorities. In evolving to the present day, the focus has mutated into an attempt to impose a worldview that emphasizes multiple, intersecting levels of oppression ("intersectionality") based on group identification.

In place of promoting universal rights and principles—the traditional remit of the left--advocates now police others on the left, including within the Democratic party, to uncritically embrace this intersectional approach, insist on an arcane vocabulary for speaking about these purportedly oppressed groups, and prohibit discourse based on logic and evidence to evaluate the assertions of those who claim to speak on the groups' behalf.

Is America really a "white supremacist" society? What does "structural racism" even mean, and does it explain all the socioeconomic problems of nonwhites? Is anyone who raises questions about immigration levels a racist? Are personal pronouns necessary and something the left should seek to popularize? Are transwomen exactly the same as biological women and are those who question such a claim simply "haters" who should be expunged from the left coalition (as has been advocated in the UK)? This list could go on.

What ties the questions together is that they are closely associated with practitioners of identity politics or adherents of the intersectional approach, who deem them not open to debate with the usual tools of logic and evidence. Politically derived answers are simply to be embraced by Democratic party progressives in the interest of "social justice."

The Democrats have paid a considerable price for their increasingly strong linkage to militant identity politics, which brands the party as focused on, or at least distracted by, issues of little relevance to most voters' lives. Worse, the focus has led many working-class voters to believe that, unless they subscribe to this emerging worldview and are willing to speak its language, they will be condemned as reactionary, intolerant, and racist by those who purport to represent their interests.

To some extent these voters are right: They really are looked down upon by substantial segments of the Democratic party—typically younger, well-educated, and metropolitan—who embrace identity politics and the intersectional approach. This has contributed to the emerging rupture in the Democratic Party's coalition along lines of education and region.

This rupture was solidified by the election of Donald Trump in 2016. By far the dominant interpretation of white working class support for Trump on the left was that these voters were racist and xenophobic, full stop. They just didn't like the loss of status and privilege allegedly attendant upon being white as America evolved to a more multicultural, multiracial democracy. This was odd since Democratic progressives had just spent the last many decades sternly denouncing the American neoliberal economic model and how it was ruining the lives and communities of all working people.

The Trump years further deepened the identity politics influence with the Democratic party, particularly in the wake of the nationwide movement protesting the murder of George Floyd. This left its stamp on the 2020 edition of the Democratic party, notwithstanding their old school standard-bearer, Joe Biden.

It has also left its stamp on how Democrats have handled difficult culturally-inflected issues since the election. They have fallen prey again and again to what I have termed the "Fox News Fallacy"—the idea that if Fox News and the like are criticizing the Democrats on such issues there must be absolutely nothing to the criticisms and the criticized policies should be defended at all costs. This approach has not served the Democrats well as Biden's term has evolved.

Start with crime. Initially dismissed as simply an artifact of the Covid shutdown that was being vastly exaggerated by Fox News and the like for their nefarious purposes, it is now apparent that the spike in violent crime is quite real and that voters are very, very concerned about it. This very definitely includes black and Hispanic voters, as indicated by polling data and confirmed by Eric Adams' support base in the New York mayoral contest. No wonder more and more Democratic politicians are running as fast as they can away from any hint of "defund the police," the slogan beloved of the activist left that was actually put on the ballot in Minneapolis...and soundly defeated, especially by black voters. Consistent with this, a recent Pew poll found that black and Hispanic Democrats are significantly more likely than white Democrats to favor more police funding in their area.

Given this, it is no surprise Republicans, according to a recent *Wall Street Journal* poll, are favored over Democrats on the crime issue by 20 points.

Another example of the Fox News Fallacy is the immigration issue. The Biden administration initially insisted that the surge at the border would go away on its own as the hot weather season arrived, a line most Democrats echoed, invoking the idea that the issue was more a Fox News talking point than a real problem.

Not so. It is now apparent that the perceived liberalization of the border regime under the Biden administration did indeed spur more migrants to try their luck at their border. An astonishing 1.7 million illegal crossings at the southern border were recorded in the 2021 fiscal year, the highest total since at least 1960, when the government first started keeping such records. In response, the administration has scrambled to deploy whatever tools it has at its disposal, including some left over from the Trump administration, to stem the tide. This has not sat well with immigration advocates, who staged a (virtual) walkout on top Biden officials in late 2021 to protest these administration policies.

These and other pressures, as well as the desire not to give in to Fox News talking points about a border crisis, has led most Democratic politicians to treat the topic of border security—and even the phrase—very gingerly (though Biden did at least allude to the need to "secure the border: in his SOTU speech). As a result, there is no clear Democratic plan for an immigration system that would both permit reasonable levels of legal immigration and provide the border security necessary to stem illegal immigration. Nothing illustrates this better than the Biden administration's current plan to end Title 42, a move that will almost certainly lead to a further surge of immigrants at the border and increased pressure on an already-overwhelmed system.

Voters have noticed. In the *Wall Street Journal* poll previously cited, Republicans are favored over Democrats by 26 points on border security. And Biden, as noted earlier, has abysmal approval ratings on the immigration issue, typically in the low '30s.

Democrats would do well to remember that public opinion polling over the years has consistently shown overwhelming majorities in favor of more spending and emphasis on border security. The uncomfortable fact is that, while this issue is being exploited by Fox News, it is still a very real problem Democrats need to address.

Finally, consider critical race theory or CRT, a particularly flagrant example of the Fox News Fallacy in that Democrats refuse to admit even grudgingly that there might be a problem here. CRT is a term originating in academic legal theory that has been shorthanded by the right as a catch-all for the intrusion of race essentialism into teacher training, school curricula and the like.

The standard Democratic comeback to criticism about CRT in the schools is simply to assert that any voters, including parents, who are concerned about CRT are manipulated by Fox News and are opposing benign pedagogical practices like teaching about slavery, Jim Crow, the Tulsa race massacre, redlining and so on. The not so subtle implication is that such voters are racists since who else would be opposed to simply teaching such historical facts?

But voters' worries about CRT cannot be bludgeoned away so easily by saying CRT doesn't really exist in the schools and parents just don't want their kids taught about slavery. Parents are far more worried about their children being arrayed into hierarchies of privilege and oppression and encouraged to see everything through a racial lens—whatever the theory is called—than they are concerned with their children learning about historical incidents and practices of racism.

This issue has importantly become caught up in general dissatisfaction with how Democrats have handled schooling issues during the pandemic. In Virginia, voters who were already upset about parental burdens and academic deficits from extended school closures became additionally concerned that an emerging focus on "social justice" pedagogy and policies was detracting from learning traditional academic subjects and rewarding high achievement. As a memo by the Democratic firm ALG Research on focus groups with suburban Virginia Biden-Youngkin voters noted:

They feel that people's ability to have a civil discussion has vanished, and that they have to walk on eggshells even on seemingly innocuous topics. This extends to discussions around race in schools, where they were less concerned with critical race theory as an idea or curriculum but expressed frustration with the black-and-white approach they see taken toward such complicated subjects....

This isn't about "critical race theory" itself, and we shouldn't dismiss that CRT isn't real and think we've tackled the issue. Many swing voters knew, when pushed by more-liberal members of the group, that CRT wasn't taught in Virginia schools. But at the same time, they felt like racial and social justice issues were overtaking math, history, and other things. They absolutely want their kids to hear the good and the bad of American history, at the same time they are worried that racial and cultural issues are taking over the state's curricula. We should expect this backlash to continue, especially as it plays into another way where parents and communities feel like they are losing control over their schools in addition to the basics of even being able to decide if they're open or not.

Again, these issues cannot be waved away simply by dismissing complaining parents as racists or, less pejoratively, as dupes of Fox News. This is particularly the case for Asian parents. It is difficult to overestimate how important education is to Asian voters, who see it as the key tool for upward mobility—a tool that even the poorest Asian parents can take advantage of. But Democrats are becoming increasingly associated with an approach to schooling that seems anti-meritocratic, oriented away from standardized tests, gifted and talented programs and test-in elite schools—all areas where Asian children have excelled.

It does not seem mysterious that Asian voters might react negatively to this approach. In fact, it would be mysterious if they didn't.

As a result of these and other cultural issues, the party's—or, at least, Biden's—attempt to rebrand Democrats as a unifying party speaking for Americans across divisions of race and class appears to have failed. Voters are not sure Democrats can look beyond identity politics to ensure public safety, secure borders, high quality, non-ideological education, and economic progress for all Americans.

Nevertheless, Biden and the Democrats must persist in attempting a rebrand in these areas because the alternative is ceding a culture wars advantage to the Republicans that will ensure not just defeat in 2022 but the continued failure of Democrats' efforts to forge a dominant majority coalition for years to come. One obvious place to try this is on the crime issue, building on Biden's recent, tentative steps in this direction.

Consider the fact that Democrats are associated with a wave of progressive public prosecutors who seem quite hesitant about keeping criminals off the street, even as a spike in violent crimes like murders and carjacking sweeps the nation. This is twinned to a climate of tolerance and non-prosecution for lesser crimes that is degrading the quality of life in many cities under Democratic control.

Economics

To the extent Democrats have an overarching economic story it is that a dramatic expansion of the social safety net and a rapid move to a clean energy economy will—eventually--result in strong growth and an abundance of good jobs. But this is a muddled story that is clearly not getting through.

A standard Democratic take on this problem is that the basic economic ideas and accomplishments are great, they simply haven't been properly communicated. But I think the problem runs far deeper than this. Consider the debacle around the Build Back Better bill.

This was the multi-trillion-dollar bill that Democrats were, until very recently, trying to wrangle through Congress. It was supposedly "transformational"—but transformation to what? Democrats talked about the care economy, a Green New Deal, and other big ideas associated with Build Back Better. But what that added up to was not clear. Would it have created a more dynamic American capitalism that could lift up broad swaths of the country that have been left behind? Instead, the bill had a "shaggy dog" quality of funneling money to a wide variety of Democratic priorities. Some of this spending would have supported useful expansions of the notably stingy American welfare system and some would have supported useful public investments not provided for in the infrastructure bill, particularly in clean energy.

But none of this seemed transformational in the sense of leading to a more productive, higher growth, and less regionally unequal American capitalism. Indeed, this did not seem to be the point; rather, it was to make the current model of capitalism a bit fairer and a bit more climate friendly. That was laudable, but it fell short of a new model of capitalism that could brand the Democrats as the party of a fast growth American future.

But it is a huge mistake to lose sight of the need for faster growth? Growth, particularly productivity growth, is what drives rising living standards over time and Democrats presumably stand for the fastest possible rise in living standards. Faster growth also makes easier the achievement of Democrats' other goals. Hard economic times typically generate pessimism about the future and fear of change, not broad support for more democracy and social justice. In contrast, when times are good, when the economy is expanding and living standards are steadily rising for most of the population, people see better opportunities for themselves and are more inclined toward social generosity, tolerance, and collective advance.

Yet much of the Democratic left still regards the goal of more and faster economic growth with suspicion, preferring to focus on the fairness of how current growth is distributed. This reflects not just an understandable and laudable focus on unequal distribution, but also a general feeling that the fruits of growth are poisoned, encouraging unhealthy consumerist lifestyles and, worse, driving the climate crisis that is hurtling humanity toward doom. The latter view is responsible for the increasing vogue on the left for the idea of "degrowth."

With such views it is not surprising that economic growth does not rank very high on the Democratic left's list of economic objectives.

Doesn't the left want to make people happy? One has to wonder. There seems to be more interest in figuring out what people should stop doing and consuming than in figuring out how people can have more to do and consume. The very idea of abundance is rarely discussed, except to disparage it.

You can also see this in the rather modest amount of attention and resources devoted to technological advance in the Democrats' other bills. The bipartisan infrastructure bill did contain some money for developing next generation energy technologies like clean hydrogen, carbon capture, and advanced nuclear, but the amount was comparatively modest. The clean energy money in the last version of the Build Back Better bill (shelved—but now revived), was mostly focused on speeding up deployment of wind, solar, and electric vehicles.

But if there is to be an abundant clean energy future, not a degrowth one, it will depend on our ability to develop the requisite energy technologies which must necessarily go beyond wind and solar. The same could be said about a wide range of other technological challenges that could underpin a future of abundance: AI and machine learning; CRISPR and mRNA biotechnology; advanced robotics and the internet of things. These technologies, just like clean energy technologies, need to be developed aggressively to unleash their potential.

That's why it's inadequate for Democrats to focus narrowly on a clean energy, Green New Deal-type future. Not only is there an excessive focus on wind and solar, but the challenges for an abundant future cannot be reduced to the need for a clean energy transition. And make no mistake: what Americans want is an abundant future not just a green one that, they are told, is mostly necessary to stave off planetary disaster. The fact is that, for better or worse, combatting climate change does not rank very high on voters' priority list (14th in a recent Pew Research poll). That suggests investment in clean energy technologies needs to be embedded in a broader "abundance agenda" (to use Derek Thompson's phrase) that drives up the supply of innovation and can deliver an abundant life for all not just the avoidance of disaster.

In short, what Americans want, and need is an abundant economy, of which a clean energy economy or a care economy are merely subsets or components. That can be a winning vision of where Democrats want to take the economy in ways that Build Back Better or a Green New Deal simply can't.

That should be the Democrats' brand: more innovation, faster progress, greater abundance. Without that, simply being fairer and greener will fail as a unifying economic offer.

Patriotism

Today's Democrats have difficulty embracing patriotism and weaving it into their political brand. It wasn't so long ago, Bill Clinton was saying "There is nothing wrong with America that cannot be cured by what is right with America." And even more recently, when Barack Obama won the Presidency in 2008, he said:

"If there is anyone out there who still doubts that America is a place where all things are possible, who still wonders if the dream of our founders is alive in our time, who still questions the power of our democracy, tonight is your answer."

For his part, Joe Biden does try to inject a little of that old time patriotism into his remarks from time to time. It's not really taking though. A big part of his party is singing a different tune and singing it loudly. As the liberal commentator Noah Smith observes:

[I]n the age of social media, the progressive movement is defined less by the President and more by the collection of journalists, professors, and lower-level politicians who dominate Twitter and major publications and news networks. And here I've seen a remarkable and pervasive vilification of America become not just widespread but de rigeur among progressives since unrest broke out in the mid-2010s....

The general conceit among today's progressives is that America was founded on racism, that it has never faced up to this fact, and that the most important task for combatting American racism is to force the nation to face up to that "history".... Even if it loses them elections, progressives seem prepared to go down fighting for the idea that America needs to educate its young people about its fundamentally White supremacist character....

[T]he version of "history" that progressives want to teach young people, generally speaking, is a cartoonish story in which America is the villain—a nation formed from racism, founded the day the first slave stepped onto our shores, dedicated thereafter to the repression and brutalization of people of color.

This "history" ignores America's deep and powerful tradition of anti-racism, the universalistic egalitarian ideals of the Declaration of Independence, the abolitionist movement that was present from the very beginning, the Founders' conception of the U.S. as a nation of immigrants, America's role in the ending of European colonialism, its position at the forefront of liberal democratic reforms and experimentation, the promotion of global standards of human rights following WW2, and so on.

Consistent with this analysis, a survey project by the More in Common group was able to separate out a group they termed "progressive activists" who were 8 percent of the population (but punch far above their weight in the Democratic party) and are described as "deeply concerned with issues concerning equity, fairness, and America's direction today. They tend to be more secular, cosmopolitan, and highly engaged with social media".

These progressive activists' attitude toward their own country departs greatly from not just that of average Americans but from pretty much any other group you might care to name, including average nonwhite Americans. Black, Hispanic and Asian Americans, in fact, are highly likely to be proud to be Americans and highly likely to say they would still choose to live in America if they could choose to live anywhere in the world.

In contrast, progressive activists are loathe to express these sentiments For example, just 34 percent of progressive activists say they are "proud to be American" compared to 62 percent of Asians, 70 percent of blacks, and 76 percent of Hispanics.

This is a big, big problem. One of the only effective ways—and possibly the most effective way—to mobilize Americans behind big projects is to appeal to patriotism, to Americans as part of a nation. Indeed much of what America accomplished in the 20th century was under the banner of liberal nationalism. Yet many in the Democratic party blanche at any hint of nationalism—one reason so many are leery of patriotism—because of its association with darker impulses and political trends. Yet as John Judis has pointed out, nationalism has its positive side as well in that it allows citizens to identify on a collective level and support projects that serve the common good rather than their immediate interests.

Given all that Democrats hope to accomplish, it makes absolutely no sense not to appeal to Americans' patriotism and love of country. That too has to be part of Democrats' rebranding. They must insist that their party is a patriotic party that believes Americans as a nation can accomplish great things. And they should not shrink from emphasizing the competitive aspect of patriotism. America is indeed in a competition with other nations like China and it is not xenophobic to say that America is a great nation that can win that competition.

A Democratic party that occupies the cultural center ground, promotes an abundance agenda and is unabashedly patriotic has a real shot at political domination given Republicans' serious problems and weaknesses. Conversely, a Democratic party that does not rebrand in this way dooms American politics to continued stalemate and polarization. That's not a pleasant prospect.

Democrats Move Left, But the Center Holds

Credit: Democratic Party on Facebook.

Per the William A. Galston "Democrats Move Left, But the Center Holds" article published in *The Wall Street Journal* in August 2020:

A June 2020 report from the Pew Research Center details the party's demographic shifts. It has become less white and more educated. In 1994, 23% of Democrats were nonwhite. Today 40% are, compared with 17% of Republicans. When it comes to education, the parties have switched places. In 1996, 22% of Democrats and 27% of Republicans had college degrees. The figures are now 41% and 29%, respectively. College-educated whites rose from 19% to 28% of Democrats, while whites without degrees fell from 58% to 30%. Non-college-educated whites now make up 57% of Republicans.

This shift has been especially pronounced among women. In 1994 nearly half of white women with college degrees identified as Republican, compared with only one-third today. White men have moved more slowly in this direction, from 59% to 51%.

Add religion to the mix, and Republicans look like the America of the 1990s while Democrats resemble projections for the 2050s. In 2008, the earliest year for which Pew has data, white Christian Democrats outnumbered religiously unaffiliated ones by 26 points. Today, unaffiliated Democrats outnumber white Christians by 12 points. By contrast, more than 6 in 10 Republicans are white Christians, and only 15% of Republicans are unaffiliated.

Then there's geographic polarization. Urban voters have increasingly identified with Democrats and rural voters with Republicans, a trend that accelerated in 2016. Twenty percent of Clinton's 1992 vote came from rural America, compared with only 9% of Hillary Clinton's, according to Boston College political scientist David Hopkins.

The battleground is the suburbs—evenly divided in the early 1990s and now. The suburban share of the presidential vote has steadily increased, to an all-time high of 56% in 2016, Hopkins finds. A pronounced suburban shift toward one party would be a decisive change in the partisan balance that could reshape American politics for a generation. Democrats have become increasingly dependent on suburban voters, whose share of the Democratic presidential total has risen to 52% from 40% while the party's urban vote share remained stable, and its rural share collapsed.

These trends are even more pronounced in congressional elections.

According to Hopkins, the share of Democratic House seats in predominantly suburban districts rose to 60% in 2018 from 41% in 1992, while the share in rural districts fell to 5% from 24%. The share of Democratic senators from predominantly suburban states rose to 79% from 55% while the share from rural states fell to 6% from 28%.

Suburbs are politically heterogeneous. Hopkins finds that Democrats have improved their presidential performance in the suburban counties surrounding the 20 largest metropolitan areas but not smaller ones

Demography and geography have reshaped the Democratic Party's ideology. As conservative rural and small-town voters shifted their allegiance toward Republicans and the suburbs became more important to the Democratic coalition, the party moved left on many issues.

Other forces contributed. Industrial labor unions, which were moderate on culture and foreign policy, have waned while more ethnically diverse, left-leaning public-employee and service-sector unions gained ground. The financial crisis of 2008-09 exacerbated doubts about the market-friendly orientation that dominated the party during the 1990s, as did rising inequality and corporate concentration. Occupy Wall Street in 2011 was a harbinger of the progressive coalition that Sen. Bernie Sanders, an independent who calls himself a democratic socialist, mobilized in his 2016 challenge to Clinton. The surprise primary victory of another democratic socialist, Alexandria Ocasio-Cortez, over a Democratic House leader turned out to be the first of several such upsets in 2018 and this year.

As the 2020 primaries began, the left had reason to hope that this would be its year. Sens. Sanders and Elizabeth Warren got off to strong starts, and early primaries made Sanders a front-runner. If African-Americans—many of whom who are more moderate than white progressives—hadn't united behind Biden in South Carolina, the Vermont senator probably would be the party's nominee.

The Biden campaign understood the need to conciliate the left—something Clinton failed to do in 2016. It set up six "Biden-Sanders unity task forces" to work out compromises on contested issues. Biden made speeches and put out briefing papers that were well to the left of positions he had endorsed during the primaries. He has sought to promote party unity without alienating either his moderate base or the suburban independents and moderate Republicans who held their noses and voted for Trump four years ago.

Biden's challenge, in short, has been to keep his balance.

Even with the left-wing insurgency, most Democrats are reformers, not revolutionaries. They want to improve capitalism, not establish socialism. They worry that social mobility has slowed and not all Americans have enjoyed the fruits of economic growth. They believe that corporate concentration has inhibited innovation and that financialization has distorted the economy. They think all Americans deserve shelter and medical care. They want to make society more inclusive. They are convinced that climate change is dangerous and human activity contributes to it. They believe that alliances and international institutions help advance American interests but pushing for regime change usually doesn't. These views are contestable but hardly radical.

The 2020 Democratic platform is evidence that the center has held. Here's a list of what it doesn't endorse: Medicare for All, the Green New Deal, reparations for slavery, defunding the police, free college for all, cancellation of all student debt, open borders, abolishing Immigration and Customs Enforcement, a national ban on fracking, deep cuts in the defense budget, and the anti-Israel boycott, divestment and sanctions movement.

Instead, it calls for reforms to existing programs aimed at making affordable health insurance available to all, reducing carbon emissions with new technologies, improving police practices, equalizing opportunity across racial and ethnic lines, reducing the costs of college, making immigration enforcement more humane, and reducing the costs of defense procurement.

Still, the Democratic Party leans further left than it did in 1992. Taken as a whole, the party's agenda would substantially expand the size, scope and cost of the federal government. That will require higher taxes on corporations, wealthy Americans, investors and estates. Other positions put the party at odds with Republicans in ways that are longstanding and familiar. Today's

Democrats aren't supply-siders, but they haven't been since Lyndon B. Johnson's administration. They continue to believe vigorous regulation is compatible with economic growth and innovation.

Democrats are more focused than ever on equality for women, racial and ethnic minorities, disabled Americans and the full range of gender identities. They are more united on social and cultural issues than on their prescriptions for the economy. Their unity presages intensified conflict with social conservatives, with no end in sight.

These Are Not Your Grandfather's Democrats

This section is courtesy of the Jim Daws American Thinker article in January 2019 titled "These Are Not Your Grandfather's Democrats."

The Democrats' obstinate refusal to fund a physical barrier on our southern border is the starkest illustration yet that they are no longer a political party dedicated to the protection and prosperity of the United States. The party has been captured by cultural Marxists who are radically hostile to America's founding principles, its history, and its people. It's no exaggeration to recognize the reality that the Democratic Party is engaged in an ideological war against the historic American nation, which many of the party's members despise.

Post-Civil War Democrats fashioned themselves as champions of America's working classes and defenders the freedoms contained in the Bill of Rights. Those Democrats were patriotic and believed that while the founders' promise had yet to be fully realized, their ideals of "life, liberty and the pursuit of happiness" were profound and sacred truths.

That all changed beginning with the cultural revolution of the 1960s, as cultural Marxists began their long march to take over America's universities, media, courts, and popular culture. These Democrats fancied themselves revolutionaries who believed that because of its flaws, America was irredeemable. Their motto was "tear it all down." While tattered remnants of those old-style Democrats survive on the margins, they are no longer an animating force within the party.

Committed civil libertarians were also jettisoned by the Democrats. Once champions of free speech, the Dems now work in myriad ways on college campuses, in popular culture, and on social media to censor opposing points of view, often through violence and intimidation.

Second Amendment rights are likewise under constant assault from the Democrats, who know that an unarmed, docile populace is a prerequisite for state control. And Fourth Amendment rights to privacy have been so violated as to now be rights in name only.

The Dems have filled the void created by the abandonment of these constituencies and once cherished beliefs with a toxic stew of grievance and identity politics. They've cobbled together a coalition of people who believe that government is their salvation and that any shortfall of their own is the fault of an oppressive, bigoted America.

Where once they believed in equal rights, they now push racial preferences and quotas. Where once they believed in free enterprise and market capitalism, they now openly advocate socialism. Belief in strong, traditional families has been replaced by advocacy of redefining marriage and men in women's sports and bathrooms. Once antiwar, they now openly advocate for endless, globalist wars of no discernible national interest for America's young men and women to fight and die in

The problem with all this is that America is still marginally a traditionally conservative nation, and none of these leftist policies enjoys majority support outside liberal coastal and big-city bastions. So the new Democrats are pretending desperately to be the Democrats of old just long enough to complete the transformation of the nation to fit their Marxist ideology.

The way Democrats mean to complete the transformation is through mass immigration—both legal and illegal. They have been importing a new electorate that has little history, understanding, or appreciation of free enterprise and civil rights. These new voters are more concerned with day-to-day economic survival than "life, liberty and the pursuit of happiness"—ironically because of the very socialist governments they are fleeing.

This is the reason why the Democrats are so adamantly opposed to a physical barrier on the border—not because they believe that it doesn't work, but because they know that it does.

Young Democrats Are Less Politically Tolerant Than Republicans, Poll Shows

A recent survey conducted by Axios shows that young Democrats are far more likely to be less tolerant of people who have different political beliefs per the Daniel Chang El American article in December 2021 titled "Young Democrats Are Less Politically Tolerant Than Republicans, Poll Shows".

The poll shows that College Democrats are far less likely than Republicans to have friends from the other side of the aisle but Republicans more likely to have Democratic friends. Clearly, younger Democrats are less tolerant than their Republican and Libertarian cohorts.

The survey showed that an overwhelming 71% of young Democrats would probably not go on a date with someone who voted for another candidate. A substantial 37% of respondents said that they will probably not be friends with someone who has a different political position. Almost a third said they would not work for someone who voted for the opposing candidate, and 41% said they wouldn't even shop at or support a business of someone from the opposing party.

In contrast, only 31% of Republicans said they would probably not date someone who voted for the other party, and less than 10% said that they would base their decision on who they work for, who are their friends, and where do they shop at, on politics. The numbers are also low for Independents, as less than 30% say they will not date someone who voted differently, 11% said they might not be friends with someone from the opposing candidate, 13% said they would not shop at a business from a supporter of the different party.

2 – Biden-Harris White House, Cabinet, Appointments, Executive Orders & Failing Agenda

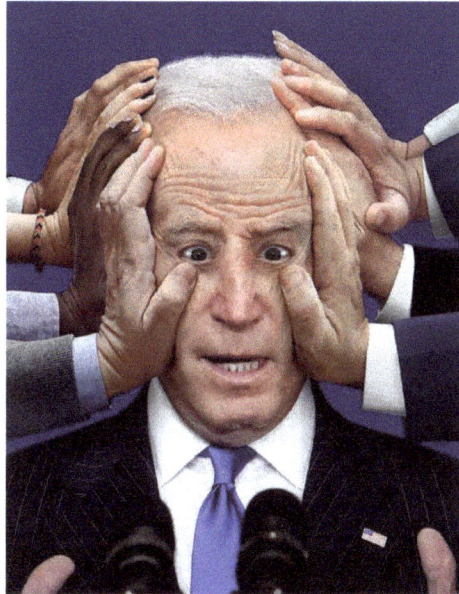

Credit: Joe Darrow/Drew Angerer/Getty Images.

Biden's victory in the Democratic Party primary temporarily wrested control of the party out of the hands of its activists and placed it back with its voters, according to the "Joe Biden's Big Squeeze" New York Intelligencer article in November 2021 by Jonathan Chait

This was the vision that entranced liberals in the heady months after Biden's inauguration. He would usher in a "New" New Deal that would end the long Reagan era in which Republicans painted government as an enemy of normal Americans. The Democrats seemed to have the means to do it: control of Congress, a pandemic-induced national emergency that cried out for robust government intervention, and relative unanimity between their warring wings.

Yet as Biden's term wears on into its second year, he has only been able to pass an infrastructure bill whittled down small enough to satisfy Republicans, the Build Back Better plan has been cut to ribbons, and his approval is in tatters. Biden's critics in the center and on the right have blamed his excessive liberalism. But the opposite is true. Biden is actually following a plan designed in direct opposition to the party's movement-driven leftward turn.

Biden's first-term strategy was predicated on a counterrevolution in Democratic Party political thinking led by an unlikely spokesperson: a data analyst and socialist named David Shor. He has become something of a cult figure on the center left for his critique of the party's leftward lurch, which he believes is out of step with the values of most of its voters.

The principles of David Shor thought boil down to a few key precepts. Shor believes the central dynamic in western politics is educational polarization: the tendency of college-educated voters to move left while those without college education move right. It follows that, as educated people have diverged from the working class, the Democratic Party's political class (which consists entirely of college-educated voters) has moved much further from the political midpoint that it once inhabited.

Shor's solution is to be vigilant about this bias and to correct for it by paying close attention to polling and speaking in plain, accessible language.

Biden's Legislative Strategy Has Closely Hewed to 'Shorist' Principles

Biden has tried to keep the political conversation framed as closely as possible around issues in which he and his party have an advantage: handling the pandemic and rebuilding the economy. His economic program has carefully avoided any controversial social debates and focused on a highly popular combination of raising taxes on the ultra-wealthy and redistributing the proceeds to the working and middle class through programs like universal access to child care, community college, and a child tax credit.

Despite his strategy, divisions among congressional Democrats remain bitter. In a leaked conference call after the 2020 elections, Democrat Abigail Spanberger lambasted progressive Democrats like AOC for allowing unpopular slogans like "Defund the police" to define the party, and she blamed those errors for the defeat of several moderate Democrats. The moderates' anger at the left wing is well grounded, but, perversely, they have taken out this anger on Biden.

Those divisions erupted into view again in early November 2021. After Democrats suffered a defeat in normally blue Virginia and a near defeat in deep-blue New Jersey, the party's centrist wing had a ready explanation: They had veered too far from the center, catering to their activists rather than the people who had elected them. "We can't go too far left," warned Joe Manchin. "This is not a center-left or a left country. We are a center—if anything, a little center-right—country; that's being shown, and we ought to be able to recognize that."

By that point in time from Manchin's, a *Washington Post* poll found Biden's approval rating dropping to its lowest level ever. Sixty-three percent of respondents said Biden had accomplished "little or nothing" or "not very much." Yet 58 percent registered support for a plan to spend $2 trillion to "address climate change and to create or expand preschool, health care and other social programs."

The dream of a Rooseveltian presidency was always grandiose, not least because Biden lacks FDR's giant majorities in Congress. Yet it was a sensible ambition in its form. Biden's goal was to demonstrate the concrete benefits of good government and, in so doing, to disprove the cynical Trumpian claim that Washington was merely controlled by wealthy elites and the Swamp.

Biden's Blunders

This section is courtesy of the Matthew Continetti "Biden's Blunders" *National Review* article in August 2021:

Every presidency has bad moments—but the president adds to the controversies he inherited. In Biden's defense, four is the number of crises Joe Biden said the nation faced when he accepted the 2020 Democratic presidential nomination. His list included the coronavirus pandemic, the precarious economy, ensuring racial equity in the aftermath of the George Floyd killing, and climate change.

By the time Biden became president, he had added to his index of emergencies the fate of democracy, truth, and America's role in the world. "Any one of these would be enough to challenge us in profound ways," Biden said during his inaugural address. "But the fact is we face them all at once, presenting this nation with the gravest of responsibilities."

Regardless, they are responsibilities that Biden cannot handle. Not only has he failed to solve the problems he identified during the campaign; he's created a whole new set of challenges that run from America's southern border to the Hindu Kush.

As a result, the public has re-evaluated his conduct and capability. The buzzwords that filled coverage of Biden's early days—"hypercompetent," "normalcy," "unity," "transformative"—now seem inappropriate and silly. The comparisons that some pundits made last spring between Biden and LBJ, FDR, and Ronald Reagan were premature at the time. Now they just look ridiculous.

What makes Biden's rough patch notable is its suddenness and contingency. Only a few months ago, it might have seemed as if he was making progress on issues such as the pandemic and the economy. Unexpected developments, as well as unforced errors on the border and in Afghanistan, have now undermined confidence in his leadership and eroded his public standing.

The Delta variant of the coronavirus, inflation, crime, illegal immigration, and national humiliation at the hands of the Taliban have done more than complicate Biden's efforts to sign into law the largest expansion of government since the Great Society. They have put Democratic control of Congress at risk—and the country in jeopardy.

Biden is president because his priorities tracked closely with those of the 2020 electorate. Take the coronavirus pandemic. The plurality of voters who rated it the most important issue in a postelection poll by Fox News supported Biden two to one. While the national exit poll conducted by Edison Research had a slightly more complicated and confusing issue breakdown, it also showed that the voters who had rated either the pandemic or health-care policy as the most important issue went for Biden by lopsided margins.

Americans gave Biden's coronavirus response high marks during the first half of the year. He took the pandemic seriously. His team ramped up production and distribution of the vaccines authorized for emergency use under his predecessor. In a March speech, Biden predicted that the summer of 2021 would "begin to mark our independence from this virus." In May, the

Centers for Disease Control announced that vaccinated individuals no longer needed to wear masks indoors. Case numbers and deaths plunged from January through July.

Then Things Got Worse

The first sign that Biden wasn't in charge of the situation came in April 2021, when the Food and Drug Administration (FDA) temporarily paused injections of the Johnson & Johnson vaccine. This decision arrested the momentum of the vaccination campaign and illustrated the dangers of bureaucratic caprice. Meanwhile, the Delta variant of the virus spread among the unvaccinated. Case numbers picked up. Hospitalizations and deaths followed. On July 27, the CDC reversed its previous guidance and recommended once again that vaccinated people in areas of high transmission wear masks indoors. The messages from public-health authorities were contradictory, confusing, and dispiriting. Biden seemed powerless.

What was once a political asset turned into a liability. Two-thirds of adults approved of Biden's handling of the coronavirus in a February 2021 Gallup poll. By August, that number had dropped 16 points. "All party groups are now more critical of Biden's handling of the corona-virus situation compared with February," wrote pollster Jeffrey M. Jones, "with approval among Republicans and independents down roughly 20 points." Moreover, independents have begun to disapprove of Biden's performance in general. As recently as June, they gave him a job-approval rating of 55 percent. Only 43 percent of independents approved in August.

The pandemic was not even the only crisis in which Biden was flailing. The economy was never his best issue—voters for whom it was the top priority in 2020 went for Donald Trump—but the gradual recovery from the coronavirus-induced recession and the passage of the $2 trillion American Rescue Plan helped Biden's standing at the beginning of his term. In the February Gallup poll, 54 percent of adults approved of his handling of the economy. By August, however, that rating had fallen to 46 percent.

The reason was inflation. Rising prices have increased the cost of living, diminished wage gains, and soured voters on the president's economic management. In a Morning Consult poll from late July, 59 percent of registered voters blamed Biden for inflation. In early August, a Hill-HarrisX poll found that inflation was registered voters' top economic worry. Around the same time, 86 percent of the registered voters surveyed in a Fox News poll said that it was a concern. The president's response has been to downplay the threat. "Our experts believe and the data shows that most of the price increases we've seen were expected and expected to be temporary," Biden said in July. He hopes so.

Neither racial inequity nor climate change has proven any easier for Biden to fix. "For the second consecutive year, U.S. adults' positive ratings of relations between Black and White Americans are at their lowest point in more than two decades of measurement," wrote Gallup's Megan Brenan in July. Judges have blocked Biden's attempt to forgive the debts of minority farmers because it violates civil-rights law. Parents nationwide have rebelled against school boards eager to import critical race theory into the classroom. The Black Lives Matter (BLM) movement has hemorrhaged support. In June 2020, as Biden planned his nomination-acceptance speech, a Yahoo News/YouGov poll of U.S. adults found 57 percent of them approving Black Lives Matter. One year later, 42 percent of Americans approved.

The public is worried about crime. In a USA Today/Ipsos poll from early summer, two-thirds of adults said that crime had grown worse over the past year. One-third of adults said that they had witnessed a crime spike in their own neighborhood. Seventy percent of adults called for additional funding for police departments. Seventy-seven percent wanted more cops on the beat. Navigator, a Demo-cratic polling company, reported in July that majorities of Democrats, independents, Republicans, blacks, Hispanics, and whites considered violent crime a "major crisis." In late June, as fears over public safety became unignorable, Biden tried to reframe the crime debate as an argument for gun control. His messaging flopped.

A similar atmosphere of irrelevance and impotence surrounds Biden's climate policy. Biden reentered the Paris climate agreement but is far from reaching a deal to limit either China's or India's greenhouse-gas emissions. He signed a nonbinding, symbolic executive order calling for half of the new auto fleet manu-factured each year to be composed of electric vehicles by 2030. He canceled the Keystone XL pipeline, paused the issuance of new drilling leases on public lands and waters, suspended oil and gas leases in the Arctic National Wildlife Refuge that the Trump administration had approved, and is under pressure from the Left to restrict U.S. exports of liquid natural gas.

Yet Biden has a rather la-di-da attitude toward carbon emissions elsewhere. He acquiesced to the Nord Stream 2 pipeline between Russia and Germany, which makes it possible for Vladimir Putin to cut off energy supplies to Ukraine without jeopardizing Western European markets. He asked OPEC to ramp up oil production, showing more concern for the domestic political cost of high gasoline prices than for the environmental and strategic costs of empowering the cartel. His negotiators in Vienna promised to drop sanctions on Iran's energy sector if the Islamic Republic reenters the 2014 nuclear deal.

Biden also made a big show of undoing his predecessor's immigration policies. He suspended construction of the border wall. He lifted the so-called Muslim ban on travel and immigration from 13 countries. He ended the "Remain in Mexico" policy that required asylum-seekers to wait there as U.S. courts adjudicated their claims. He exited the "safe third country" agreements with Guatemala, Honduras, and El Salvador that instructed migrants to apply for asylum in the first nation they entered. He exempted minors from "Title 42" protocols that allow for rapid deportation during public-health emergencies.

Guess what happened next. The number of individuals detained on the southern border swelled. Every month broke records. July was the busiest month on the border in 21 years. Never has the United States taken into custody more family units and unaccompanied minors. When the fiscal year ends on September 30, more than 1 million illegal migrants will have been detained. Many of them have been released into the U.S. interior.

Biden can neither explain nor stop the deluge. At first, he said that the surge was seasonal. It wasn't. Then Vice President Harris traveled to Guatemala and told migrants not to come. They kept coming. Secretary of Homeland Security Alejandro Mayorkas recently told Border Patrol agents that "we can't continue like this, our people in the field can't continue and our system isn't built for it." Note his use of the present tense. The Trump administration did build a system that mostly secured the southern border. Biden wrecked it.

The unfolding disaster in Afghanistan is another direct consequence of Biden's ineptitude. His failure to plan for the chaos that would follow America's exit resulted in a humanitarian disaster and a potential mass-hostage situation as some 6,000 U.S. troops evacuated tens of thousands of U.S. citizens and Afghan partners from a single airport in Kabul ringed by Taliban checkpoints. Biden's word has been exposed as worthless. He said that the Afghan army wouldn't fall to the Taliban. It did. He said that al-Qaeda is not in Afghanistan. It is. He said that our allies haven't questioned America's credi-bility. They have. The British parliament held the withdrawal in contempt, and former British prime minister Tony Blair called the logic behind it "imbecilic."

That's an understatement. As the 78-year-old Biden gets ready to exit the political arena, he seems intent on recreating the conditions that prevailed when he entered it a half century ago. Inflation, crime, American retreat—these hallmarks of the 1970s have returned. And they have joined postmodern threats, such as a worldwide pandemic, unchecked migration, climate change, and the global jihadist-Salafist movement. Biden has been president for less than a year. The number of crises buffeting American politics, economics, society, and culture already has multiplied beyond his control.

In the run-up to the 2020 campaign, President Obama reportedly told a fellow Democrat, "Don't underestimate Joe's ability to f*** things up."

The Kamala Harris Problem

Kamala Harris is the single best argument for Democrats trying to prop up Joe Biden no matter what. She has been a disaster as vice president, even as she's done nothing particularly noteworthy either good or bad. She's simply a political black hole, whose abysmal ratings reflect not just Biden's troubles but her own profound, inherent flaws as a political figure.

Per the Rich Lowry *National Review* article "The Kamala Harris Problem" in June 2022: Kamala Harris has the authenticity of Hillary Clinton, the charm of Al Gore, and the common touch of Adlai Stevenson.

She could have been engineered in a lab as a conviction-less opportunist lacking basic political horse sense—and she more or less was. She came up in a California where the dominance of TV ads makes retail politicking all, but unnecessary, and internal Democratic politics is largely based on identity politics. Compared to her, Biden really is Middle Class Joe. The contrast with Chuck Schumer, another Democratic leader from a deep-blue state, is instructive—Schumer had a tough statewide race against a Republican within memory and is aware that not all voters are extremely online "woke" progressives.

Harris could have run as an ideologically interesting, tough-minded former prosecutor in the 2020 Democratic nomination fight—a little like Eric Adams in the New York City mayoral primaries last year. Instead, she got sucked into the idea that the winning lane would be a couple of ticks to the right of Bernie Sanders. She co-sponsored his "Medicare for All" proposal, before making a confusing hash of her position when she realized the political implausibility of the plan.

She seemed defensive about her record as a prosecutor, which came under withering assault from Representative Tulsi Gabbard from the left.

Her signature moment—attacking Joe Biden for his opposition to busing based on her own experience getting bused—didn't pay the expected dividends because of its self-evident calculation.

Harris is a politician who always seems to be reading stage directions out loud. Her laugh, a target of critics, usually sounds forced and highly deliberate, at times bordering on inappropriate affect. It's a valuable political skill to seem at ease even when reaching for the brass ring at the highest level of American politics. Bill Clinton, George W. Bush, and Barack Obama all had this ability. Harris has shown no indication that she has it or will develop it.

Biden has done her no favors with her assignments as vice president. Given the foolhardiness of the underlying Biden policies, there was no realistic way she was going to diminish migration at the southern border. Nor was she going to do anything to get a voting-rights bill passed. That said, Harris hasn't mastered any particular issue area and gives the impression of seeking tableaus that will lend to her gravitas without ever succeeding.

On top of all this, she hasn't managed to secure a close, trusted relationship with the president.

Any rational observer could have predicted that Biden's VP pick was going to be particularly sensitive given that, as de Gaulle famously said, "Old age is a shipwreck." Instead, Biden played identity politics by choosing Harris, and it's understandable now that some Democrats would like, against all evidence, to bank everything on Biden's youthful vigor.

The Democrats Have a Kamala Harris Problem

Per the Charles C.W. Cooke *National Review* article in May 2021 titled "The Democrats Have a Kamala Harris Problem" he states:

Americans have never much liked Kamala Harris. Despite being theoretically well-placed to dominate the 2020 Democratic primary, she dropped out of the race in December of 2019 with just 3 percent support nationally and about 7 percent support in her home state of California.

Now holding the vice presidency, Harris remains impressively unbeloved. Per a recent YouGov poll, her net approval rating is ten points underwater among all voters and 25 points underwater among independents, 44 percent of whom say they have a "very unfavorable" opinion. For a vice president to engender such feelings—especially at this stage in the cycle—is unusual, to say the least.

Still, that Harris is unpopular should come as no great surprise, given that she somehow manages to combine into a single package a transparent insincerity, an unvarnished authoritarianism, and a tendency toward precisely the sort of self-satisfied progressivism that helped the Republicans to limit their losses at the last general election.

If her apologists wish to, they can pretend that the reaction Harris yields is "gendered" or "systemic" or "inequitable" or whatever other bastardized academic term is fashionable this week, and they should feel free to knock themselves out doing so.

Deep down, though, they must know that America isn't the problem here. The problem is that Harris is a phony.

A Cabinency of Dunces

As the nation sinks inexplicably into self-created crisis after crisis, debate rages whether President Joe Biden is incompetent, mean-spirited, or an ideologue who feels the country's mess is his success.

This section is courtesy of the Victor Davis Hanson *Epoch Times* May 2022 article "A Cabinency of Dunces": A second national discussion revolves around who actually is overseeing the current national catastrophe, given Biden's frequent bewilderment and cognitive challenges.

But one area of agreement is the sheer craziness of Biden's Cabinet appointments, who have translated his incoherent ideology into catastrophic governance.

Secretary of Homeland Security **Alejandro Mayorkas** has essentially nullified federal immigration law. More than 2 million foreign nationals have illegally crossed the southern border without audit—and without COVID-19 vaccinations and tests during a pandemic. Mayorkas either cannot or will not follow federal law.

But he did create a new Disinformation Governance Board. To head his new Orwellian Ministry of Truth, he appointed **Nina Jankowicz**—an arch disinformationist who helped peddle the Russian collusion, Steele dossier, and Alfa Bank hoaxes. While Jankowicz's adolescent videos and past tweets finally forced her resignation, Mayorkas promises his board will carry on.

In the days before the recent Virginia election, grassroots parent groups challenged critical race theory taught in the schools. In reaction and under prompts from teachers unions, Attorney General **Merrick Garland** directed both the FBI and the Justice Department to establish a special task force apparently to "investigate threats" from parents against school board members.

The FBI recently has been knee-deep in political controversies. It illegally doctored a FISA application to entrap an American citizen. Its former directors, under oath before Congress, either claimed faulty memory or admitted lying to federal investigators.

The last thing a scandal-plagued FBI needed was to go undercover at school board meetings to investigate parents worried over their children's education.

We are in a fuel price spiral that is destroying the middle class.

Yet when Energy Secretary **Jennifer Granholm** was asked about plans to lower gas prices, she laughed off the idea as "hilarious." Later, Granholm preposterously claimed, "It is not the administration policies that have affected supply and demand."

Apparently haranguing those who finance fossil-fuel production, canceling the Keystone pipeline, suspending new federal oil and gas leases, and stopping production in the Arctic National Wildlife Refuge all had nothing to do with high fuel prices.

Currently, supply chain disruptions are paralyzing the U.S. economy.

The huge Port of Los Angeles has been a mess for more than a year. Since last fall, dozens of cargo ships have been backed up to the horizon. Thousands of trucks are bottlenecked at the port.

During the mess, Transportation Secretary **Pete Buttigieg** was not at work. Instead, at the height of the crisis, he took a two-month paternity leave to help out his husband and two newborn babies.

Such paternal concern is a noble thing. But Buttigieg is supposed to ensure that life-or-death supplies reach millions of strapped Americans.

This winter, trains entering and leaving Los Angeles were routinely looted in the Old West style of train robbing—without much of a response from Buttigieg's transportation bureau.

In Senate testimony, Secretary of the Interior Secretary **Deb Haaland** refused to explain why her department is slow walking federal oil and gas leases at a time when Americans are paying between $5 and $6 a gallon for gas.

Haaland was unable to provide simple answers about when new leases will result in more supplies of oil and gas. Her panicked aides slid talking points to her, given that in deer-in-the-headlights fashion, she seemed incapable of providing senators with basic information about U.S. energy production on federal lands.

Biden's National Economic Council deputy director **Brian Dreese** had argued that inflation was actually a good thing, and the entire administration had pushed the notion that the best prescription to alleviate inflation was more big progressive spending—part of a broader trend of Democrats saying utterly absurd things about the economy.

Treasury Secretary **Janet Yellen** admitted in an interview with CNN that her past views on how inflation in the United States would progress were faulty. Yellen, along with Federal Reserve officials, had previously insisted that inflation was temporary. However, with inflation now near four-decade highs, many have been forced to change their stance on the matter.

"I think I was wrong then about the path that inflation would take," Yellen said in the May 31, 2022 interview. "As I mentioned, there have been unanticipated and large shocks to the economy that have boosted energy and food prices and supply bottlenecks that have affected our economy badly that I didn't—at the time, didn't fully understand, but we recognize that now."

The common denominator to these Biden appointees is ideological rigidity, nonchalance, and sheer incompetence. They seem indifferent to the current border, inflation, energy, and crime disasters. When confronted, they are unable to answer simple questions from Congress, or they mock anyone asking for answers on behalf of the strapped American people.

We don't know why or how such an unimpressive cadre ended up running the government, only that they are here, and the American people are suffering from their presence.

Here Are the Trump Reversal Executive Actions Biden Signed in His First 100 Days

This section is courtesy of the April 2021 CNN article "Here Are the Executive Actions Biden Signed in His First 100 Days" by Christopher Hickey, Curt Merrill, Richard J. Chang, Kate Sullivan, Janie Boschma and Sean O'Key:

President Joe Biden signed a flurry of executive actions in his first 100 days in office, primarily aimed at curbing the coronavirus pandemic and dismantling many of former President Donald Trump's policies.

The executive actions include halting funding for the construction of Trump's border wall, reversing Trump's travel ban targeting largely Muslim countries, imposing a mask mandate on federal property, ramping up vaccination supplies, canceling the Keystone XL pipeline, ending federal use of private prisons and reversing Trump's ban on transgender Americans joining the military.

In his first 100 days in office, Biden signed more than 60 executive actions, 24 of which are direct reversals of Trump's policies. Biden has defended the number as necessary to undo what he considers "bad policy" inherited from Trump, especially on immigration.

To date, 10 of his 12 actions on immigration are reversals of Trump's policies.

"And I want to make it clear—there's a lot of talk, with good reason, about the number of executive orders that I have signed—I'm not making new law; I'm eliminating bad policy," Biden said as he signed a series of actions on immigration from the Oval Office on February 2. "What I'm doing is taking on the issues that—99% of them—that the president, the last president of the United States, issued executive orders I felt were very counterproductive to our security, counterproductive to who we are as a country, particularly in the area of immigration."

So far, Biden has signed more executive orders and memorandums reversing those of his predecessor Trump than any of the last three presidents as the list below shows:

04/16/2021   Immigration: Reverses the Trump policy banning refugees from key regions and enables flights from those regions to begin within days. Declares that the 15,000 annual refugee cap set by Trump will be raised to a number to be determined by May 15.

04/01/2021   Other: Revokes a Trump executive order that authorized sanctions on International Criminal Court officials.

02/24/2021   Economy: Revokes a series of seven Trump administration actions that had eased regulatory requirements, as well as actions that called for withholding funding from cities for allowing protests in support of Black Lives Matter, that imposed stricter work requirements to be eligible for federal welfare and that promoted "beautiful federal civic architecture."

02/24/2021   Immigration: Revokes a Trump-era proclamation that limited legal immigration during the Covid-19 pandemic.

02/17/2021   **Labor:** Revokes a Trump administration order creating an industry-led apprenticeship program.

02/04/2021   **Immigration:** Expands the United States Refugee Admissions Program and rescinds Trump policies that limited refugee admissions and required additional vetting.

02/04/2021   **Immigration:** Directs relevant agencies to ensure LGBTQI+ refugees and asylum seekers have equal access to protections, requires the Department of State to lead a standing group to respond quickly to international LGBTQI+ human rights abuses and to report annually to Congress on global LGBTQI+ abuses, directs agencies to review Trump administration policies and rescind those that are inconsistent with this memo within 100 days.

02/02/2021   **Immigration:** Revokes Trump's order justifying separating families at the border and creates a task force that recommends steps to Biden to reunite separated families.

02/02/2021   **Immigration:** Aims to address economic and political causes of migration, works with organizations to provide protection to asylum seekers and ensures Central American asylum seekers have legal access to the United States. Rescinds Trump administration policies and guidelines and also initiates a review of policies "that have effectively closed the U.S. border to asylum seekers."

02/02/2021   **Immigration:** Rescinds Trump's memo requiring immigrants to repay the government if they receive public benefits. Elevates the role of the executive branch in promoting immigrant integration and inclusion, including reestablishing a Task Force on New Americans. Requires agencies to review immigration regulations and policies.

02/01/2021   **Economy:** Reinstates tariffs applied under the Trump administration to aluminum imports from the United Arab Emirates, citing the need for domestic production of aluminum for national security and reviving industry.

01/28/2021   **Health Care:** Rescinds the "Mexico City Policy," a ban on US government funding for foreign nonprofits that perform or promote abortions.

01/25/2021   **Coronavirus:** Reinstates Covid-19 travel restrictions for individuals traveling to the United States from the Schengen Area, the United Kingdom, Ireland and South Africa.

01/25/2021   **Equity:** Reverses the Trump administration's ban on transgender Americans joining the military.

01/22/2021   **Economy:** Restores collective bargaining power and worker protections for federal workers, and lays the foundation for $15 minimum wage.

01/20/2021   **Coronavirus:** Stops the United States' withdrawal from the World Health Organization, with Dr. Anthony Fauci becoming the head of the delegation to the WHO.

01/20/2021   **Environment:** Rejoins the Paris climate accord, a process that will take 30 days.

01/20/2021   **Environment:** Cancels the Keystone XL pipeline and directs agencies to review and reverse more than 100 Trump actions on the environment.

01/20/2021   **Equity:** Rescinds the Trump administration's 1776 Commission, directs agencies to review their actions to ensure racial equity.

01/20/2021   **Census:** Requires non-citizens to be included in the Census and apportionment of congressional representatives.

01/20/2021   **Immigration:** Reverses the Trump administration's restrictions on US entry for passport holders from seven Muslim-majority countries.

01/20/2021   **Immigration:** Undoes Trump's expansion of immigration enforcement within the United States.

01/20/2021   **Immigration:** Halts construction of the border wall by terminating the national emergency declaration used to fund it.

01/20/2021   **Regulation:** Directs OMB director to develop recommendations to modernize regulatory review and undoes Trump's regulatory approval process.

Alejandro Mayorkas, Architect of DACA, Tapped to be DHS Secretary

Per the Ira Mehlman FAIR December 2020 article "Alejandro Mayorkas, Architect of DACA, Tapped to be DHS Secretary":

Concerns that President-elect Biden will pursue a radical immigration agenda after taking office were heightened in November when he tapped Alejandro Mayorkas to serve as Secretary of the Department of Homeland Security (DHS). The nation's immigration enforcement agencies— Customs and Border Patrol (CBP) and Immigration and Customs Enforcement (ICE)—as well as the U.S. Citizenship and Immigration Services (USCIS), all fall under the auspices of DHS.

Mayorkas has a long history on immigration policy matters, including serving in the Obama administration as the director of USCIS, and even as U.S. Attorney for California under President Bill Clinton. Most crucially, as an advisor to former President Obama, Mayorkas was the architect of the de facto amnesty program implemented in 2012, known as Deferred Action for Childhood Arrivals (DACA), under which some 700,000 illegal aliens (many well into adulthood) have been granted exemption from removal and work authorization in direct contradiction to federal statutes.

President Trump sought to end DACA, but his efforts were stymied by numerous legal challenges, some of which are still pending in the courts even as he prepares to leave office. President-elect Biden has indicated that he will move to fully restore DACA once he takes office, and it is likely that Mayorkas will be tasked with spearheading this effort as well as others aimed at protecting people who are in the country illegally.

More concerning is that Mayorkas will lead the effort to undo many Trump-era policies that have at least partially stemmed the flood of migrants entering the country illegally. In accepting his nomination to head DHS, Mayorkas announced his intention to "advance our proud history as a country of welcome"—a high-minded declaration, but one, based on Mayorkas' history, that is likely to extend to welcoming millions of people who violate our immigration laws. High on his agenda is likely to be the actual or de facto canceling of Trump agreements with Mexico and Central American governments that were essential to stanching the surges of migrants entering the United States by making specious claims for political asylum.

House Republicans Call on Senate Leaders to Reject Biden DHS Picks, Warn They Won't End Border Crisis

Per the Adam Shaw Fox News June 2021 report titled "House Republicans Call on Senate Leaders to Reject Biden DHS Picks, Warn They Won't End Border Crisis":

More than 30 House Republicans wrote to Senate leaders in both parties, urging them to reject President Biden's nominees for key Department of Homeland Security agencies—warning that they will not "make the decisions necessary" to end the ongoing crisis at the southern border.

In a letter to Senate Republican Leader Mitch McConnell and Democratic Leader Chuck Schumer, the 31 Republicans say the nominees "either helped develop the policies that have produced the crisis or have shown an unwillingness to enforce immigration law."

The Biden administration has been facing a surge in migration at the border, with more than 178,000 migrants encountered in April alone, including more than 13,000 unaccompanied children. The crisis has overwhelmed border facilities and led to shocking scenes at the border.

While the administration has blamed a combination of "root causes" in Central America and a lack of preparation from the Trump administration, Republicans have blamed the rolling back of Trump-era border protections such as border wall construction and the Migrant Protection Protocols (MPP), as well as a narrowing of interior enforcement and a push for a path to citizenship for illegal immigrants.

As the debate rages on, the Senate is currently considering three nominees to key DHS positions: Ur Jaddou to lead the U.S. Citizenship and Immigration Services (USCIS), Chris Magnus to serve as head of Customs and Border Protection (CBP) and Sheriff Ed Gonzalez to lead Immigration and Customs Enforcement (ICE.)

The lawmakers note that Jaddou led the Biden transition team's review of DHS, in which they say, "she developed the policies that created the current crisis at the southern border." Meanwhile, they point to Magnus' defense of "sanctuary" policies—that restrict cooperation with federal immigration enforcement—as police chief in Tucson, Arizona.

They also note that Gonzalez, when he served as Sheriff of Harris County, terminated cooperation agreements with ICE, and also opposed ICE raids of illegal immigrants in his jurisdiction—forbidding his officers from participating.

"The policies that these nominees promoted in their previous positions clearly demonstrate the nominees will be unwilling to make the decisions necessary to enforce the law and end the current border crisis," the lawmakers write. "Confirming these nominees would endorse the policies that created the crisis."

The letter was led by Reps. Andy Biggs, R-Ariz., and Brian Babin, R-Texas, who chair the House Border Security Caucus and have been intensely opposing the Biden administration's policies on immigration and asylum—arguing that it has fueled the massive migration wave they say is putting Americans in danger, and that Biden should reinstate the Trump-era policies it ended.

"Each of these candidates has a history of making dangerous policy decisions, ignoring immigration law, and perpetuating the open borders narrative," he said. "These agencies are vital to the safety and security of our country, and we deserve for them to be led by people who will honor that responsibility."

3 – GOP's Useful Idiots: Biden, Harris, Clinton, Schumer, Pelosi, AOC & 'Dem' Others

Credit: CNN.com - Prominent Democrats Warren, Pelosi, Sanders, Schumer, and Biden.

For many, electing Joe Biden represented a return to normality, moderation, unity and competence. Unfortunately, his presidency has only ushered in hyper-divisiveness, immoderate policy, venality and staggering incompetence. Furthermore, the president was dealt an excellent hand and has played it terribly. He has no one to blame for the sorry state of his administration but himself.

Per the Kyle Smith *National Review* June 2022 article "Biden Made His Own Mess":

You'd think someone whose career in national politics goes all the way back to 1972 would have noticed this, but apparently President Biden hasn't: Unpopular presidents tend to complain that they were dealt a bad hand, and then grouse that the media are making things look worse than they are. But Biden was dealt an excellent hand; he has no excuses for the mess he's in.

When Biden took office, the U.S. was already bouncing back from economic calamity, and tens of millions of vaccine doses were in the pipeline. If he had made smart decisions, the U.S. would be doing fine right now. Instead, he is the primary cause of the crises that are swamping his presidency. The media could scarcely be more inclined to spin things in his favor, and yet even they can't entirely ignore the dispiriting facts.

A less measurable crisis is the nationwide sense of being browbeaten into submission by woke politics. Biden has been the Vladimir Putin of this culture-war bombardment, nominating far-left candidates for key regulatory posts, attempting to set up a Ministry of Truth within the Department of Homeland Security, blasting away at Florida for stopping schools from teaching eight-year-olds about sexuality, endorsing sex-change procedures for children, siccing the FBI on parents who dare to speak out against school boards, and going easy on woke terrorists.

Meanwhile, Biden's administration refers to mothers as "birthing people." If the president would like to stop looking ridiculous, he could start by criticizing the Oberlin-meets-Newspeak lingo his appointees favor.

Joe Biden's Growing List of Failures

Per the November 2021 Larry Alexander *Newsweek* report "Joe Biden's Growing List of Failures" the list of Biden's failures is long, and it grows daily. Here are the highlights of that list.

First, of course, is the disastrous withdrawal from Afghanistan. Biden pulled out our troops before getting out our civilians, green card holders and allies, then had to send troops back in to help them get out. Yet even then, Biden failed to get everyone out, despite promising to do so. And in addition to stranding people, the evacuation left billions of dollars' worth of arms, vehicles and equipment in the hands of the Taliban, abandoned a strategic base in the fight against terrorism and allowed the release of imprisoned hard-core terrorists.

Another Biden disaster happened at the southern border. The number of illegal immigrants that streamed into the country this year, all because of Biden's refusal to enforce our immigration laws, is stunning. That number includes thousands of so-called amnesty seekers, who are generally released into the country with an order that they show up for a hearing in the distant future—an order that often goes ignored. It also includes people who are unvaccinated or infected with COVID-19, as well as gang members, drug traffickers, sex traffickers and even individuals on terrorism watchlists. The president's primary duty is to "take care that the laws be faithfully executed." Biden has willfully failed to do so. That is an impeachable offense.

Right up with these two disasters is that of inflation. Prices are rising steeply, with no end in sight. On top of what already amounts to a cruel tax on the poor and those on fixed incomes, Biden wants to spend trillions more, which will just make inflation even worse. Moreover, the economy is suffering from massive supply chain bottlenecks, with ships waiting weeks to get into ports, and a shortage of workers and truck drivers to deal with them once they get in.

A principal cause of the current inflation is high energy prices—the product of Biden's energy policies. Upon assuming office, Biden immediately canceled the Keystone XL pipeline, which would have employed some 11,000 people. The oil that would have come through the pipeline will still come in, though by costlier and more polluting means (trucks and rail).

At the same time, Biden gave his approval for the Nord Stream pipeline from Russia to Germany. At the same time he was restricting domestic oil and gas production, leading to higher gas and heating prices, Biden called on OPEC and Russia to supply more oil and gas in order to reduce those prices.

Biden has fully embraced identity politics in the federal bureaucracy. Many of his appointees have been selected based on their race, sex, LGBT status and so on, and not because they were the most qualified persons available. Biden has also reinstated critical race theory training for federal employees. His administration thus reinforces rather than rebuts the poisonous lies now spread throughout our educational system and in the body politic.

Another Biden failure has been his mishandling of the COVID-19 pandemic. Biden inherited the enormous benefit of coronavirus vaccines produced by the Trump administration's Operation Warp Speed. His response to the COVID pandemic thereafter has been characterized by frequent policy reversals. The most recent of which is the unconstitutional ordering of vaccine mandates—a move that, previously, the president said he would never make. As a result, the country is faced with the resignation and firing of police officers, firefighters, health care workers and armed forces personnel. Even worse is that, despite the availability of vaccines, more people have died of COVID-19 during Biden's presidency than during Trump's.

Biden has thoroughly politicized the enforcement of federal law. His Justice Department fails to treat equal offenders equally. It meted out harsh punishments and lengthy pre-trial detentions to those who on January 6 broke into the Capitol, few of whom engaged in any violence or destruction of property. They were, at most, guilty of trespass and obstructing a governmental proceeding, offenses which have been frequently committed by left-wing groups (recall, for example, the Kavanaugh hearings).

Contrast the treatment of the January 6 defendants with, for example, the DOJ's treatment of Antifa and BLM rioters who tried to burn down a federal courthouse in Portland, a much more serious federal crime. And now the DOJ has turned its attention to parents complaining about schools' racializing and sexualizing their children.

The military has been similarly politicized under the Biden administration. Its function is to be a lethal threat to foreign adversaries, not a political partisan or a social experiment in woke ideas. But the generals and admirals in charge know that the Biden administration is in thrall to identity politics; so, to further their careers, they bring woke concepts into the military at the expense of its basic function. And with respect to that basic function, Biden—while backing major spending increases in many domestic programs—has left the military with a reduced budget, in terms of purchasing power. At the same time, our adversaries are rattling their sabers.

Finally, it is worth commenting on Biden's character. Biden is prone not just to embellishing the truth, but to outright lying. His campaign lied about his son Hunter's laptop—saying that well-substantiated reports of its contents was Russian disinformation. He lied about Hunter's business dealings, including possible influence peddling, with the Chinese. He lied about what Donald Trump said regarding the Charlottesville protests. He lied about Kyle Rittenhouse, claiming the teenager was a white supremacist before his trial even began. Throughout his political career, he has plagiarized and told whoppers about things he is supposed to have done (but didn't do).

Biden has attained virtually no successes as president. But as the above list attests, he has produced a lifetime's worth of major failures in less than a year.

Harris's Office Undergoes Difficult Reset

Per the Brett Samuels and Amie Parnes *The Hill* December 2021 article "Harris's Office Undergoes Difficult Reset":

Kamala Harris's office is undergoing a reset after a difficult first year, which saw a rocky start for the vice president. The reset, which includes the departure of Symone Sanders—the most recognizable official in the office—is the result of Harris's public stumbles, a streak of bad press and staff squabbling, particularly in the communications office, according to sources familiar with the vice president's office.

The turmoil has raised worries among Democrats about her prospects as a presidential candidate. "No one seems happy," said one source close to the vice president's office.

News of Sanders's departure was followed by reports that two more press aides would depart in the coming weeks: Peter Velz, the vice president's director of press operations, and Vince Evans, the deputy director of the Office of Public Engagement and Intergovernmental Affairs for Harris, are planning to leave those positions soon, a source confirmed.

Those planned exits became public a few weeks after Harris's office confirmed her communications director, Ashley Etienne, would leave the position at the end of the year. Sources suggested the close of the year provided a natural time for some officials to transition out, but acknowledged a reset could be helpful.

"They had to turn over the office," said one Democratic operative familiar with the dynamics in the vice president's office. "Too much dissatisfaction."

One source said it's clear that Harris "feels adrift without her people" including her sister Maya, who was a senior adviser on her presidential campaign. The source said decision making in the office is also "really slow" with every decision passing through chief of staff Tina Flournoy.

Harris has a history of cycling through staff, dating back to her years as California attorney general. Staffing problems also plagued Harris's presidential campaign, which folded before the Iowa caucuses after initial enthusiasm. But those familiar with her operation say it's a larger problem than simply replacing some staff.

"It's obvious things aren't in a great place, so I understand the urge to sub in a new team but that misdiagnoses the problem," said one source familiar with Harris's operations. "The problem is there has never been a coherent strategy. It has always been an operation that lurches from one chaotic moment to the next."

The source said it's not necessarily a problem with Harris but rather "the way she runs things does not necessarily set her up for success. She relies on a small group of people for everything and because they only have so much bandwidth the 'urgent' frequently crowds out the 'important.' "

The tensions and departures have fueled chatter in Democratic circles about whether Harris would remain as Biden's heir apparent to run for president in 2028, or in 2024 should the 79-year-old president opt not to seek reelection.

Cackling Kamala

Per the Kyle Smith *National Review* October 2021 article titled "Cackling Kamala":

Kamala Harris is a heartbeat away from becoming the first woman president, the first Asian president, the first woman-of-color president. Big wins all around, right? So why are the Democrats so nervous? They appear to be on the verge of calling in the Henry Wallace treatment and dumping Harris before Joe Biden runs for president again, this time with the election weeks before his 82nd birthday, in 2024.

"People think she's f***ing up, maybe she shouldn't be the heir apparent," one Democratic operative told Axios. White House aides use earthy language like "sh**show" to describe Harris's "poorly managed" office. It's "an abusive environment," a staffer "with direct knowledge" told Politico, adding, "It's not a healthy environment and people often feel mistreated. It's not a place where people feel supported but a place where people feel treated like sh**."

What if Biden should decline to run for reelection as an octogenarian? Harris, as his lady in waiting, would almost have to be the party's designated successor because she is black and female. To replace her, according to the party's prevailing thought codes and its media enablers, would be racist and sexist. Yet the prospect of riding into battle behind Kamala Harris's generalship has every Dem in D.C. reaching for the Maalox, if not the Ativan or maybe the hemlock.

Dems including "many current senior administration figures," says Axios, do not think she could beat any potential foe, from Lord Voldemort to Ernst Stavro Blofeld to Donald Trump. If the options facing the American voter on a future ballot turn out to be "Kamala Harris" and "Literally Anyone Else," Harris is going to be not just an underdog but a longshot.

She's a lady whose trademark gambit—the deranged cackle, which she Jokerishly emits anytime she can't answer a question—makes Hillary Clinton seem as lovable as a litter of golden-retriever puppies.

Unlike Hillary, Harris does not make people feel sorry for her for having been ritually humiliated in her marriage to an intern-abusing lech. Unlike Hillary, Harris doesn't make people think "She earned it" or "She paid her dues."

The voters understand that Harris is in the position she currently occupies for a completely unearned reason. She is a woman of color, Biden promised Dem primary voters he'd run with a woman, then a woman of color, and this wild-eyed, tone-deaf, unbelievably toxic and yet somehow colorless candidate was the best he could grab from a very limited menu of offerings.

The Biden administration seems at a loss about what to do with Harris. Everything she touches crumbles to dust. When Biden made her "border czar" in March and COVID-infected illegal immigrants began flooding into the country, she laughed and informed interviewers that she was in no hurry to go down and see things for herself.

When Lester Holt of NBC pressed her on the question of why she hadn't gone to the border, she famously replied, "And I haven't been to Europe. And I mean, I don't—I don't understand the point that you're making." Laughing dismissively, responding with a non sequitur, and then confessing she doesn't understand the rudiments of politics (even the easiest rules, such as the one about appearing to take problems seriously while photographers snap away).

She didn't even bother with a perfunctory toe-touch in El Paso until June, and the crisis continues to boil over. Several high-level Biden-administration officials, including the attorney general, the secretary of state, and the head of DHS, attended a border-security meeting in Mexico City on October 8; Harris spent the day posing for photos at a day-care center in New Jersey.

Team Kamala thinks Biden doesn't want competition from his No. 2. So Joe Biden is setting her up to fail? If so, that would appear to be Biden's one unambiguous success.

AOC Is the Gift That Keeps Giving

Rep. Alexandria Ocasio-Cortez doesn't think much of the agencies that keep America safe according to the Karl Rove *Wall Street Journal* in July 2019 titled "AOC Is the Gift That Keeps Giving":

New Yorker editor David Remnick recently asked about her call to abolish U.S. Immigration and Customs Enforcement. Couldn't ICE be reformed? No, replied the freshman Democrat. "The core structure of ICE" and "the entire Department of Homeland Security" are "large threats to American civil liberties."

Remnick asked: "Would you get rid of Homeland Security, too?" Ocasio-Cortez replied, "I think so, I think so." She called the department's formation one of the George W. Bush administration's "egregious mistakes," described her call for its abolition as "a very qualified and supported position," and added: "We never should have created DHS."

The idea of abolishing the Department of Homeland Security is moronic, stupid, naive and dumb.

Should the U.S. really shut down the agency in charge of air-transportation security, so hijackers armed with box cutters or bombs can board planes? Do Americans want our borders to be left unprotected against illegal aliens, traffickers, drugs and terrorists? Would America be safer or more free without capabilities like disaster emergency services, terrorism-prevention fusion centers, biological-warfare defense, the Coast Guard, programs to stop domestic deployment of weapons of mass destruction, and protective services for government facilities?

All these are Homeland Security functions.

Ocasio-Cortez doesn't believe the department is needed to keep America safe, Rove told Fox News Channel's Martha MacCallum last week, the congresswoman should talk to the Democratic chairmen of the House Homeland Security and Intelligence committees. She should talk to the police department of the city she represents. The NYPD will tell her the Department of Homeland Security has helped foil terrorist plots against the Big Apple.

If AOC remained intent on abolishing the department, Rove suggested she visit with constituents who lost a loved one on 9/11. Ask if they believe Homeland Security should be abolished so that other American families might suffer the pain they have. The department's creation was a great bipartisan accomplishment, Rove told MacCallum—a new way to meet the 21st century's challenges. Those challenges haven't gone away, whatever Ocasio-Cortez thinks.

Shortly after this exchange on Fox, Ocasio-Cortez appeared on Twitter to say that 132 representatives voted against creating the department in 2002. Calling it "ill-conceived," she wrote that "discussing reorganization shouldn't be out of the question" and "it's really not that radical."

Except that she hadn't said she advocated "reorganization." She called for abolishing the department.

Rove responded on Twitter, reminding her that more than twice as many representatives—295—voted to create the department and that the Senate vote was 90-9. Rove pointed out her transparent flip-flop and suggested that upon sober reflection, even she might have decided it was nutty to get rid of the department. If she hadn't really changed her mind, Rove challenged her to show us her bill to undo what she called an "egregious mistake." Then we could all see how many co-sponsors her "very qualified and supported position" drew.

Crickets. No response. There's nothing she can say that makes her look good.

But the incident shows that the draft of the Green New Deal she issued in February 2021 wasn't an aberration. That's the draft with references to cow flatulence, unspecified constraints on commercial air travel, and a collection of left-wing nostrums to transform America into a new Venezuela. Her chief of staff told the truth last week: The Green New Deal isn't mainly about climate—it's about making America socialist.

Rep. Ocasio-Cortez is not a serious legislator but an unusually shallow poseur, the product of social-media culture. She offers slogans cribbed from the latest socialist bull session; wild utterances that receive enthusiastic nods from "woke" Democrats and looks of astonishment from much of Middle America.

There are reasons why AOC, "The Squad" of her running buddies on the House's far-left fringe, and their operatives are characterizing some less-liberal Democratic representatives as akin to 1940s Southern segregationists, threatening them with primary challenges, and even castigating Speaker Nancy Pelosi as a racist. They're convinced the shock value of their attacks and radical ideas will give their movement dominance over the Democratic Party and the country.

AOC Slams Clinton Strategist James Carville

From the Geoff Earle DailyMail.com November 2021 "AOC slams Clinton strategist James Carville for blaming 'stupid wokeness' on the Democrats' crushing election defeats because it is 'a term almost exclusively used by older people'" article:

Democratic Rep. Alexandria Ocasio-Cortez has hit back at Clinton strategist James Carville for suggesting 'stupid wokeness' caused the wave of crushing Democrat defeats.

'There are limits to trying to mobilize a campaign with a 100% moderate strategy without mobilizing the base. (I) said nothing abt "wokeness" which is a term almost exclusively used by older people these days btw,' The Squad Member wrote on Twitter.

'The average audience for people seriously using the word "woke" in a 2021 political discussion are James Carville and Fox News pundits. So that should tell you all you need to know,' she added. Veteran Democrat Carville tore into 'stupid wokeness' as the root of Terry McAuliffe's defeat in the Virginia governor's race and said some members need to go to 'woke detox'.

Carville, who helped steer Bill Clinton to victory in 1992 aimed squarely at cultural clashes over race, education, and police funding as the heart of the matter, after Republican Glenn Youngkin took down McAuliffe by winning over suburban areas that had gone for Joe Biden just a year ago.

Carville, who boosted Clinton with his 'It's the economy, stupid' mantra, weighed in even as 'squad' member Rep. Ilhan Omar retweeted a message saying progressives would get blamed for McAuliffe's loss, suggesting he didn't run left enough.

'What went wrong is just stupid wokeness. Don't just look at Virginia and New Jersey. Look at Long Island, look at Buffalo, look at Minneapolis, even look at Seattle, Washington,' Carville said as he ticked off election results in an appearance on PBS News Hour.

'I mean, this "defund the police" lunacy, this take Abraham Lincoln's name off of schools. I mean that—people see that,' he said. He said Terry McAuliffe got 'caught up in something national' and blamed it for his loss (McAuliffe also has deep Clinton ties).

AOC Roasted for 'Sexual Frustrations' Tweet About GOP Critics: Taking Up the 'Plight of the Super-Hot'

From the Lindsey Ellefson The Wrap January 2022 article "AOC Roasted for 'Sexual Frustrations' Tweet About GOP Critics: Taking Up the 'Plight of the Super-Hot'":

Rep. Ocasio-Cortez suggested Republicans who critique her vacation are "projecting their sexual frustrations" on her. A chat on CNN's "New Day" revolved around Republicans and their "sexual frustrations," ultimately ending with conservative commentator Mary Katherine Ham joking that Rep. Alexandria Ocasio-Cortez has taken up the fight for "the plight of the super-hot."

To understand how this segment came about, turn to Ocasio-Cortez's Twitter. She responded to right-wing criticism of her New Year's vacation to Florida by writing, "If Republicans are mad they can't date me they can just say that instead of projecting their sexual frustrations onto my boyfriend's feet. Ya creepy weirdos. It's starting to get old ignoring the very obvious, strange, and deranged sexual frustrations that underpin the Republican fixation on me, women,& LGBT+ people in general. These people clearly need therapy, won't do it, and use politics as their outlet instead. It's really weird."

Though Ocasio-Cortez's tweet racked up 19,000 retweets and 175,000 likes compared to Cortes' 3,000 and 9,000, respectively, Ham was not among those who were amused by the defense.

"First of all, I woke up like this," she joked on CNN's "New Day." "So I think you have the authority on people being sexually frustrated by my mere existence. It happens all the time. I'm glad to be able to discuss this important issue with you. The plight of the super-hot in America has long been ignored and AOC has started a national conversation about this."

Biden's Got Problems. Is Chuck Schumer One of Them?

Per the A.B. Stoddard Real Clear Politics March 2021 article "Biden's Got Problems. Is Chuck Schumer One of Them?":

There is a lot Schumer is likely doing right. Yet he is gratuitously alienating Republicans in a 50-50 Senate where—while he is technically majority leader—Democrats preside over the chamber without truly controlling it. An evenly split chamber does not "change America in a big, bold way." On most votes the vice president cannot break a 50-50 tie, so 10 Republicans are required for 60 votes to overcome a filibuster. For now Schumer is making it harder to find those Republican votes, not easier.

No one knows better than the four-term senator that the entire Biden presidency now revolves around the decisions made by fellow Democratic Sen. Joe Manchin, who is feeling quite comfortable bashing his own leader for refusing to court Republicans.

"I haven't seen an effort by any of our leadership to go sit down and work with them," Manchin said last week. "Just make that effort. Make a little bit more of an effort with him and Mitch McConnell and make an effort with the leadership. John Thune's a very good guy. Roy Blunt, I hate to see Roy leaving. These are all good people."

It was a one-two punch, not only fingering Schumer for failing to reach across the aisle but complimenting Republicans.

So far Schumer seems far more focused on pleasing progressives than cooperating with Republicans, impressing Rep. Alexandria Ocasio-Cortez, who would represent the most serious threat to Schumer in any field of left-wing Democrats, has said she hasn't made up her mind about challenging the incumbent next year, but that she is pleased the idea of her running has pushed Schumer left.

Since Schumer won't "just make that effort" to reach out to Blunt or McConnell or Thune or Collins, as Manchin urges, it seems that failure is actually an option for the majority leader—as long as he wins his primary.

Petulant Nancy Pelosi is Everything Wrong With Democratic Party

From the Miranda Devine *New York Post* February 2020 article "Petulant Nancy Pelosi is Everything Wrong With Democratic Party: Devine" comes her report:

Nancy Pelosi looked like a malfunctioning Stepford wife as she sat behind President Trump during his State of the Union address in 2020. Her lower face twitched, she muttered to herself, shook her head, smiled inappropriately, gazed around, chewed her lip or remained glued to her seat during standing ovations in honor of special guests.

It was a bizarre enough performance before she rose to her feet and dramatically ripped up her copy of the president's speech in what will go down in history as the most unseemly display of partisanship in this partisan era.

That moment was when the myth of the "master political strategist" was busted, and we saw Pelosi, 79, for what she is. Pretending to be classy and prayerful when she is full of petty hatreds and is incapable of holding her party together, a woman who parades her Catholicism while advocating no-holds-barred abortions, feigning to pray for the president while deriding him as "sedated."

She told reporters that ripping up the speech was "a very dignified act … the courteous thing to do, considering some of the other exuberances within me." But her petulant vandalism was the opposite of courteous, quite obviously. Pelosi showed no contrition for ripping up the speech, nor for the political catastrophe of her failed impeachment drive.

57 People From Bill And Hillary Clinton's Inner Circle Have Died In Strange Circumstances

Per the Gwen Farrell Evie May 20 2022 post "What Is Going On? 57 People From Bill And Hillary Clinton's Inner Circle Have Died In Strange Circumstances In The Last 30 Years":

The Clintons have been a bulwark of Democratic politics since the late 1970s, when Bill was attorney general of Arkansas, later governor, and then elected the 42nd president. As most of us know, Hillary was previously a senator for the state of New York, former first lady, secretary of state, and candidate for president in 2016.

Neither of their careers has been without scandal, though—Bill's infamous sexual relationship with White House intern Monica Lewinsky and sexual assault allegations levied against him by Paula Jones and Juanita Broaddrick eventually led to his impeachment in 1998, after he was found guilty by the House of obstruction of justice and lying under oath.

However, these pale in comparison, starting with the early to mid-1990s accusations and investigations against the Clintons about the mysterious deaths of their well-connected associates really began, and most of it originated with "The Clinton Chronicles," a documentary released in 1994 and produced by an organization out of California called Citizens for an Honest Government. The documentary, which was heavily promoted by political commentator Larry Nichols and Rev. Jerry Falwell, only distributed around 300,000 copies.

"The Clinton Chronicles" first suggested the Clintons' association with the odd deaths of individuals in their inner circle.

Though it has since been labeled a "conspiracy theory" and even "anti-Clinton propaganda," The Clinton Chronicles, which specifically lobbied allegations of gross criminal behavior against Bill like sexual assault, drug running and money laundering, was really the first source to openly introduce the concept of the Clintons' possible association with the odd or unexplained deaths of individuals within their inner circle.

The documentary specifically covered the apparent suicide of White House Deputy Counsel Vince Foster, who grew up across the street from Bill in Little Rock and shot himself in a park in 1993 (though his fingerprints were never found on the weapon, which detractors have long pointed to as evidence of outside involvement).

The Clinton List

Sometimes called the Clinton List or the Clinton Body Count, a quick search online (depending on your browser, of course) yields a whole host of pretty intriguing results. Though Vince Foster and Clinton fundraising guru Ed Willey were likely the first suicides the List took notice of, they weren't the last. Additionally, disgraced financier and sex trafficker Jeffrey Epstein's less-than-credible suicide is probably the most famous one to be associated with the Clintons, but it certainly isn't the only one.

Forbidden History on Twitter summarizes the Body Count succinctly: of the 57 people on the List, "15 of them committed suicide, eight died in car and plane crashes, and 14 were killed under mysterious circumstances."

A post on the Reddit thread dives into the List more in-depth, specifically in naming almost 50 individuals, their connections to the Clintons, and their cause of death. As part of the pair's inner circle the majority of them had potentially damning information to share, and even those who didn't plan to come forward and share their inside knowledge were part of Clinton's attorney general, gubernatorial, or presidential administration, or connected intimately with those who were.

For example, of the 57 names, 11 of them, all men, were former Clinton bodyguards. Another, John Ashe (former head of the UN General Assembly), died from a crushed windpipe while lifting weights at home. One man, James Milan, was decapitated—though "the Coroner ruled his death was due to 'natural causes.'" Another young woman, who was murdered at a Starbucks in Georgetown, was a former White House intern who was allegedly going to release her accounts of sexual harassment during her time in the White House before she was killed.

No matter how the so-called left biased fact-checkers attempt to explain away or debunk the sky-high body count, no one can statistically explain away or debunk the exponential high number of unusual deaths by Clinton associates, from any causes—compared to the average number of "unusual" deaths in the general population.

Bernie Sanders' Permanent Revolution

From the August 2019 issue of *The Economist* article "Bernie Sanders' Permanent Revolution":

Democratic presidential candidate Sen. Bernie Sanders of Vermont inspired millions of loyal supporters, some of whom chose not to support Hillary Clinton in the general election in 2016. Democratic politicians still believe Sanders's 2016 insurgency showed the party had moved in a big way to the left.

Not since Eugene McCarthy in 1968 have Democrats faced such an anomaly. After the unexpected success of his 2016 presidential run, Sanders has developed an almost cult-like hold on a small but meaningful minority of the Democratic electorate.

Thereafter, an unreconciled Sanders become a general-election problem for Democrats. His aggrieved minority was easily sufficient to deny their candidate victory in close-fought states such as Michigan or Wisconsin. Thus did McCarthy help ensure Hubert Humphrey's defeat by Richard Nixon in 1968—and Sanders help ensure Hillary Clinton's to Donald Trump?

To help answer that question, fully 12 percent of people who voted for Sen. Bernie Sanders, I-Vt., in the 2016 Democratic presidential primaries voted for President Trump in the general election. That is according to the data from the Cooperative Congressional Election Study—a massive election survey of around 50,000 people.

These numbers show that after a bitter Democratic primary, more than 1 in 10 of those who voted in the 2016 primaries for the very progressive Sanders ended up voting for the Republican in the general election, rather than for the Democratic candidate, Hillary Clinton.

Elizabeth Warren: The Bonfire of the Democrats

Per the Rich Lowry Politico February 2019 article "Elizabeth Warren: The Bonfire of the Democrats":

Being a progressive hero of long-standing doesn't afford any protection. Consider Sen. Elizabeth Warren. She certainly deserves all the grief she gets for her laughable identification of herself over the years as an American Indian. But for the identity-politics Left, her fault runs deeper: In trying to rebut the allegedly racist mockery of her as "Pocahontas," she herself committed a racial offense.

After taking a DNA test to prove her (distant) Native American ancestry, she stood accused in the words of a member of a tribe in South Dakota of "privileging nonindigenous definitions of being indigenous." According The *New York Times*, she had also tread "too far into the fraught area of racial science—a field that has, at times, been used to justify the subjugation of racial minorities and Native Americans." Not to mention how she had given "validity to the idea that race is determined by blood—a bedrock principle for white supremacists and others who believe in racial hierarchies.

Yes, Warren stood exposed as implicitly in league with the oppressors of Native Americans—and here she had just wanted Donald Trump to stop referring to her by a derisive nickname. Cherokee Nation activist Rebecca Nagle told CNN that Warren needed to apologize "to the tribes that she has harmed and to Native people broadly."

Sure enough, she apologized, and presumably will keep on doing it as long as she's running.

Georgia Voting Explosion Marks Beginning of the End for Stacey Abrams

From the Joe Concha *The Hill* May 2022 report titled "Georgia Voting Explosion Marks Beginning of the End for Stacey Abrams":

And then there's two-time Georgia gubernatorial candidate Stacey Abrams (D), who alleged that the Georgia law purposely suppresses minority turnout. "There are components of it that are indeed racist because they use racial animus as a means of targeting the behaviors of certain voters to eliminate their participant and limit their participation in elections," Abrams said in Senate hearings after the law was passed in 2021.

"Jim Crow 2.0 is about two insidious things: voter suppression and election subversion. It's no longer about who gets to vote; it's about making it harder to vote. It's about who gets to count the vote and whether your vote counts at all. It's not hyperbole; this is a fact."

That was President Biden during a speech in Georgia pushing the Democrats quest to federalize voting rights. Biden has played the Jim Crow 2.0 card multiple times, during his presidential campaign and while in office. His vice president, Kamala Harris, was tapped to lead the administration's "voters rights" effort after doing such a fine job (he's being sarcastic) fixing the border crisis. "I don't want an America of the future for my kids to be in an America where we … are suppressing the right of the American people to vote," Harris declared in echoing her boss.

Georgia has become the front lines of the voting debate. In 2021, Republican leaders made some changes to existing laws to restore public confidence in the system. Democrats, followed by major corporations in the Peach State including Coca-Cola and Delta Air Lines, cried foul while making laughable claims that the voting law changes would make voting noticeably harder in the state. Major League Baseball even moved its annual All-Star game out of Atlanta that summer.

But a funny thing happened in the month of May 2022 in Georgia. Early voting records were set. More people voted in a primary than ever before. In three weeks of early voting, more than 857,00 votes were cast, marking a 212 percent jump over the 2020 presidential primaries and a 168 percent jump over the 2018 gubernatorial primaries in Georgia, according to Secretary of State Brad Raffensperger.

Stacey Abrams just lost her signature issue and she'll be facing off with Gov. Brian Kemp again in 2022.

Beto O'Rourke Confronts Texas Governor at School Shooting News Conference

Per the KCRA May 2022 news story "'This is on you': Beto O'Rourke confronts Texas governor at school shooting news conference":

Beto O'Rourke confronted Texas Gov. Greg Abbott in the middle of a news conference following the mass shooting that killed multiple people, including 19 children, at an elementary school in Uvalde, Texas, shouting, "This is on you!"

Sen. Ted Cruz told O'Rourke to "sit down" as he approached the stage where officials were offering new information on the shooting. Lt. Gov. Dan Patrick told the candidate that he was "out of line and an embarrassment," and motioned for local law enforcement to stop him.

"The time to stop the next shooting is right now, and you're doing nothing," O'Rourke said as a law enforcement officer shooed him away from the stage. As O'Rourke continued to speak off-mic, Uvalde Mayor Don McLaughlin told authorities to get him out of the auditorium and repeated "Sir, you are out of line." The mayor then said, "I can't believe you're a sick (expletive) that would come to a deal like this to make a political issue."

O'Rourke started to shuffle out of the auditorium before stopping halfway where he started speaking again. While not all of his comments were audible, he could be seen pointing at the stage saying, "It's on you." McLaughlin fired back by saying, "it's on (expletives) like you. Why don't you get out of here?" As O'Rourke exited, a few people shouted from the crowd for about a minute before Abbott continued the news conference.

O'Rourke, who won the Democratic primary back on March 1, 2022, by carrying over 90% of the vote, will face off against Abbott for the Texas governorship in November. Already a staunch advocate before the Uvalde shooting, O'Rourke is certain to make gun control a central theme of the race. According to FiveThirtyEight's most recent polling aggregation, Abbott currently holds a 10-point lead over O'Rourke.

4 – Policy Failures: Inflation Immigration, Energy, Voting, Pandemic, Infrastructure & More

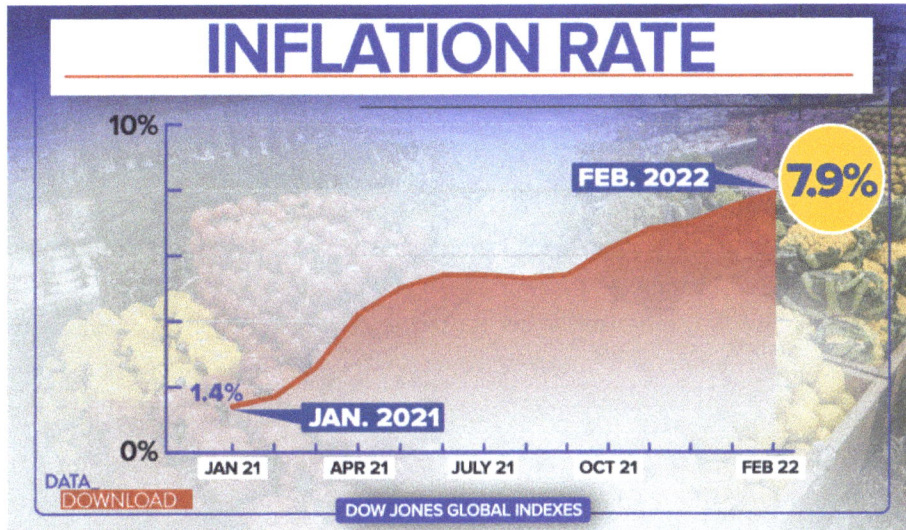

Credit: NBC News.

From the Kyle Smith *National Review* June 2022 article "Biden Made His Own Mess":

The single biggest problem Biden faces—inflation—is clearly his fault. Congress passed trillions of dollars' worth of stimulus in 2020 during the end of Trump's term. By the time Biden took office, the economy had rebounded energetically, growing 33.4 percent and 4.1 percent, respectively, in the last two quarters of 2020, and it was already roaring along at a 6.4 percent growth clip for the first quarter of 2021.

Yet Biden pushed for more stimulus and got it, pouring $1.9 trillion worth of kerosene on the fire. And then he pushed for even more of the same, spending the rest of the year advocating trillions in infrastructure spending (which he got) and trillions more in spending on the so-called Build Back Better agenda (which he didn't).

Gasoline prices are not as directly linked to Biden's actions as inflation, but he can hardly blame exogenous forces (like Putin) for the spike in the cost of fossil fuel when disrupting its supply has been a nakedly stated objective of the bureaucracy he put in place.

Supply-chain problems? Biden is responsible for some of them, and the labor-union allies whose influence he wishes to expand are to blame for some others. Biden's failure to waive the nonsensical Jones Act, which severely limits maritime trade, has prolonged and worsened the crisis. Meanwhile, Biden's own bureaucrats at the FDA are responsible for the baby-formula shortage because it's the FDA that decrees, again nonsensically, that the baby formula used by millions all over Western Europe is not up to U.S. standards.

Biden is the primary author of the humiliating retreat from Afghanistan that first caused his approval ratings to sag. His softness on illegal immigration is the obvious cause of the ongoing border crisis. And his inability to get through even a heavily stage-managed appearance without looking as clueless as Grandpa Simpson is the reason Americans doubt his fitness to lead. These last 18 months could have given us a story of American renewal and recovery. Instead, they've given us a damning story of presidential mismanagement.

Democrats' Opposition to Fossil Fuels is Political

Per the joint Masooma Haq and Paul Greaney *Epoch Times* April 2022 article titled "Democrats' Opposition to Fossil Fuels is Political: Grover Norquist":

President Joe Biden has said climate change is an existential threat and that his administration is committed to mitigating the damage caused by carbon emissions, and therefore he will not support the fossil fuel industry in the United States. He has instead opted to import oil and gas from places like Russia and the Middle East.

The Biden administration has said its goal is to "create a carbon pollution-free power sector by 2035 and net-zero emissions economy by no later than 2050." However, in 2021, Biden's climate czar, John Kerry, admitted that even if the United States meets its emission goals, that would not be enough to impact climate change.

"He also knows that Paris alone is not enough," Kerry told reporters at a White House press briefing in 2021 while talking about the reason President Joe Biden reentered the Paris Climate Agreement. "Not when almost 90 percent of all of the planet's emissions—global emissions—come from outside of U.S. borders. We could go to zero tomorrow and the problem isn't solved," Kerry conceded.

While Republicans want to enhance U.S. fossil fuels production and use an all-of-the-above energy approach, Democrats want to replace fossil fuels with renewable energy because they would have control over that industry and those companies would vote for their party, Norquist said.

How Biden's Tunnel Vision on Oil and Gas Encouraged Putin's Invasion of Ukraine

In just over a year, per the Carrie Sheffield NBC News March 2022 news report "How Biden's Tunnel Vision on Oil and Gas Encouraged Putin's Invasion of Ukraine," Biden buckled under pressure from domestic environmentalists to halt the Keystone XL pipeline, block new oil and gas leases and push through burdensome new, legally dubious Securities and Exchange Commission climate regulations.

Biden also issued new greenhouse gas rules to expand how what is called the "social cost of carbon" is calculated. The measure has been opposed in court by 10 Republican-led states in a lawsuit that argues that the methodology the administration relied on was flawed and points to possible violations of federal law during the rule-making process.

Biden and Western economies are scrambling to reverse this through measures like Biden's announcement, with the European Union, of a natural gas-exporting deal to reduce Europe's reliance on Russia. But in many ways, the die had already been cast. This casting likely contributed to Putin's heinous calculus while he planned his deadly, horrific Ukraine invasion. Putin knew he had significant leverage against the West and that America was helping Russia gain even more leverage by weakening U.S. oil and gas.

Germany is a leading indicator of where the U.S. is heading under Biden. In recent years, Germany spent heavily on failed "green energy" initiatives that missed its climate goal because of their limited carbon-cutting results. Not to mention that in the first half of 2021, the country had the highest household electricity price in the E.U. Who suffers the most when that happens? Poor and middle-class families.

Even as Biden undermines the U.S. oil and gas industry, he has asked foreign countries to produce more fossil fuels—a craven political move, since Democrats see the writing on the wall for November's elections. Americans aren't buying Biden's claim that Putin is to blame for gas price hikes—inflation increases predominantly occurred before Ukraine's invasion.

Democrats' Recent Rejection of COVID Insanity Will Not Save Them This Fall

Per the Josh Hammer *Epoch Times* February 2022 report "Democrats' Recent Rejection of COVID Insanity Will Not Save Them This Fall":

In a desperate attempt to stave off, or at least mitigate, a veritable electoral bloodbath, Democrats have conveniently decided that now is the time to finally stop obsessing over COVID. Yes, now—right as other polling evinces a majority of Americans want to cease or seriously lessen COVID-induced lifestyle restrictions.

New York Gov. Kathy Hochul just announced an end to the Empire State's statewide masking requirement for businesses, although a mask mandate regrettably remains in place at schools and health care facilities. What's more, New Jersey, Connecticut, Delaware, Oregon, and California—all of which, like New York, are Democratic-governed—announced early February 2022 their own plans to lift indoor mask mandates either later in February or in March.

These Democratic leaders have invariably pointed to receding caseloads, and perhaps "the science," more generally, to justify their obviously coordinated reversals on mask mandates. To be sure, mask mandates (for inefficacious masks) and vaccine mandates (for vaccines that do not stop transmission) are bad public policy. So, good for Democrats for finally catching up. Welcome to the party, guys; some of us have been here for a while already.

But Democrats cannot plausibly pretend that "the science" has changed in any meaningful way. All that has changed is their ever-plummeting polling and ever-sinking expected fortunes this fall. Hochul and California Gov. Gavin Newsom have not had some sort of grand epiphany. There will be no "mea culpa," no acknowledgment that Republican Florida Gov. Ron DeSantis had it right on COVID all along.

There will be no apologies for the ways that divisive vaccine mandates and pointless mask mandates harm our social fabric and undermine the common good. If Democrats could still politically get away with imposing their will, they would do so. It just turns out they can't.

The Build Back Better Blues

Per the Justin Haskins *The Hill* December2021 article "Joe Manchin Just Killed Build Back Better—and Saved the US Economy in the Process":

Despite repeated promises from President Biden that original version of their Build Back Better(BBB) bill will cost "zero dollars," the nonpartisan Congressional Budget Office (CBO) has estimated that the bill would add $365 billion to the national deficit over the 2022-2031 period, not including $207 billion in additional revenues that could be added by increasing tax enforcement measures and expanding the Internal Revenue Service (IRS).

This, however, is a wildly misleading estimate, because the CBO's calculation assumes that many of BBB's largest programs and tax credits would be allowed to expire, in some cases after only a single year. This is incredibly unlikely and gives the false sense that BBB is much more affordable than it actually is.

According to budget watchdogs such as the Committee for a Responsible Federal Budget, BBB's real price tag—one that includes true 10-year cost estimates for the bill's most important provisions—is nearly $5 trillion, and the impact on the federal deficit would likely be closer to $3 trillion.

The additional $3 trillion in debt would need to be covered through tax increases or, more realistically, money printing. In either case, the economy would suffer dramatically.

Build Back Better would, as originally written, impose large tax increases on wealthier families, investors and corporations. The costs for many of these increases would almost certainly be passed on to consumers and workers in the form of higher prices, reduced product or service quality, and/or layoffs.

Printing money to pay the additional $3 trillion in costs could be even more catastrophic for the economy. The United States is already facing an inflation crisis fueled by record levels of government spending and money-printing related to the COVID-19 lockdowns and recovery.

Democrats Would Be Shortsighted to Nuke the Senate Filibuster

Per the Josh Hammer *Newsweek* March 2021 article "Democrats Would Be Shortsighted to Nuke the Senate Filibuster":

"You'll regret this, and you may regret this a lot sooner than you think," then-Senate Minority Leader Mitch McConnell (R-Ky.) told then-Senate Majority Leader Harry Reid (D-Nev.) in 2013 upon Senate Democrats' invoking the "nuclear option" to prevent Senate Republicans from filibustering all lower-court judicial nominations.

And so it was: In 2017, facing fierce Democratic opposition on the nomination of then-Judge Neil Gorsuch to replace Justice Antonin Scalia on the Supreme Court, then-Majority Leader

McConnell galvanized Republicans to extend Reid's precedent to Supreme Court nominees. Gorsuch, Brett Kavanaugh, and Amy Coney Barrett all ended up benefiting by means of razor-thin confirmation margins on the Senate floor that would not have been possible with traditional filibuster rules in place.

To be sure, ending the Senate filibuster is hardly a fait accompli. Sens. Joe Manchin (D-W.Va.) and Kyrsten Sinema (D-Ariz.) have expressed reservations, and in a 50-50 deadlocked Senate, Democrats cannot afford to lose a single vote. But if they end up yielding to the already-escalating grassroots pressure and join their colleagues to end or "reform" the filibuster—more likely than not, this columnist thinks—Democrats may enjoy short-term gains but will regret their move just as quickly as they came to regret its 2013 predecessor.

Nuking the Senate filibuster—something Republicans notably eschewed during their own Trump-era control of the Senate—would undermine the American political order, in which counter-majoritarian measures are deeply woven. But it would also be a shortsighted move, even from a cynical, partisan perspective. If dedication to James Madison doesn't prevent Democrats from embarking on this misplaced crusade, perhaps their own long-term self-interest will.

Democrats Introduce Bill to Expand Supreme Court, But Reception Is Tepid

From the Zachary Stieber *Epoch Times* April 2021 article titled "Democrats Introduce Bill to Expand Supreme Court, but Reception Is Tepid":

The "Judiciary Act of 2021" would add four seats to the nation's top court, effectively flipping the balance from 6–3 in favor of conservative-appointed justices to 7–6 in the opposite direction. Republicans decried the proposal as one of a number of Democrat attacks on institutions, including efforts to eliminate the filibuster.

"Last week, President Biden, who was marketed to the country as a moderate and an institutionalist, jumped in with both feet, set up a pseudo-academic commission to study the merits of packing the Supreme Court, just an attempt to close this transparent power play in fake legitimacy. But, alas, the far-left cannot even wait for the fake theatrics of the fake study to play out," Senate Republican Leader Mitch McConnell (R-Ky.) said on the Senate floor.

House Minority Leader Kevin McCarthy (R-Calif.) accused Democrats of promoting a "plan to dismantle a government institution in pursuit of their socialist agenda. Never in my time in politics did I ever believe they would go this far," he added in his weekly press conference on Capitol Hill. "I question: is there a moderate Democrat left in the party?"

Congress can adjust the number of seats on the Supreme Court with legislation, but it has been at nine seats since 1869. The last major effort to change the number, by President Franklin Roosevelt, a Democrat, was rejected in 1937 by Congress.

Democrats face an uphill battle in getting the bill passed.

House Committee Approves Another Attempt to Grant DC Statehood in Party-Line Vote

Per the Janita Kan *Epoch Times* April 2021 article "House Committee Approves Another Attempt to Grant DC Statehood in Party-Line Vote":

Democrats in the House Oversight Committee have voted along party lines in April 2021 to pass a bill seeking to make the District of Columbia the 51st state, sending their bill to a full House vote.

The panel voted 25-19 to advance H.R. 51, also known as the "Washington, D.C. Admission Act," to grant statehood to residents in the district after a lengthy debate over the constitutionality of the effort. The Democrat-led House passed a similar bill in 2020 but the Democrat effort was effectively shot down by the then-Republican-led Senate.

If successful, the bill would see D.C. residents be able to elect two more Senators to represent the Democrat-leaning state. The federal district, to be controlled by Congress, would be limited to two square miles surrounding the White House, Capitol, Supreme Court, and National Mall to be named the "Capital."

The Democrats' efforts have been opposed by Republicans, who argue that the efforts are unconstitutional and characterized the push as a "power grab" that would tip the scales in the Senate in the Democrats' favor.

Similarly, 22 Republican attorneys general vowed to challenge any attempt to make D.C. the 51st state.

Democratic Discontent Brews With Federal Reserve

Per the Tobias Burns *The Hill* May 2022 article "Democratic Discontent Brews With Federal Reserve":

Discontent with the Federal Reserve is brewing among Democrats, even those who voted earlier this month to confirm Fed chairman Jerome Powell for another four-year term.

With inflation at 40-year highs and the prospect of a recession looming large over midterm elections later this year, Democrats are worried the economy could cost them their majorities. And the feeling in the party is that if the Fed had acted quicker, Democrats might not be facing such tough headwinds.

Specifically, Democrats say the Fed started raising interests too late following the onset of the pandemic, missing an opportunity to curb the inflation that's weighing on Democratic hopes for reelection.

The idea that the Fed acted too late to raise interest rates to lower inflation has support among a chorus of economists, who say it was overly stimulative and too focused on propping up demand deep into the pandemic even as deeper issues affecting supply chains went unaddressed.

The GOP argument is getting some backing from economists who see the stimulus from Congress, the administration and the Fed as having had a snowball effect upon inflation.

"In 2021, there had already been a huge stimulus package, and Biden added another $2 trillion, or to be precise, $1.9 trillion or 8 percent of GDP. Powell should have been beginning to put on the brakes, if not in March of 2021 when Biden introduced that package, then at least a few months later," Desmond Lachman, an economist with the right-leaning American Enterprise Institute, a Washington think tank, said in an interview.

"Instead, he kept interest rates at zero and kept flooding the market with liquidity, so he set us up and played a big role in getting the high inflation," he said.

To bring inflation down, the Fed increased interest rates earlier in May 2022 by half a percent, or 50 basis points, to 0.83 percent, saying it "anticipates that ongoing increases in the target range will be appropriate." The interest rate hikes have hit stock markets hard, with some either in or near bear territory that represents a 20 percent fall from peaks.

The deeper worry is that the rising interest rates could lead to a recession, though a number of economists think that is unlikely until at least 2023. The Fed is hoping it can tame inflation without triggering a recession.

Biden's Plan to Punish the Responsible

From the Jim Geraghty *National Review* April 2022 report titled "Biden's Plan to Punish the Responsible":

President Biden is on the verge of rewriting a longstanding social contract by deciding that taxpayers should repay significant portions of student loans, instead of the borrowers who took out those loans and received the education. The biggest beneficiaries would be white Americans under the age of 40 who have graduate degrees and live in high-income, majority-white neighborhoods—in other words, extremely online Democrats.

If you borrow money and sign a contract promising to pay it back, then you must pay it back, or you will suffer serious long-term financial consequences. Or at least, that's the way it used to work until Democrats decided they could win a lot of votes by just waving a magic wand and declaring that people didn't have to pay their student debt back.

Joe Biden is on the verge of crossing out that part of the social contract with a red pen and declaring that taxpayers will pay back those debts instead   or at least a significant chunk of them for his preferred demographics—the Democratic Party's activist class, and that will exacerbate the already-bad inflation crisis.

The president shared his plans during a 90-minute White House meeting with members of the Congressional Hispanic Caucus, participants in the exchange tell CBS News. The move could affect more than 43 million borrowers who hold more than $1.6 trillion in federal student loan debt, the second-largest debt held by Americans, behind mortgages.

The federal government has postponed repayments of student loans seven times since the start of the pandemic; no one has been required to pay back a student loan since March 13, 2020.

Interest rates on those loans during this period dropped to zero, and collections on defaulted loans stopped.

The total outstanding balance for federally owned student loans—including the defaults—in December 2021 was $1.38 trillion. A study from the Federal Reserve Bank of New York determined a lot about who would benefit the most from Biden's proposal:

Forgiveness of $10,000 per borrower would forgive a total of $321 billion of federal student loans, eliminate the entire balance for 11.8 million borrowers (31.1 percent), and cancel 30.5 percent of loans delinquent or in default prior to the pandemic forbearance.

Increasing the forgiveness amount increases the share of total forgiven debt for higher credit score borrowers and those living in richer neighborhoods with a majority of white residents.

In other words, without an income cap, forgiving $10,000 per borrower would most benefit whites under the age of 40 who have graduate degrees and live in high-income, majority-white neighborhoods. This is one of the most Democratic-leaning and outspoken progressive demographics in the country.

This is a wealth transfer from taxpayers to the Democratic Party's Twitter class.

A Recap of Joe Biden's 6 Biggest Failures During His First Year as President

This section is courtesy of the Inigo Alexander *Newsweek* January 2022 article "Joe Biden's 6 Biggest Failures During His First Year as President":

President Joe Biden's first year in the Oval Office has come to a close today and, as is to be expected of an administration's freshman year, the president has had a tumultuous path so far.

The series of challenges presented to Biden's administration have made the 46th president's inaugural year at the White House a difficult one, having to deal with record inflation, the ongoing COVID pandemic and political division.

As Biden came to an end to his first year in office, *Newsweek* looked back over some of the president's failures over the course of the last year.

1) Failed Build Back Better Act

President Biden's flagship Build Back Better Act has failed to get passed in law, despite his commitment to pass the bill by Christmas. The Build Back Better Act is a central piece of the administration's objectives and was originally drafted with a budget of $3.5 trillion that included provisions and support for infrastructure and social policies. Eventually, the bill's budget saw itself slashed to $1.75 trillion.

The proposed bill was initially passed by the House in November, though has been stalled in the Senate since. The Build Back Better Act also lost the crucial support of Democratic senators Joe Manchin and Kyrsten Sinema, all but killing the bill as it needs the support of all 50 Democratic senators.

President Biden could now be forced to sacrifice key components of the bill in order to maneuver through the divided Senate.

Biden might have to compromise on issues such as the extension of the enhanced child tax credit, universal preschool and increased climate change funding in hopes of passing his flagship bill.

2) Stalled Voting Legislation

Other central elements of the Biden administration's agenda for his inaugural year have also met a deadlock.

Democrats also failed to pass voting rights legislation, which their Republican counterparts have successfully opposed. This follows the introduction of new voting restrictions in Republican-led states in the aftermath of the 2020 election, and former president Donald Trump's false claims of voter fraud.

In order to successfully pass the voting rights legislation, the Biden administration would also have to reform the Senate filibuster, which Manchin has repeatedly opposed.

3) Failure to Cancel Student Debt

On the campaign trail, Biden vowed he would cancel at least $10,000 of student loan debt per person in an effort to undo individual burdens the loans imposed.

The President has extended the interest-free pause on federal student loan repayments that was introduced amid the pandemic, though the measure is by no means a forgiveness of standing loans. The pause is scheduled to lift in February, and payments will resume.

His primary actions on this front are primarily built on existing promises on the topic made by previous administrations. Much debate has been had about the president's authority to personally write off student debts, with certain factions of the Democratic party urging the president to use executive action to resolve the issue.

However, Biden himself expressed his doubt towards that approach, and said in April: "I don't think I have the authority", a sentiment echoed by House Speaker Nancy Pelosi.

4) COVID Mismanagement

Biden has long been aware of the severity of the COVID pandemic and the need for effective measures to manage the crisis, and in the opening months of his tenure he oversaw a mass vaccination campaign.

However the emergence of the Delta variant over the summer and the recent wave of Omicron has stalled Biden's initial progress on the COVID front. The administration's lack of preparation for new variants was reflected in the sharp surge in cases nationwide, as well as in the shortage of testing kits.

The surge in infections saw an average of over 750,000 daily new COVID cases reported over the last week, according to data from John Hopkins University. The number of daily COVID deaths has also seen a rise in the past week, with 1,796 deaths reported last according to John Hopkins data.

A number of Biden's fellow Democratic senators criticized his approach for being "reactive, rather than proactive." Additionally, Biden recently saw the Supreme Court block Biden's vaccine mandate for businesses, which intended to enforce vaccine-or-test requirements for large private companies.

Criticism was also leveled at the CDC for its guidance recommending mask use in schools for children over the age of two. Scientists raised concerns over the method's effectiveness, while fellow international bodies offered contrasting advice to the CDC.

Consequently, more U.S. citizens than ever now disapprove of Biden's handling of the pandemic, with 48 percent of the public dissatisfied.

5) Record Inflation

President Biden's economic accomplishments have been bittersweet. On the one hand, the Biden administration approved a hefty $1.9 trillion COVID relief package and passed a $1.2 trillion bipartisan infrastructure law. Additionally, a record 6.4 million jobs were created which saw unemployment drop to just 3.9 percent last December.

On the other hand, national inflation rose to a record 6.8 percent, the highest level in 40 years. This has consistently driven up the prices of basic goods and services such as gas, food and housing. The upshot in prices seen in December represented the sixth consecutive month of price increments.

In November, gas prices skyrocketed by 58 percent, the largest increase recorded over a 12-month period since 1980.

Rising inflation was also compounded with supply chain shortages and delays, further aggravating the issue for consumers. The White House has deemed the rising prices to be "transitory," a temporary effect as a result of increased pandemic-related costs. and expects the surge to settle over the coming months. In a statement at the time, Biden said the ongoing inflation was not representative of "today's reality".

"It does not reflect the expected price decreases in the weeks and months ahead," Biden said in the statement.

6) Immigration Debacles and Remain in Mexico

In Biden's opening year in the White House, the issue of migration and the administration's mismanagement at the US-Mexico border has become a constant headache.

Biden had vowed to undo many of Trump's heavily criticized immigration policies in a bid to guarantee increased protection and care for asylum-seekers and migrants entering the country. However, his administration's handling of the issue has left a lot to be desired.

Despite his campaign trail promises, Biden has reinstated the Trump-era Remain In Mexico program and has also upheld a controversial policy known as Title 42.

Title 42 has been heavily criticized for using the pandemic to enable veiled human rights violations and pre-emptively remove migrants found at the border. The policy has also led to family separations at the border, as many blocked from entering the country chose to send their children through alone in a bid to guarantee their safety.

Meanwhile, the Remain In Mexico program has been slammed by critics for denying migrants entry to the U.S. while keeping them in bureaucratic limbo at makeshift border camps in Mexico.

The administration's negligence at the border has also resulted in increased hostility. In the opening 10 months of Biden's presidency, over 7,647 cases of rape, torture, murder, kidnapping and violent assault towards asylum-seekers at the border have been recorded.

The administration has faced fierce criticism for their mismanagement at the border, with the United Nations urging Biden to lift the repressive policies.

More Pills the Democrats Will Find Hard to Swallow

Per the Dan McLaughlin *National Review* November 2021 article "More Pills the Democrats Will Find Hard to Swallow":

As McLaughlin wrote in October, "Ruy Teixeira is the co-author . . . of the 2002 book The Emerging Democratic Majority. He is probably more responsible than anyone for the rise of smug Democratic projections that demography would sweep them into power and consign Republicans to the dustbin of history."

However, he has been raising ever-increasing alarms that Democrats are now fatally out of step with ordinary voters by virtue of their capture by "woke" academic cultural leftism. As he writes in a recent newsletter, "It's not a good look for the party of the working class to be losing so much working class support that it's no longer, well, the party of the working class. But of course it goes way beyond the look to the realities of electoral performance and political power. Put simply, there's just no way Democrats can maintain a consistent hold on political power with this level of working class support."

Teixeira has some very good advice for Democrats:

- A Democratic brand reset is clearly in order to stop the bleeding among working class voters, along the lines suggested by the Jacobin study. A good way to start would be to embrace widely-held American views and values that are particularly strong among the multiracial working class.

- Equality of opportunity is a fundamental American principle; equality of outcome is not.

- America is not perfect, but it is good to be patriotic and proud of the country.

- Discrimination and racism are bad, but they are not the cause of all disparities in American society.

- No one is completely without bias but calling all white people racists who benefit from white privilege and American society a white supremacist society is not right or fair.

- America benefits from the presence of immigrants and no immigrant, even if illegal, should be mistreated. But border security is still important, as is an enforceable system that fairly decides who can enter the country.

- Police misconduct and brutality against people of any race is wrong and we need to reform police conduct and recruitment. But crime is a real problem so more and better policing is needed for public safety. That cannot be provided by "defunding the police."

- There are underlying differences between men and women but discrimination on the basis of gender is wrong.

- There are basically two genders but people who want to live as a gender different from their biological sex should have that right and not be discriminated against. However, there are issues around child consent to transitioning and participation in women's sports that are complicated and not settled.

- Racial achievement gaps are bad, and we should seek to close them. However, they are not due just to racism and standards of high achievement should be maintained for people of all races.

- Language policing has gone too far; by and large, people should be able to express their views without fear of sanction by employer, school, institution or government. Good faith should be assumed, not bad faith.

Besides positively embracing these views it is necessary for major Democratic officeholders and candidates to actively dissociate themselves and their party from the woke stances that contradict these views and tarnish their brand among working class voters. That entails not just saying that one does not endorse now-familiar strands of cultural leftism but in some well-chosen places directly criticizing by name some who hold extreme views that are associated with the Democrats. That will be of great assistance in getting the message through to average working class voters.

Teixeira predicts that some Democratic politicians will be smart enough to take a good deal of this advice at the state, local, and House district level, but not until they receive a 1988-style national repudiation is the party's elite likely to truly internalize the message.

5 – The Progressivism Socialism Madness of the Democratic Party and the Coming Mid-Terms

Credit: Carlos Barria/Reuters - Bernie Sanders.

From *The SAPIENT Being* we start this chapter with the Dr. Raymond M. Berger "Marxism and Progressivism: A Play in Two Acts" article published in June 2018:

Today's progressive movement—different from the American Progressive movement of the late nineteenth century—has repackaged Marxist theory into Critical Race Theory (CRT) with new actors and injustices but the same old drama.

The epic struggle between bourgeoisie and proletariat is replaced by the morally laden struggles between privileged and oppressed actors with new names. In this contemporary version of Marxist drama, people of color are pitted against a white male power structure supported by a mysterious but powerful force of institutional racism. Women are pitted against a male patriarchy that invades not only the workplace but intrudes into the very intimacy of the home to wreak injustice.

As the blinders of the new false consciousness fall from the eyes of the oppressed, new oppressed groups emerge. Some are based on "sexual minority status"—gay people, transsexuals, intersex, non-gender conforming—others on physical traits—the disabled, the unattractive, fat people. In place of an exploitive bourgeoisie there are heterosexists, cis-gender persons, those who exploit the disabled and those who engage in "lookism," that is, those who exploit others due to their appearance.

Added to these colorful actors are the multitude of colonized people of the third world and their exploitive evil colonizers. Because this is a drama, the respective roles of colonizer and colonized are always simplified, with few benefits but much evil attributed to colonization. And even long after the departure of the colonizers from formerly colonized lands, the injustice of the original colonial sin is said to persist, as every problem of the newly independent peoples is attributed to the legacy of colonialism.

In the same way, injustices based on race and ethnicity are said to live on, in the form of the legacy of racism, even after much of the oppression is alleviated.

More recently the world has seen a northward migration of millions from impoverished and violent lands in the south. Amidst the confusion of roles—are these immigrants, migrants, or refugees?—these folks join the long line of oppressed people who are unjustly exploited and abused in their adopted countries. There is nothing more dramatic and poignant than these huddled masses, to use the words of poet Emma Lazarus.

These are new actors (through the lens of CRT) in an old drama around the struggle between persecutor and victim, between exploiter and exploited. Marx's focus on labor has now extended to every conceivable human difference, as if the very existence of difference is morally wrong.

Progressivism as the New Marxism

As shown in *The SAPIENT Being*, in Marx's older drama, the moral imperative of progressives is to once again "set things right." In Marx's time this was the task of revolutionaries. Today this task falls to progressive politicians and activists, social justice reformers, civil rights workers, cultural appropriation enforcers, diversity, and inclusion warriors and the like who have spread into the media, government, college campuses, non-profits, neighborhood organizations and workplaces.

Marxist revolutionaries sought to set things right by leading a revolution to overthrow the capitalist system and replace it with a just economic system. Progressives want to set things right through social change in order to create a just society. In a just society everyone is equal: men and women, immigrants and native-born, persons of various racial and ethnic groups, heterosexuals, and homosexuals, first and third world people, disabled and able-bodied.

This will be a society free from the "isms" of sexism, nativism, racism, heterosexism, colonialism, and ableism.

To the progressive, the success of the newly liberated oppressed person must not be limited by the extent of their talent or effort. Success is merited by the very existence of their membership in an oppressed group. As in Marxist theory—"from each according to his ability, to each according to his needs"—-even people of lesser abilities and efforts deserve equal outcomes.

The progressive sees anything less than this as failure. And worst of all, an unsuspecting American audience has not figured this out yet, but the SAPIENT Being has, as well as other sapient journalists, news casts, and organizations.

How the New Religion of Progressivism Leverages Victimization

As noted in *The SAPIENT Being*, according to the tenets of progressivism—victimization accrues power. Per the Scott Allen twelve post series "Toxic New Religions at The Cultural Roots of Campus Rage," here's how it works:

First, progressives sees reality entirely within the Marxist framework of oppressor and oppressed. Further, the principal oppressors are white, Christian, or Jewish heterosexual males. They are uniquely oppressive, "white supremacists" who have abused cultural power and privilege at the expense of every other group.

These are givens. They function as "core doctrines" of the new religion. Try arguing these points with adherents; they will be incredulous, as if you were asserting a flat earth. These are simply "self-evident" realities. If you are not white, male, Christian/Jewish, heterosexual, you are, by definition, a victim, and victimization accrues power. Ben Shapiro explains how this works:

Progressives rank the value of a view not based on the logic or merit of the view but on the level of victimization in American society experienced by the person espousing the view. An LGBT black woman is automatically considered more correct than a straight white male, before any speech exits either of their mouths.

The fact that victimization accrues power helps explain the wild exaggeration and hyperbole employed by so-called victim groups. The more victimized and oppressed you paint yourself, the more your voice counts.

Progressivism Madness by Way of Postmodernism

As shown in *The SAPIENT Being*, Allen demonstrates how the next "core doctrine" of progressivism builds on the concept of Postmodernism which denies the existence of transcendent, objective truth or morality, so each identity group defines its own reality and morality, not subject to critique by outsiders. This is known as cultural relativism, or multiculturalism.

Even something as simple as enjoying food, clothing, or music from another ethnic group is taken to be an "act of oppression," or in the parlance of the new religion of progressivism, "cultural appropriation."

If a particular Muslim group practices female genital mutilation or honor killing, multiculturalism forbids any value judgment from outside that culture. After all, it is their culture—it is their reality. Who are we to judge? Somali-born Ayaan Hirsi Ali routinely challenges this belief.

At many American universities today, any critical examination pertaining to Islam, including Shariah and the treatment of women in Islam, is declared to be out of the realm of scrutiny. Examinations (i.e., freedom speech) frighten universities more than the litany of honor killings and wholesale abuse of women in so many parts of the Islamic world.

If some racial or ethnic groups suffer from higher rates of poverty, unemployment, drug addiction, or divorce, multiculturalism disallows laying blame on the beliefs or actions of those within the group. In keeping with the first "core doctrine" of group identity, individual belief or action isn't available for consideration.

Rather, the blame must, by default, lie in the larger historical, social, or structural forces. This is why progressives are seemingly obsessed with "systemic or structural" oppression or racism. To attribute negative outcomes to the beliefs or actions of those within the community is "blaming the victim," the cardinal sin for progressives.

Alexandria Ocasio-Cortez (AOC): The Millennial face of Progressivism madness.

Western Civilization as the Ultimate Source of Oppression

There is one major exception to the non-judgmental approach demanded by cultural relativism.

The Judeo-Christian belief system comes in for very harsh critique, usually in the form of attacks against "Western civilization." Because America's history is part of the larger story of Western civilization, this explains the overwhelmingly critical view that adherents of the new religion of Progressivism have towards America and its history.

To progressives, American history and culture, rooted in Judeo-Christian beliefs, is viewed as uniquely oppressive. That is the third "core doctrine," or unquestioned given of the new religion.

If this seems inconsistent, it will make more sense when you realize that this particular view is grounded less in postmodernism, and more in a neo-Marxist ideology. We'll explore this further in the next section.

As Allen explains: To see the world through the lens of Marxism, either in its old or new form, is to see the world exclusively in terms of power relationships—a merciless, zero-sum world of domination, subjugation, and oppression.

In its original form, Marxism was framed in economic terms. The oppressors were bourgeois property owners and capitalists, and the oppressed were the subjugated "workers of the world."

The newer form of Marxism thriving today on university campuses worldwide identifies Western civilization, rooted in a Judeo-Christian belief system, as the ultimate source of oppression. After all, it was this particular culture that gave rise to the capitalist economic system viewed by Marxists new and old as rapacious and destructive.

Western civilization (including the history and culture of the United States) is held by adherents of progressivism to be uniquely oppressive, imperialistic, colonial, racist, sexist, classist, and patriarchal. It has created (in the words of a student activist at Claremont's Pomona University), "interlocking systems of domination that produce the lethal conditions under which oppressed peoples are forced to live."

You might think he's describing life in North Korea, but you'd be wrong. He's talking about life for minorities in America, from his vantage point as a student at one of America's most elite institutions.

Redemption is Available, But Only Under Certain Conditions

If you happen to be a white, Christian (or Jewish), cisgender, heterosexual male, and you have anything positive to say about the contributions of Western civilization to human flourishing, expect to be labeled a "white supremacist." You are imbued with a deep-seated cultural superiority and subconscious racism, sexism, and host of "phobias." You have "privileges" that people of "marginalized identities" do not share, and you continue to enjoy these privileges at their expense.

You must confess and renounce your unconscious racism and white privilege. You must denounce America for her oppressive and violent history, and commit to working for her fundamental transformation, a sort of reverse pledge of allegiance to the flag (or at least a refusal to participate in that exercise which, for generations, marked the beginning of every school day).

You must also actively "ally" with America's many oppressed victims. This is what was seen in the 2020 Democratic Party debates and primaries.

Everyone who is not a white, Christian, heterosexual male, is by definition, an oppressed victim. Women, Muslims, "people of color," LGBTQ+ identity groups—all are victimized in a multitude of ways by the stealthy and diabolically oppressive systems and structures imposed by Western civilization. And while all non-white groups are oppressed, they are not oppressed equally.

"Intersectionality" is the trendy new word coined to describe the complex matrix of oppression. A white woman is oppressed (because she is a woman), but she is not as oppressed as much as a black woman. A black woman who is also a lesbian is still more oppressed still.

According to The Hudson Institute's Heather MacDonald, "individuals who can check off multiple victim boxes experience exponentially higher and more complex levels of life-threatening oppression than lower-status single-category victims." And because victimhood accrues a host of benefits, including status and power, there is a kind of perverse competition—a "victimhood Olympics"—to be seen as the most oppressed of all.

"Victim" identity is critical to the Democrats' success at the ballot box.

If you are an American who does not see yourself as a "victim" of capitalism, racism or misogyny, you likely will be a Republican. But if you view yourself in any way as a "victim" you will likely be a Democrat. Most all of the welfare programs we have are designed for "victims." Democrats love people who become dependent upon government as they know that dependency creates voters. The Black Lives Matter movement was embraced by Democrats, and they even ridiculed anyone who felt that all lives matter. Single mothers with kids are also "victims" as married mothers with kids more often vote Republican.

Identity Politics in Context

From the Frank Newport Gallup December 2021 report "Identity Politics in Context," a key aspect of identifying and controlling the various demographics of victimization is Identity politics.

Identity Politics generally refers to people evaluating issues through the lens of their association with a specific group. This in turn means that approaches to issues, politicians and political parties revolve around how those things affect the relevant group or groups. This can include the conviction that one's group is being oppressed or discriminated against either by larger groups or by society as a whole. Identity politics can also create backlashes among those who disagree with what it means for the rest of society.

No Shortage of Groups With Which to Identify

There are many different groups with which Americans can identify, ranging from those based on ascriptive characteristics (traits we are born with, such as race, ethnicity, sex and social class positioning of one's parents) to those based on circumstances and choices that develop as people move through life, including political party, religious affiliation, geographic location, socioeconomic status, and club and group memberships.

The groups most commonly associated with identity politics in today's political environment center on race, ethnicity, religion, gender and sexual orientation.

An interesting reference point in this regard comes from Joe Biden's 2020 campaign website, on which he listed 19 different identity groups for which he had specific plans. These included tribal nations, women, people with disabilities, Black Americans, military families, union members, rural Americans, older Americans, the LBGTQ+ community, veterans, the Catholic community, students/young Americans, immigrants, the AAPI (Asian American Pacific Islander) community, the Indian American community, the Jewish community, the Muslim American community, the Latino community and the Arab American community. Others would point out that White conservatives or political liberals can also constitute political identity groups.

Criticisms of identity politics tend to center not so much on the idea that people's group identity should be important in their politics, but on ways in which identity politics has been manipulated by its advocates—the progressive and socialist wings of the Democratic Party.

Democrats Embracing Socialism is Dangerous for America

Per the Paris Dennard *The Hill* August 2018 article "Democrats Embracing Socialism is Dangerous for America":

In less than a decade, what at one time seemed to be a small subsection of the Democratic coalition has become its loudest voice. In 2016, the Democratic base came close to handing avowed socialist Sen. Bernie Sanders (I-Vt.) its party's nomination. Reflecting on that election, Hillary Clinton claimed being a capitalist "probably" hurt her campaign. But we all know there was a lot more to point to than being a capitalist that led to her defeat to President Trump.

In June 2018, Alexandria Ocasio-Cortez defeated 10-term incumbent Rep. Joe Crowley in the Democratic primary for New York's 14th Congressional District. Ocasio-Cortez ran on a full-blown socialist platform, which included calls for universal single-payer healthcare, "free" education for all, housing as a human right, guaranteed jobs, and abolishing Immigration and Customs Enforcement. Watch any number of her recent interviews and you will see she even struggles with articulating how to implement her own socialist ideas in our system of government.

When Sanders introduced his socialist healthcare plan—Medicare for All—in Sept. 2017, 16 of Sanders' Senate Democratic colleagues signed on as co-sponsors to the bill. Those cosponsors included other rumored presidential contenders such as Sens. Kirsten Gillibrand of New York, Cory Booker of New Jersey, Kamala Harris of New York, and Elizabeth Warren of Massachusetts.

A number of high-profile Democrats are also embracing the idea of a job guarantee as expressed by Ocasio-Cortez's extreme platform. Booker has devised such a plan, as has Sanders. Gillibrand has also expressed her support for the proposal.

Some Democrats are backing the idea of universal basic income, a policy that is now officially part of the California Democratic Party's platform. Former President Obama recently said that he supports such a policy.

The Democratic Socialists of America (DSA)—to which Ocasio-Cortez belongs—are fast becoming the new face of the Democratic National Committee (DNC). They have already emerged as its loudest voice. The group advocates for things like the abolition of capitalism, the abolition of prisons, socialist healthcare, and calls for the boycott of Israel. In the 2017 local elections, 15 candidates affiliated with DSA were elected on the Democrat ticket.

Socialism Madness is Consuming the Democratic Party

Outlined in the Peter Wehner "The Democratic Party Has Become Radicalized And Their Socialist, Pro-Death And Anti-Israel Agenda Should Be Truly Terrifying To All Americans" Before It's News report in April 2019:

If you want to understand just how radicalized the Democratic Party has become in recent years, look at the ascent of Senator Bernie Sanders of Vermont. A self-proclaimed socialist, Sanders served as mayor of Burlington, Vermont, and was then elected to the House in 1990 and the Senate in 2006. It's hard to overstate just how left-wing Sanders's views have been, at least by the standards of American politics.

For most of his career, Sanders—who identified as an independent but who caucused with Democrats—was treated like a curiosity and even a bit of a crazy uncle by Democrats, who considered the label *socialist* to be a smear.

No more.

The most prominent socialist in America, Sanders has gained a following, and in 2016, he challenged Hillary Clinton for the presidential nomination. He eventually lost, of course, but not before winning roughly 13 million votes and 23 primaries and caucuses against Hillary Clinton, who got 17 million votes and won 34 contests. He electrified Democratic audiences in ways she could not, drawing a crowd of nearly 30,000 in Portland. The hashtag "Feel the Bern" exploded in popularity in 2016. Sanders particularly inspired the younger generation, drawing far more votes in the primaries from those under the age of 30 than did Clinton and Trump combined.

He's not kidding, and he's not alone. Among the freshman class of House Democrats, Alexandria Ocasio-Cortez—now the second-most-famous democratic socialist in America—is the unquestioned star among the base. According to Dan Balz of *The Washington Post*, Ocasio-Cortez is "the titular leader of a progressive grass-roots movement pushing the party to the left." (The mere mention of her name elicits spontaneous applause on programs like "The Late Show With Stephen Colbert.")

To grasp the leftward lurch of the Democratic Party more fully, it's useful to run through some of the ideas that are now being seriously talked about and embraced by leading members of the party—ideas that together would be fiscally ruinous, invest massive and unwarranted trust in central planners, and weaken America's security.

- **The Green New Deal**, a 10-year effort to eliminate fossil fuels "as much as is technologically feasible" that would completely transform the American economy, put the federal government in partial or complete control over large sectors, and retrofit every building in America. It would change the way we travel and eat, switch the entire electrical grid to renewable energy sources, and for good measure "guarantee" high-paying jobs, affordable housing, and universal health care. It would be astronomically costly and constitute by far the greatest centralization of power in American history.

- **Medicare for all**, which would greatly expand the federal role in health care. Some versions would wipe out the health-insurance industry and do away with employer-sponsored health plans that now cover roughly 175 million Americans. This would be hugely disruptive and unpopular (70 percent of Americans are happy with their coverage), and would exacerbate the worst efficiencies of an already highly inefficient program.

- **Make college tuition-free and debt-free,** with the no-debt promise including both tuition and living expenses—a highly expensive undertaking ($50 billion a year or so just for the federal government)—that would transfer money from less wealthy families whose children do not attend college to wealthier families whose children do. It could also have potentially devastating effects on many private, not-for-profit colleges.

- **Increase the top marginal tax rate** to 70 percent from its current rate of 37 percent for those making more than $10 million, unwise in the 21st-century economy and far above the average top rate for OECD nations; and impose a "wealth tax" that would levy a 2 percent annual tax on a household's assets—including stocks, real estate, and retirement funds—above $50 million. It isn't even clear whether a tax on wealth rather than income would be constitutional, but that almost seems beside the point.

- **Abolish the U.S. Immigration and Customs Enforcement (ICE),** which upholds immigration laws; protect "sanctuary cities" (local jurisdictions that don't fully cooperate with federal efforts to find and deport unauthorized immigrants); and take down existing walls on the southern border, walls which Speaker Nancy Pelosi has referred to as "an immorality." These policies signal that Democrats don't really believe in border security and are mostly untroubled by illegal immigration.

- **Eliminate the Senate filibuster**, pack the courts, and put an end to the Electoral College. The effect of these would be to weaken protections against abuses of majority power.

- **Reparations for African Americans** to provide compensation for past injustices like slavery, Jim Crow laws, and redlining. (Senator Elizabeth Warren believes Native Americans should be included as well.) Reparations would pose countless practical problems and create unintended consequences, as David Frum argued in these pages.

- **Opposition to any limits on even third-trimester abortions**, and opposition to the Born-Alive Abortion Survivors Protection Act, legislation clarifying that babies who survive attempted abortions must receive medical care. Abortion is a very difficult issue that requires empathy on all sides—but for many of us, this stance of Democrats is morally incomprehensible.

- **Increasing antipathy aimed at Israel**, one of the most estimable nations in the world. Two freshmen Democrats, Representatives Ilhan Omar and Rashida Tlaib, have embraced the boycott, divestment, and sanctions movement targeting Israel, and House Democratic leaders faced a fierce backlash in their efforts to condemn the anti-Semitic remarks by Omar, who has a record of anti-Semitic comments and who most recently accused supporters of Israel of dual loyalties. (The Democratic House, unable to pass a measure that focused solely on anti-Semitism, eventually passed a resolution condemning "hateful expressions of intolerance.")

To be sure, these views are not embraced by all Democrats—but they are ideas that are gaining adherents, including among several 2020 presidential candidates, and are fundamentally reshaping and radicalizing the Democratic Party.

On every front, the Democratic Party is moving left, and the power of the left can be seen in the fact that even Democrats who oppose some of these policies are wary of attacking them. When it comes to challenging the progressive wing, Democratic candidates act as if they are walking on eggshells.

Biden is Handing the Midterms to the GOP

From the Timothy Head *The Hill* March 2022 article "Biden is Handing the Midterms to the GOP":

President Biden is losing voters from key groups left and right, and this exodus of voters shouldn't surprise anyone who has been paying attention. He made a lot of big promises to win in 2020 and has delivered on very few of them. Take a look at his State of the Union address, and you'll find a long list of problems for which he failed to take responsibility.

All of these voters, it seems, are abandoning Biden because they're tired of failure.

Due to the adverse effects of progressivism and socialism on the Democratic Party, a growing number of people in politics—including many from the left—believe that both the Biden/Harris White House and the Democratic Party are damaged brands. Granted, in politics the negative can often be flipped back to the positive in a matter of weeks or months.

Biden promised to unite the country, but more than half of Americans think he is divisive. He vowed to end the pandemic; instead, he sent small businesses around the country into a financial crisis by prolonging pandemic-related restrictions. He pledged he would solve the crisis at America's southern border, but he has just tried to hide it. He promised economic prosperity, but inflation has hit a 40-year high and gas prices just broke the national record.

Ordinary Americans are bearing the brunt of this.

That said, people are expressing legitimate concerns about President Biden's cognitive health; the continuing staff exits from Vice President Kamala Harris's team, combined with stories of dysfunction in her office; ongoing fallout from the pandemic and the policies associated with it; escalating inflation; punishing fuel costs; supply shortages; rising crime in major cities; serious security and immigration issues at our southern border; the seeming dismissal of parental rights with the regard to the education of children; and a Democratic Party held hostage by the "woke" fringe of its base.

All this would seem to indicate that such a turnaround for the current occupants of the White House is unlikely.

You Don't Need to Be a Fortune Teller: Signs Point to GOP Sweep This Year

Per the Alan Greenblatt *Governing* May 2022 report "You Don't Need to Be a Fortune Teller: Signs Point to GOP Sweep This Year":

The president's party always loses seats in midterms. This year, just about everything—fundraising, voter enthusiasm, demographic shifts, the issues mix—is going the right way for

Republicans. For Democrats this year, the only real question is whether the elections will be only moderately bad or completely terrible.

If you think like a weather forecaster, all kinds of data point to a major storm. By basically every metric you can think of—fundraising, candidate recruitment, voter enthusiasm, demographic shifts—a big wave is forming that will sweep hundreds of Democrats out of office, up and down the ticket.

The main reason isn't hard to figure out. Every president can count on his party losing seats in midterms, but President Biden's approval ratings are particularly bad. On average, 41 percent of Americans approve of the job he's doing, compared with 54 percent who disapprove. "That is one of the lowest marks of any president since World War II," says Henry Olsen, a conservative analyst at the Ethics and Public Policy Center. "Unless that changes, I would expect a solid Democratic defeat."

Granted, President Donald Trump's approval ratings were similarly bargain basement in 2018—but then, Republicans lost control of the House that year, along with seven governorships. The more important comparison, at any rate, is not with Trump but with Biden himself. Biden won the presidency in 2020 by 4.5 points. If he's down 13, that represents a huge drop in support, which seriously imperils his party.

Swing voters have swung hard against Biden. His net approval rating among independents is roughly minus 20. That's a group he carried in 2020 by 13 points, according to exit polls.

We've already witnessed a demonstration of how the president's numbers can drag down other Democrats. Last November, Biden's net disapproval numbers were 12.5 percent points lower than his victory margin in 2020. Guess what? The swing from Biden's share of the vote to that won in 2020 by the Democratic candidates for governor was 12 points. Gov. Phil Murphy managed barely to hold on in New Jersey, but Democrat Terry McAuliffe lost the governorship to Republican Glenn Youngkin in Virginia—a state Biden had carried a year earlier by 10 points.

Now, Biden's numbers are even lower than they were back in November. This means any Democrat who won their last election by less than double-digit margins should be nervous. That certainly includes vulnerable governors such as Tony Evers of Wisconsin and Laura Kelly of Kansas.

"The president's dismal ratings are what people care about the most," says GOP consultant David Carney. "It could be a bloodbath up and down the ballot, from the school board to Congress."

There are several known unknowns that could shift the landscape between now and Nov. 8. Inflation might tick lower and the war in Ukraine may have played out in a way that helps Biden politically. Perhaps the school shooting in Texas will activate voters in a way that other mass shootings have failed to do. An NPR/Marist poll released last week found that the expected Supreme Court action to overturn Roe v. Wade should help energize Democrats. Sixty-six percent of Democrats said it would make them more likely to vote this fall, versus 40 percent of Republicans.

"There are two big things that we don't know yet how they will play: The first one is the Jan. 6 committee and its hearings, and the second one is this abortion decision," says Lara Brown, a political scientist at George Washington University. "Depending on how those capture the attention of the country and different demographics, I do think that can impact the magnitude of whatever wave the Republicans are looking at."

But in the weeks since Justice Samuel Alito's majority opinion on abortion law was leaked, there's been no evidence of a surge in Democratic participation in primaries or early voting. Not even any real uptick.

"I'd be surprised if Roe v. Wade did not energize the marginal Democratic voter, the sort that would usually vote in the presidential race but not necessarily in the midterm, but that only gets you so far," Olsen says. "The real game is the swing voter."

Undoing Obama's Coalition

Biden's old boss, Barack Obama, put together a winning coalition during his presidency, combining college-educated whites with young, Black and Latino voters. The danger for Democrats is that Biden appears to be unraveling that coalition. About the only groups still solidly in his camp are dedicated members of the Democratic base, such as Black voters and college-educated women.

Biden carried close to two-thirds of Hispanic voters in 2020, but their shift toward Trump, compared to 2016, was notable, especially in states such as Florida and Texas. In the Texas primaries in March this year, participation in GOP primaries was up dramatically in heavily Hispanic portions of South Texas that traditionally have been overwhelmingly Democratic.

An NPR/Marist poll released last month found that 52 percent of Latinos say they're more likely to support Republican candidates for Congress; just 39 percent favor Democrats.

Young voters have been a particular problem for Biden. Voters under 30 favored Biden over Trump, 60 percent to 39 percent, in 2020, but they've soured on him since. Biden's approval rating among young voters has dropped by 18 points over the past year, according to a Harvard Institute of Politics poll—which is in line with what other pollsters are finding.

Even as Democrats shed support among Latinos, young voters and parents, the party's longstanding problem with working-class white voters continues to worsen. The April NPR/Marist poll found Democrats are only favored by a third of white voters without college degrees, compared to 55 percent who say they are likely to support Republicans.

"The people who are left backing Biden are the people who would back any Democrat under anything except extreme circumstances," Olsen says. "That's a terrible place to be in for an election. You've lost America's middle."

Generically Bad

Regarding the 100-seat Senate, which is currently tied, if there are relatively few Democratic seats in play this year, meaning each race will count enormously. Still, Republicans have enough opportunities not only to win the majority but come away with a total of perhaps 53 or 54 seats.

The GOP needs only five seats to take control of the 435-member House. Redistricting has turned out to be more or less a wash, but on net Republicans gained a slight advantage. A lot of GOP-tilted seats have been fortified against all but the worst-case scenarios, while Democrats hold more seats that are marginal.

They'll have little protection in a wave year. There's hardly any ticket-splitting, with voters favoring candidates of one party or the other up and down the ballot. There are only 16 seats in the House where the district voted one way for president in 2020 and the other for Congress.

The players matter, but sometimes the playing field matters more. In the most competitive House districts, generic Republicans are leading generic Democrats by 47 percent to 39 percent. That's according to internal polling by the Democratic Congressional Campaign Committee.

Messaging and Money

The gap between the numbers of Democrats and Republicans retiring from Congress is the highest it's been in decades. At the legislative level, Republicans are leaving fewer seats open than Democrats.

Republicans raised $170 million from January to March through WinRed, an online fundraising platform. That still lags the Democrats' ActBlue, which has traditionally been much more robust, but represents nearly a one-quarter jump for WinRed over the same period in 2020. The Republican Governors Association raised $33 million in the first quarter of the year, which was nearly $10 million more than the Democratic Governors Association. The Republican State Leadership Committee brought in just over $10 million, compared with $6.5 million for the Democratic Legislative Campaign Committee.

Who Will Turn Out?

In the end, voter behavior matters most of all. Again, the GOP has a big advantage.

A slew of polls have showed large and indeed growing gaps in terms of levels of enthusiasm about voting this year between Republicans and Democrats. But we don't have to rely strictly on polls any more. We're still relatively early in the primary season, but Republicans are showing up in ways that Democrats are not.

In the first 10 states to hold primaries in 2022, Republicans received 61 percent of the total vote, according to an analysis by GOP pollster John Couvillon. The party generating more enthusiasm in primaries has fared quite well in the last few midterms. Democrats received 54 percent of the primary vote in 2018—a solid midterm year for them—while Republicans got 55 percent in both 2010 and 2014, landslide years for the party.

It's true that primary turnout isn't a perfect measure, since not all races are equally competitive. For example, Stacey Abrams was unopposed for the Democratic nomination for governor of Georgia, while GOP Gov. Brian Kemp faced a contentious, if ultimately easy, contest against former Sen. David Perdue. Turnout on the GOP side increased by a half-million votes, compared to the 2018 primary.

But looking at the total picture, it's clear more Republicans are turning out. A lot more Republicans. Overall Republican primary turnout is up 32 percent, while Democratic turnout has actually declined 3 percent.

All this paints a pretty grim picture for Democrats. They're running behind on the issues that concern voters most. Their leader is losing support among key constituencies. Their potential candidates are less likely to run, while their voters are less likely to turn out.

It's clear that Republicans will be stronger at the end of the year than they are now. It's not yet possible to say how much stronger, but if anyone offers to bet you Democrats will retain power in Congress, take their money. At the state level, GOP victories may not be as momentous, but that's only because they already hold majorities among governors, legislators and legislative chambers.

For Republicans, it's beginning to look a lot like Christmas will fall early this year, on Nov. 8.

6 – The Mainstream Media's Democratic Party & White House Collusion, Fake News & Lies

Wide partisan differences in views about social media companies labeling posts from elected officials as misleading or inaccurate

% of U.S. adults who say they ___ of social media companies labeling posts on their platforms from elected officials as inaccurate or misleading

	Disapprove	Approve
U.S. adults	46	51
Rep/Lean Rep	71	27
Dem/Lean Dem	25	73

% of U.S. adults who say they have ___ (of) confidence in social media companies to determine which posts on their platforms should be labeled as innaccurate or misleading

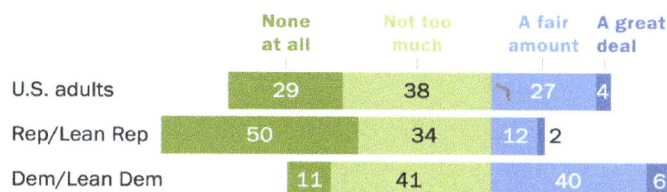

	None at all	Not too much	A fair amount	A great deal
U.S. adults	29	38	27	4
Rep/Lean Rep	50	34	12	2
Dem/Lean Dem	11	41	40	6

Note: Strongly/somewhat approve or disapprove responses are combined. Those who did not give an answer are not shown.
Source: Survey of U.S. adults conducted June 16-22, 2020.
"Most Americans Think Social Media Sites Censor Political Viewpoints"

PEW RESEARCH CENTER

From *Fake News Madness*, a recent 2020 landmark poll of 20,000 citizens undertaken by the Knight Foundation and Gallup found that Americans' hope for and trust in an objective media is all but lost. They see not only an ever-growing partisanship in news reporting but a determination by the mainstream media to push a political agenda instead of honestly disseminating the news.

While generic faith in the media has been gradually declining over recent decades, the precipitous drop in trust and questions about what motivates the mainstream media can be traced to June 2015 and Donald Trump's entry into the presidential sweepstakes.

This latest poll is the most devastating indictment of the media in polling history. Some highlights:

- 84% of surveyed Americans lay either a moderate or a great deal of the blame for today's partisan hostility at the feet of the media.

- Further, 82% believe news outlets are either deliberately "misrepresenting the facts" or are "making them up entirely".

- This is further amplified as 79% of those surveyed say media outlets are trying to persuade people to adopt a certain opinion about an issue or an individual.

- Similarly, while the respondents in the poll believe that the media is "critical" or "very important" to democracy, 86% say they have witnessed either a fair amount or a great deal of bias in news reporting. Damningly, 78% feel that this bias is reflected in the spread of fake news which "is a major" problem" that exceeds all other in the mainstream media environment.

- By contrast, in 2007 62% of respondents in a Pew Research poll claimed to have witnessed either a fair amount or a great deal of bias in news reporting; in another Pew Research poll in 2012, that result increased slightly to 67% as compared to 86% today. How did the mainstream media sink to this abysmal level of distrust and disdain?

Donald Trump's entry into the presidential field in 2015 was a godsend to the mainstream media that had been hemorrhaging red ink for many years. The denizens of the mainstream media hierarchies knew that unremitting coverage of Trump, a global celebrity, would dramatically increase viewership, clicks on the internet and newspaper readership and thus their bottom line.

However, Donald Trump, during the campaign, continuously pointed out the left-wing bias and misreporting in the mainstream media and popularized a phrase that is now part of the American lexicon: fake news. With ridicule and mockery, he succeeded in making the media a potent campaign issue and a focal point of voter resentment.

While the vast majority of those in the mainstream media seethed at this disparagement, they, certain in the final outcome of the election, continued their unrestrained reporting and coverage of his every movement and utterance as their ratings and readership went through the roof.

No entity in the United States was more devastatingly affected by the 9.0 magnitude political earthquake that took place on November 8, 2016 than the mainstream media. Not only had they contributed mightily to the election of Donald Trump, a man they loathed, but they had willingly allowed him to make them the target of national derision and contempt.

The Hunter Biden Story Goes Mainstream

Per the Judson Berger *National Review* April 2022 article "The Hunter Biden Story Goes Mainstream":

By now, it is abundantly clear that American news outlets—and the social-media giants that determine their reach—not only missed but actively suppressed one of the biggest stories of the 2020 election.

Recall, for a moment, how the *New York Post* was treated after breaking the news on the trove of data recovered from a laptop left with a Delaware repair shop, showing details of Hunter Biden's financial dealings in Ukraine and with Chinese energy company CEFC. Andrew McCarthy, in NR's latest issue, gives the recap of that episode:

Twitter locked the account of the Post—the nation's oldest continuously published newspaper and its fourth largest by circulation—as well as accounts of Trump advocates who attempted to circulate reports on Hunter's laptop. Other social-media platforms followed suit. Journalists speculatively questioned the provenance of the laptop data and former intel officials simultaneously pushed the claim that this might all be the work of Russian disinformation artists. That was enough to kill it. End of story.

Until now. The *New York Times* has authenticated key files from Hunter Biden's abandoned laptop. So has the *Washington Post*, while noting that this level of confidence extends to thousands of emails but not other chunks of data in its possession purportedly from Hunter's laptop. (*The Washington Post's* verification efforts in 2020 apparently were stymied in part by Trump allies' refusal to cooperate.) The *Wall Street Journal*, meanwhile, says a federal tax probe into Hunter is "gaining momentum," and prosecutors are looking at his sources of foreign income. The *Times* says the tax inquiry has widened to include possible violations of "foreign lobbying and money laundering rules."

So the story was a story after all. We're getting lab-leak déjà vu over here. Andy says the president's son is likely looking at indictment, one way or another, even if his back taxes are paid up now.

The latest reports are careful to note that evidence does not at this stage demonstrate wrongdoing or knowledge by the president concerning various transactions by his son. White House chief of staff Ron Klain has defended Hunter while also stressing that his dealings "don't involve the president."

But the focus is turning to President Biden, and it's not hard to understand why.

This week, we learned that a grand-jury witness reportedly has been asked to ID the individual referred to as the "big guy" in an infamous email discussing equity distributions for those involved in a deal with CEFC China Energy Co. The email seemingly discussed the possibility of a 10 percent cut for said "big guy," and one former partner has alleged that this referred to Joe Biden. Andy flags another emerging detail here, concerning a college recommendation letter, that raises suspicion about the elder Biden's level of awareness of his son's business pursuits.

As for what made this case newsworthy in the first place, the *Washington Post's* multi-article treatment of Hunter's name-trading reprises the cringey details: Nearly $5 million paid by the "Chinese energy conglomerate and its executives" to "entities controlled by" Hunter and his uncle. An agreement to represent a CEFC official later convicted in the U.S. in a bribery scheme. A getting-to-know-you diamond gift. Rich Lowry calls the particulars "jaw dropping":

The company sought to extend Chinese influence as part of Beijing's "Belt and Road" initiative. The founder of CEFC, Ye Jianming, roped in Hunter Biden, infamously giving him a 2.8-carat diamond after their first meeting. Everyone knew the score.

Big Tech Stole the 2020 Election by Weaponizing Platforms

From the Corinne Weaver Free Speech America December 2020 "SPECIAL REPORT: Big Tech Stole 2020 Election by Weaponizing Platforms" article: Big Tech companies, outraged at President Donald Trump's win in 2016, put everything they had into ensuring that he would lose in 2020.

In seven key swing states, one in seven Biden voters (14 percent) said they primarily relied on sites such as Facebook or Twitter for their election news, according to a survey from the Media Research Center (MRC) conducted by The Polling Company, which polled 1,750 Biden voters in seven swing states. But on Twitter and Facebook, conservatives, Trump supporters, and news that damaged the Biden campaign were regularly stifled, especially in the months leading up to the 2020 election.

Campaign messages only have value when they are heard. Trump and his campaign suffered the most in the censorship melee. Before the election, Twitter and Facebook had censored them 65 times but left former Vice President and Democratic presidential nominee, Joe Biden, unscathed. Twitter was the bulk of the problem, with 98 percent of all the instances of censorship.

A bombshell *New York Post* report implicating former Vice President Joe Biden and his son, Hunter Biden, in corrupt dealings in Ukraine was almost immediately suppressed on both Facebook and Twitter. The Post reported on "smoking-gun email[s]" that purportedly revealed "how Hunter Biden introduced Ukrainian businessman" to his father, the then vice president.

Polling showed that if all Biden voters had known about this story, enough would have changed their votes to swing the election to Trump. The same story that the Post was banned for is in every publication now, from *The New York Times* to CNN. After the election, of course.

A similar incident happened when the Post released a story showing Biden's corrupt dealings with China. In a separate national survey, four percent of all Biden voters, had they known the story, would not have voted for Biden.

According to an Analysis Done by *Newsweek*, the Suppression Worked

The *Post's* story only reached roughly half the audience that other viral news stories reached on Facebook. Anti-Trump stories like The *New York Times* story on Trump's taxes reached roughly 5.37 million people, while the *Post* story only reached about 1.94 million.

The denial of facts from the liberal media left voters in the dark. Many Biden voters were not aware of the broad censorship Big Tech companies used to silence conservatives and Trump supporters.

Thirty-four percent of Biden voters were not aware that Trump had been censored by Twitter and Facebook, while Biden was not censored at all, according to the poll from The Polling Company. Fifty-two percent of Biden voters were not aware that Antifa pages were allowed on Facebook, while many conservative pages had been taken down. Sixty percent of Biden voters were not aware that Facebook and Twitter prevented users from mocking or posting satire of Biden and his campaign.

But Big Tech denies it censors conservatives every time while finding new ways to suppress, label, and remove information posted on their platforms. The liberal media insist that tech companies are not removing content, but still urge Facebook, Twitter, and Google to do more to remove ideas and opinions that go against their established narrative. From criticism of mail-in ballots to satirical posts about Biden, Big Tech took them all down. YouTube's latest policy that will ban content that contests the 2020 election results is proof of the overwhelming direction toward censorship.

Big Tech Strongly Supported Biden

Companies like Facebook, Google, and Twitter picked sides before the election and used all their power to further the win.

Ninety percent of donations from Twitter and Facebook employees went to Democratic campaigns, according to OpenSecrets.org. Facebook contributed 91.68 percent ($2,409,464 out of $2,628,040) of its donations to Democrats collectively between individual donations ($2,400,269) and PAC donations ($234,000) equaling $200 or more.

Affiliates of Alphabet, Inc., Microsoft, Amazon, Facebook, and Apple donated $10,243,589 to the Biden campaign during the 2020 presidential race, according to OpenSecrets. Trump received only $427,047 from the aforementioned Big Tech companies.

When the left embraced mail-in ballots, so did Big Tech. But that meant a hasty suppression of any criticism of mail-in voting. A letter from the Biden campaign, obtained by Axios, proclaimed that Donald Trump Jr.'s public statements of concern over mail-in voting were dangerous to democracy itself. Biden specifically condemned the platform for allowing "this dangerous claptrap to be spread to millions of people."

The liberal media, including CNN and TechCrunch, previously had warned about the dangers of mail-in ballots. "Yet votes cast by mail are less likely to be counted, more likely to be compromised and more likely to be contested than those cast in a voting booth, statistics show," wrote The *New York Times* in 2012.

Trump was fact-checked by Twitter for condemning "Mail-In Ballots" as "substantially fraudulent" in May 2020. GOP Chairwoman Ronna McDaniel called out Twitter for censoring critiques of mail-in voting earlier this year: "Twitter falsely claims there is no evidence of mail-in ballot fraud." She added: "That's odd since NJ's all-mail primary this month was 'plagued' by fraud concerns, with 3,000 votes set aside." The censorship seemed to come as a response to criticism from the Biden campaign.

Big Tech Censorship and Mediacrats Collusion

Mediacrats is an often used term throughout the *MADNESS* textbooks to mean that the liberal media and Democrats are closely aligned in their philosophical views and association with each other. Big Tech companies wield an incredible amount of power when it comes to informing and influencing their users. They knew it and abused that power to help steal a presidential election.

Google Responsible Innovation Head Jen Gennai was caught on camera by Project Veritas in 2019 saying, "We're training our algorithms, like, if 2016 happened again, would we have … would the outcome be different?" Gennai bragged that Google was going to prevent "the next Trump situation."

Forbes wrote that "72% of U.S. citizens of voting age actively use some form of social media." More than 172 million potential voters were subject to the subtle changes online. Feeds were manipulated, conservative politicians were censored, and stories were suppressed in order to affect these voters in some way.

Both Facebook and Twitter continued to manipulate what they allowed users to see even after the election. Facebook modified its feed to restrict conservative sites and emphasize traditional news outlets who pride themselves on being against Trump.

It affected voters, according to the MRC survey: One of every six Biden voters surveyed (17%) said they would have abandoned the Democratic candidate had they known the facts about one of eight key stories about either Biden or Trump. The Hunter Biden story was the strongest example out of the eight and 9.4 percent of those surveyed said that would have caused them to change their vote—if they had known about it.

Big Tech proved that they were out to influence the election by continuing to hammer Trump into the ground with censorship even after all was over. Trump and his campaign have been censored at least 486 times on Twitter, with more than 400 of those instances occurring after November 3.

If liberal Big Tech companies have so much power and influence to manipulate an election, can any election really be fair? That's the question that both political parties, Congress and the federal government must address. Before the next election.

NewsGuard Ratings System Heavily Skews in Favor of Left-Wing Outlets

From the Joseph Vazquez Free Speech America December 2021 article "STUDY: NewsGuard Ratings System Heavily Skews in Favor of Left-Wing Outlets":

A new analysis reveals the extraordinary left-wing bias of website ratings firm NewsGuard (a left leaning biased content rating service being used by many organizations unsapiently), which should concern every American given that it is expanding its reach into cable and broadcast TV news. Liberal outlets were rated 27 points higher on average than news organizations on the right.

MRC Free Speech America analyzed the NewsGuard ratings of media outlets based on a list compiled by AllSides classified by their "bias" on a left-to-right scale. The average NewsGuard score for the "left" and "lean left" outlets—which included leftist outlets like Jacobin and *The Nation*—was 93/100. While the average rating for "right" and "lean right" outlets—which included Fox News, *Washington Times* and *New York Post*—was a low 66/100. That's a 27 point disparity.

According to NewsGuard's skewed ratings, left-leaning outlets have substantially more "credibility" on average than right-leaning outlets which is clearly not the case as documented and proven in *Fake News Madness: A SAPIENT Being's Guide to Spotting Fake News Media & How to Help Fight and Eliminate It (Winter 2021)*.

There were 31 total outlets listed as "left" or "lean left" and 24 outlets listed as "right" or "lean right" by AllSides. AllSides included the opinion sections of news websites separately. MRC Free Speech America excluded any outlet that was characterized as "opinion" to keep the focus on news organizations for the analysis.

NewsGuard's Skewed Ratings Are Very Disturbing

The trend is very disturbing, given that NewsGuard is reportedly expanding its partnership with IPG Mediabrands to co-create "the first-ever tool to evaluate and rate individual broadcast and cable news programs and networks," according to a press release. "The new rankings will encompass 117 shows on 27 networks and will launch in spring 2022."

Even the liberal Poynter Institute cited two media experts who shared "praise for the stated methods for rating bias" by AllSides. Poynter is the same institution that attempted to blacklist 29 conservative outlets in 2019 and is funded by prominent liberal billionaires, including George Soros and Pierre Omidyar. However, AllSides including Deseret News in its "lean right" list is disputed by MRC research.

The breakdown of the lists of outlets is even more revealing in terms of their individual grades. Socialist site Jacobin scored an astonishing "92.5" by NewsGuard. The same outlet published Marxist propaganda in October headlined: "Socialism Isn't Just About State Ownership—It's About Redistributing Power." In April 2020, Jacobin published a piece celebrating how "[s]ocialism is back on the agenda in the United States, thank God. And today's newly minted socialists shouldn't be afraid to embrace Marxism."

By comparison, The Federalist, posted in the "right" AllSides list, was scored the worst with a ridiculous "12.5" on NewsGuard. A predominant reason for the abysmal rating, according to NewsGuard, was that The Federalist questioned the efficacy of mask mandates for COVID-19, even though liberal CNBC (not on the AllSides list, but has a "95" NewsGuard rating) cited a study showing that cloth masks were only 37 percent effective at filtering out virus particles. Another August preprint study did not find an "association between mask mandates or use and reduced COVID-19 spread in US states."

That's not all. *The Nation*, which also scored a high "92.5," is the same outlet that published a 2020 piece defending "property destruction" as integral to the success of a left-wing "uprising" following the murder of George Floyd. The piece advocated for property violence: "Given that capitalism largely restricts pleasure to the consumption of goods, we should be able to entertain the idea that this taking of unnecessary things—while not a recognizably political act—is understandable or even a [sic] justifiable." [Emphasis added.]

Leftist outlet *Mother Jones* even managed to secure a notable "87.5" rating by NewsGuard. In a report headlined, "The media's epic fail," Axios slapped down the liberal media for pushing the discredited 2017 Steele dossier used to tie former President Donald Trump to Russia. Axios called the occurrence "one of the most egregious journalistic errors in modern history, and the media's response to its own mistakes has so far been tepid." *Mother Jones*, one of the outlets that the FBI reportedly used to corroborate the dossier, was stiff-necked and deflected responsibility away for pushing the Steele falsehoods. According to Axios:

Mother Jones Washington bureau chief David Corn began reporting about the dossier prior to the 2016 election. Asked by [*Washington Post* media critic Erik] Wemple whether he planned to correct the record, Corn said, 'My priority has been to deal with the much larger topic of Russia's undisputed attack and Trump's undisputed collaboration with Moscow's cover-up.' Corn did not respond to a request to speak on the record with Axios.

Liberal Fake News and Mediacrat Publications Receive Biased Scores

One of Corn's reports promoting Christopher Steele in 2017 remains on the *Mother Jones* website with no editor's note correcting the record. Still, NewsGuard rewarded *Mother Jones* with a strong grade of "87.5." This is damning, given that one of NewsGuard's five criteria for "credibility" includes: "Regularly corrects or clarifies errors." [Emphasis added.]

In addition, "[t]he site makes clear how to report an error or complaint, has effective practices for publishing clarifications and corrections, and notes corrections in a transparent way." *Mother Jones* was given a green checkmark for this criteria in its rating.

Here's a real doozy: BuzzFeed News, which "made waves in 2017 by publishing the entire [Steele] dossier, sa[id] it has no plans to take the document down." According to Axios, "[The dossier] is still online, accompanied by a note that says, 'The allegations are unverified, and the report contains errors,'" even though a key source for the document was charged with "lying" to the FBI. NewsGuard still awarded the outlet a perfect "100" score.

Liberal magazine *The Atlantic*, whose editor-in-chief Jeffrey Goldberg became notorious for publishing a shoddy report in 2020 that dubiously claimed Trump called veterans "losers" and "suckers," scored a perfect "100." Anti-Trumper and former Trump national security advisor John Bolton reportedly slammed Goldberg's propaganda as "'simply false.'" The magazine even absurdly attacked satire site The Babylon Bee for mocking leftists in a piece headlined: "The Christians Who Mock Wokeness for a Living."

In fact, some of the most notorious liberal outlets in the AllSides chart received a string of "100" scores for their so-called "credibility": *The New York Times, The Washington Post,* NBC News, Politico, *The New Yorker, TIME,* Yahoo! News, *The Guardian, The Economist* and *USA Today*. To quote billionaire Oprah Winfrey, "You get a car! You get a car! You get a car!"

Only two "lean-right" outlets on the AllSides list were given "100" scores by NewsGuard, both of which happen to be the Democrat-favoring Deseret News and the anti-Trump Reason magazine. Another anti-Trump outlet listed in the "lean right" AllSides list was The Dispatch, which received a "92.5" score from NewsGuard. It appears NewsGuard is more willing to award great scores to "lean right" sites that ironically publish pro-liberal content it approves.

The liberal HuffPost, which published an attack piece on then-conservative talk radio host Rush Limbaugh following his death headlined "Rush Limbaugh, Bigoted King of Talk Radio, Dies at 70," scored a "87.5" by NewsGuard.

The 'Fox News Fallacy' Explains a Lot

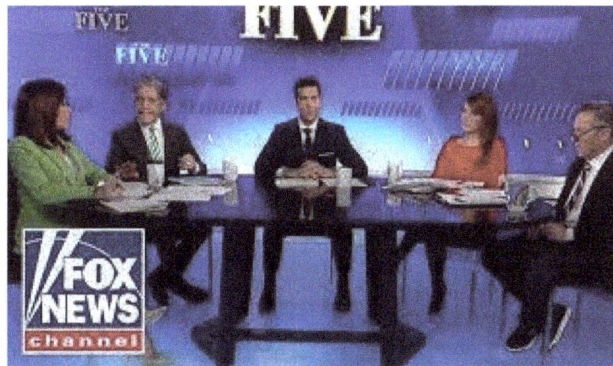

Credit: Fox News - The Five newscast.

Per the Judson Berger *National Review* April 2022 article "The 'Fox News Fallacy' Explains a Lot":

Ruy Teixeira, co-author of 2002's *The Emerging Democratic Majority*, warns his own party that it is out of step with voters and in "deep trouble" if it can't course-correct. He pinpoints three areas where the Democratic brand suffers most: culture, economics, and patriotism. He also has coined a term that explains a lot. It's called, in his words, the "Fox News fallacy."

Teixeira explains what he means by the Fox News fallacy:

The Trump years further deepened the influence of identity politics on the Democratic Party, particularly in the wake of the nationwide protest movement following the murder of George Floyd. That left its stamp on the 2020 edition of the Democratic Party, notwithstanding their old-school standard-bearer, Joe Biden.

It has also left its stamp on how Democrats have handled difficult cultural issues since the election. They have fallen prey to what I have termed the "Fox News fallacy"—the idea that, if Fox News and the like are criticizing the Democrats on an issue, the criticism must be unsound, and the disputed policy should be defended at all costs. That reflex has not served the Democrats well as Biden's term has evolved.

Spot on. I used to work at that company. Do Fox News programming and articles aggressively highlight Democratic liabilities and play up issues that constitute political problems for them? Why yes, yes they do. That's the model, essentially the inverse of what CNN did through the Trump era.

But Democrats fell into the pattern that Teixeira describes, using the Fox News gaze as reason alone to discount the problems being spotlighted—never mind that Fox has a robust news division, verifying and reporting out the stories that later serve fodder to prime-time.

Teixeira ticks off several examples of the fallacy in action, including with critical race theory, saying, "Democrats refuse to admit that there might be a problem here." Fox News aireth, ergo it's not really happening. That, or, the logic goes, the network is applying the Hubble telescope to a match to simulate a firestorm.

For instance, one Media Matters piece, published three weeks before Terry McAuliffe lost his gubernatorial battle in Virginia, echoed the Democrat's insistence that concerns about CRT in the schools were overblown. How did they know? Fox News, that's how.

Dems Need 'Fox News Shock Therapy' Sessions

From *Fake News Madness,* overall, using a more recent confirmation of this analysis, in August 2020, Media Research Center (MRC) President Brent Bozell responded to the new nationwide survey confirming that Americans overwhelmingly trust the Fox News Channel more than any other network per his report as follows:

"The proof is in the pudding. Americans want balanced news, not liberal advocacy." Fox offered them 'fair and balanced' journalism, and America has embraced them. "In terms of quantity, Fox has been pulling the highest numbers for quite some time."

"Now comes the quality meter, the new polling data showing that Fox News is also the most trusted name in news," states Bozell. "In fact, no one comes close. Fox is trusted a staggering 10 percentage points above any other network. And it is the only network to earn more trust (49%) than distrust (37%) among those polled.

"Liberal politicians and liberal journalists who regularly bash Fox News need to realize it is *they* who are completely out of touch with the American people. The bottom line is that Americans now trust Fox far more than any other network. Liberal bias has come back to bite the networks where it hurts.

The poll was conducted by the Public Policy Polling between January 18—19, 2020, and found that among the 1,151 registered voters they surveyed, Fox crushed the other networks in trust as follows:

- 49% trusted the Fox News Channel, 10 percentage points more than any other network.

- 39% said they trusted CNN.

- 35% said they trusted NBC and sister cable network MSNBC.

- 32% said they trusted CBS.

- 31% said they trusted ABC.

Fox News is also the only network to be trusted more than distrusted:

- Both ABC and CBS were not trusted by 46% of those surveyed.

- And NBC/MSNBC was not trusted by 44%.

- Only 37% did not trust Fox, the lowest level of distrust among all the networks recorded.

The SAPIENT Being's Definition of Fake News

From *Fake News Madness,* fake news has many definitions and is a broad term. However, at the SAPIENT Being, the term collectively includes media bias manifested in many different ways in mainstream journalism, social media, and illiberal establishments that in principle and practice are antithetical to an intellectually vibrant and viewpoint diverse sapient being mindset.

Per Andrew Klavan's edited definition, fake news can be further defined as follows:

Mainstream American news is ALL fake because the major news outlets are so consistently biased toward the left that whether any given story they report is factual or not, their overall reportage is essentially liberal, progressivism, or leftist propaganda. They can counter the right-wing slant of Fox News, but it's futile—because left-wing ABC, CBS, NBC, MSNBC and CNN have, combined, almost ten times the viewers.

Only seven percent of American journalists identify as Republican and the rest claim that despite the fact they're all Democrats, they can be objective. As previously noted, psychologists and the Heterodox Academy have shown that when people associate almost exclusively with those who agree with them, they suffer from groupthink, viewpoint orthodoxy, and confirmation bias—and lose their ability to see events clearly and objectively.

Ten Prevalent 'Mediacrat' Fake News Stories and Agendas

From *Fake News Madness,* unfortunately, we live in a world these days gone mad and turned up-side down it seems. Much like a witch-hunt, or where you're guilty first until proven innocent later, or simply a lack of free speech, many people cannot seem to separate their opinions from facts. Have you had enough of the idiocracy of illiberalism and fake news madness?

As the time-tested saying goes, "Everyone is entitled to their own opinions, but they're not entitled to their own facts." Facts are facts, the truth is the truth, but they can be skewed and manipulated for disingenuous methods and false narratives. We don't do that at the SAPIENT Being. In fact, we'll go out of our way to point out and correct such fallacies. This is part of the higher calling of being a journalist and a sapient being.

However, the principles are sorely lacking with the Mediacrats. To illustrate this point, here are ten powerful and relevant examples of fake news stories and false agendas that fail the criteria set in the SAPIENT Being's Journalism Code of Ethics, Practical Logic & Sapience and they also comprise the bulk of fake news stories and journalism seen and read today.

Many of the SAPIENT Being's *MADNESS* titles tackle head on these subject areas and by having a clear, truthful, and sapient understanding of these issues, one can make sense of them and make smarter choices and decisions at the ballot box and public policy.

FYI: There are many more than these ten Mediacrat examples below that are covered in detail in *Fake News Madness*.

1. Mediacrats refusing to Accept There is 'No' Gender Pay Gap.

2. Mediacrats promoting the Myth of Democratic Socialism Over American Capitalism.

3. Mediacrats unverifiable and Incorrectly Painting Trump as a Racist.

4. Mediacrats denying Black Lives Matter is a Marxist Organization.

5. Mediacrats censoring 2020 Antifa and Leftist Violence & Destruction .

6. Mediacrats denying Anti-White Racism & Victimization.

7. The SpyGate 'Soft' Coup Against Trump That Mediacrats Fail to Cover.

8. Mediacrats push Fake News About Trump's Pandemic Management.

9. Mediacrats trash Trump 2020 Election and the Republican Party.

10. Mediacrats lockdown on the Hunter Biden Scandal.

Columbia University's Trinity of Fake News Journalism, Leftist Pulitzer Prize Choices & Soros Foundation Funding Connections

From *Fake News Madness,* why the extreme ugly categorization? The ratings below are from the Media Research Center (MRC) and show the enormous, and "enormous" is no exaggeration, influence this Ivy League university has on the mainstream, social, and journalistic mediums in the United States and is key factor in Mediacrat bias.

In America there is NO other concentration of power, influence, and bias—from one over-arching organization as Columbia University. In the past century, the Columbia University School of Journalism was considered America's most respected liberal journalism programs along with their *Columbia Journalism Review (CJR)* and Pulitzer Prize choices. However, their ideology and focus has shifted ever more leftward over the course of the last two decades to a dangerous and unacceptable leftist bias with many negative consequences (covered below)—that qualifies them with the worst fake news madness rating.

Combine their past liberal and now leftist influence from the Columbia University School of Journalism and its *CJR,* their past liberal and now leftist Pulitzer Prize winner choices, and their immense financial backing from the leftist and anarchist George Soros Foundation—they're a fake news leftist behemoth without equal!

When Trump is Right, He's Right—But Many Refuse to Admit It

Per the Douglas MacKinnon *The Hill* June 2022 article "When Trump is Right, He's Right—But Many Refuse to Admit It":

If Donald Trump laid his right hand upon a Bible and swore, "The sky is blue, the sun rises in the East and sets in the West, and the New York Yankees have the most World Series titles, with 27," many in the media and on the left still might call him a "liar."

Trump has been out of the Oval Office for more than 16 months, and yet, he seems to be living rent-free in the minds of many Americans and international elites who have come to loathe him. But, facts are facts. Just because many people hate Trump does not mean that he can't be correct sometimes—or even, often.

For example: Trump reached out to the Pulitzer Prize administrator to rescind the 2018 prizes for national reporting awarded to The *New York Times* and The *Washington Post* for their investigative reporting of the then-alleged Trump-Russia interference into the 2016 presidential campaign.

Said the former president to the Pulitzer office: "There is no dispute that the Pulitzer board's award to those media outlets was based on false and fabricated information that they published. The continuing publication and recognition of the prizes on the board's website is a distortion of fact and a personal defamation that will result in the filing of litigation if the board cannot be persuaded to do the right thing on its own."

Now, all but the most partisan Democrats realize that the rumors, charges and investigations of Trump's alleged coercion with Russia during the campaign were suspect from the start. These allegations were tainted by troubling partisan connections to the Clinton campaign and Obama administration officials—including, sadly, some in the FBI and the Department of Justice.

The *Times* and the Post should have uncovered that the "shameful smears" against him were political and partisan in their investigations, Trump pointed out.

That raises an important question: Did those news organizations do honest investigations, or were they simply hoping the charges were true because of some journalists' inherent biases against Trump, which were exhibited in hundreds of negative stories they printed about him?

With regard to the Pulitzer Prize—or the Nobel Prize, for that matter, awarded to President Obama in 2009 for nothing more than inspiring "hope"—it's becoming clear that the award is generally given to those on the left, by the left.

Maybe the *Times* and the *Post* would be better served investigating the Pulitzer and Nobel committees for ignoring conservative voices. In the meantime, they should display the ethical good grace to return awards given under false premises.

Democrats Need a Day of Atonement for the Truth About Their Party

Per the Cal Thomas *Epoch Times* June 2021 article "Democrats Need a Day of Atonement":

With the creation of June 19th ("Juneteenth") as a federal holiday, Democrats have one more claim to be the party of civil rights and equal opportunity for African Americans, though most Republicans also voted for the holiday. That claim has been promoted for decades by a compliant media, academia, and high-profile politicians (the Mediacrats), but the facts say otherwise.

From Abraham Lincoln's Emancipation Proclamation in 1863 to the mid-20th century, members of the Democratic Party, dominant in the South due to its opposition to civil and political rights for African Americans, were on the wrong side of civil rights.

Federal troops finally brought the news of emancipation to Galveston, Texas on June 19, 1865, meeting resistance from plantation owners. This is the same year the Ku Klux Klan was founded. Nathan Bedford Forrest, a Confederate Army general and a Democrat, was the first grand wizard of the KKK, though he tried disbanding it in 1869 after growing critical of its "excessive violence."

The Klan, which numbered 4 million members at its peak, dedicated itself as History.com notes, "to an underground campaign of violence against Republican leaders and voters (both Black and white) in an effort to reverse the policies of Radical Reconstruction and restore white supremacy in the South."

The *Washington Examiner* cited 12 examples below of how Southern Democrats historically opposed civil rights while Reconstruction-era Republicans favored them.

- The newspaper noted Democrats voted against "every piece of civil rights legislation in Congress from 1866 to 1966."

- Congressional Democrats opposed the 13th Amendment, which officially freed the slaves in 1865. Only four Democrats voted for it.

- Republicans passed the 14th Amendment in 1866, which granted American citizenship to former slaves.

- Not one of the 56 congressional Democrats voted for the 15th Amendment in 1869, which gave former slaves the right to vote.

- Republicans backed all the civil rights laws of the 1860s, including the Civil Rights Act of 1866 and the Reconstruction Act of 1867. Their party was founded on an anti-slavery platform.

- Fast-forward to the 1960s. President John F. Kennedy was reluctant to push too hard for civil rights for fear of losing Southern support. After his assassination, President Johnson claimed Kennedy was passionately for civil rights and used his death to advance legislation in Congress. Once again, powerful Democrats in the South opposed every bill.

- The *Examiner* noted a PBS program that stated, "The Democratic Party was responsible for passing Jim Crow laws, in addition to Black Civil Codes that forced Americans to utilize separate drinking fountains, swimming polls, and other facilities in the 20th century."

- Chief Justice Earl Warren, a Dwight Eisenhower appointee, read the unanimous opinion in Brown v. Board of Education, declaring segregated schools unconstitutional. Eisenhower also ordered federal troops to Little Rock, Arkansas, in the face of opposition to integrating Central High School by Gov. Orval Faubus, a Democrat.

- Republican Senator Everett Dirksen of Illinois wrote several bills that banned discrimination in housing, culminating in the Civil Rights Act of 1968.

- Richard Nixon, a Republican, introduced the Philadelphia Plan, the precursor to affirmative action.

- Republican Ronald Reagan signed legislation establishing the Martin Luther King Jr. national holiday.

While Democrats are now claiming another victory for themselves, they might want to consider establishing an additional special occasion. Given their party's deplorable civil rights record, it could be called a day of atonement.

7 – The Party of Crime by Way of Urban Decay, Soros, Leftist District Attorneys, BLM & Antifa

Credit: Capital Research Center - George Soros and four district attorneys he helped elect (clockwise from the top left): Kimberly Gardner, George Gascon, Larry Krasner, and Kim Foxx.

David Kupelian shows how today's radicalized Democrats are the real coup plotters per his "The Party of Insurrection" WND January 2022 article:

One year after the Jan. 6 2021 Capitol riot, President Joe Biden gravely informed the nation that the incident, during which exactly one person, an unarmed female pro-Trump protester, was killed—unnecessarily shot to death at close range, without warning, by a Capitol Hill policeman—was "the most significant test of our democracy since the Civil War."

Biden delivered this extraordinary assessment immediately after Vice President Kamala Harris solemnly equated the out-of-control D.C. protest to both the Dec. 7, 1941 attack on Pearl Harbor that killed 2,403 Americans and injured 1,178, and the Sept. 11, 2001 terror attacks that killed 2,977 Americans and injured over 6,000. The Civil War killed an estimated 750,000 Americans.

How, wonder normal Americans, is it possible that the nation's top political leaders could make such obviously insane statements? More important, what do such bizarre pronouncements say about where the progressive elites are secretly leading the nation?

Although today's Democratic Party does indeed seem completely deranged and therefore unpredictable—insisting men are actually women if they think they are, claiming Biden's multi-trillion-dollar spending programs and wild currency creation will "reduce inflation," engineering a full-scale invasion of the American homeland by millions of illegal aliens so Democrats can stay in power forever, and so on—there actually is one reliable way both to determine with uncanny accuracy what these revolutionary-minded Democrats are up to right now, and to gauge what they are secretly planning for the future.

Here's the rule: Whatever the Democrats are falsely accusing their critics of doing and planning, that is precisely what they themselves are actually doing and planning.

And since today's super-radicalized Democratic Party is continually accusing conservatives both in and out of government of carrying out an "insurrection" against America's constitutional system of government, you can be sure—as we will soon see—that insurrection is exactly what they themselves are maniacally pursuing.

But first, understand that those on the revolutionary Left are, and always have been, slaves of projection: the compulsion to accuse others of the very sins and crimes of which they themselves are guilty. It's in their nature, they can't help it, it's reflexive and automatic.

Soft on Crime

Per the Rafael A. Mangual *City Journal* Winter 2021 article "Soft on Crime":

A Biden administration policy of weak policing and lax prosecution would be a disaster for the nation's cities. Criminal justice in America is at a crossroads. The ongoing debate about racial justice in policing, incarceration, and prosecution became a national fixation following the May 2020 death of George Floyd in police custody in Minneapolis. Since then, it has remained a flash point in our politics.

The election of Democrat Joe Biden, whose party is aligned with Black Lives Matter, who called Antifa "an idea," and who cites "systemic racism" as the major problem facing black Americans, will make the next four years challenging for proponents of effective policing. This challenge will be felt not only by those on the thinning blue line but also by those living in deteriorating urban enclaves that saw homicides and shootings spike in the second half of last year.

Most law-enforcement policies are a function of decisions made by state and local governments, many of which have acted in recent months to hamstring cops and hack away at policing budgets. But the incoming Biden administration will have significant influence over how the debate plays out on the ground.

The next attorney general will set the agenda at the Department of Justice (DOJ), and there is every reason to expect the agenda to go backward, reverting to Obama-era practices. The Obama DOJ, for instance, initiated numerous "pattern-and-practice" investigations of police departments based on racial disparities in various enforcement outcomes.

The Progressive-Prosecutor Movement

The last national "reckoning" on race and policing didn't just broaden the influence of Black Lives Matter; it also gave birth to the "progressive-prosecutor" movement. In urban jurisdictions around the country, defense attorneys and self-styled criminal-justice reformers began targeting district, state, and county attorney races.

That bid has proved extremely successful, thanks in part to the financial resources poured into those races by George Soros. The movement has helped install Larry Krasner in Philadelphia, Kim Foxx in Chicago, Rachel Rollins in Boston, Marilyn Mosby in Baltimore, Chesa Boudin in San Francisco, George Gascon in Los Angeles, John Creuzot in Dallas, Wesley Bell in St. Louis County, Kim Gardner in the City of St. Louis, and Eric Gonzalez in Brooklyn.

Local prosecutors have upended the system by dropping or diverting more cases, requesting bail and pretrial detention less often, supporting more parole bids, and adopting policies of non-prosecution for whole categories of crimes.

In some of these cities, U.S. attorneys have sought to mitigate the harms of these policies by stepping up to prosecute cases in which the federal government has concurrent jurisdiction. If the progressive-prosecutor movement expands into the federal government with the appointment of soft-on-crime U.S. attorneys, we could see a decline in the number of cases brought against violent criminals and drug dealers, as well as more leniency when it comes to charging decisions and plea bargaining. We have every reason to expect such a shift to affect crime rates in those jurisdictions.

A Biden administration could also decide to reduce or eliminate federal aid to local police departments already under new financial pressures as cities around the country (including Los Angeles, New York, and Minneapolis) move to cut funding to law-enforcement agencies. One program that could be on the chopping block is the 1033 program, which provides surplus military equipment (rifles, body armor, armored personnel carriers, and so on) to local departments.

Progressive critics say that the 1033 program represents the "militarization" of local police and leads to a perception of cops as an occupying force in communities. But denying local police equipment will only make it harder for them to do their jobs during a time of increasing violent crime.

The Joe Biden of 1994 is gone. Before announcing his presidential candidacy, he repudiated his role in passing the then-popular-but-now-infamous crime bill. His campaign website featured all the race-focused rhetoric that one would expect to see from far-left police critics. Incoming vice president Kamala Harris has worked to rehabilitate her public image, recasting herself as a "progressive" prosecutor.

These shifts in tone and approach reflect the real pressure that advocacy groups like Black Lives Matter, their financial backers, and their allies in the Democratic Party have exerted. The only question is whether, and to what degree, those shifts will manifest themselves in more consequential policy decisions. Public safety hangs on the answer.

Living Room Pundit's Guide to Soros District Attorneys

This section Is from the detailed outline in the Parker Thayer Capital Research Center January 2022 report titled "Living Room Pundit's Guide to Soros District Attorneys":

The Kyle Rittenhouse trial, the Jussie Smollet hoax, the attack on the Waukesha Christmas parade, the organized mob lootings in San Francisco, and now the indictment of the Baltimore district attorney have each attracted national attention and spotlighted an issue that many in law enforcement and politics have been warning of for years: the threat of activist district attorneys (DAs).

Specifically, the public imagination has been captured by the stories of activist DAs backed by the shadowy figure of George Soros. Many have heard of him, and most understand that he spends millions on U.S. politics, but very few know the specifics. As a result, Soros has become something of a folklore monster whose reputation often exceeds reality.

But when it comes to Soros's involvement in backing left-wing district attorneys, Soros really is the archvillain that rumor makes him out to be.

In fact, Soros's influence on left-wing DA candidates is often wildly underestimated. Since 2016, when Soros first began to back the campaigns of district attorneys (presumably as part of the "Resistance" to the Trump administration), CRC researchers have tracked more than $29 million in funding from Soros through a personal network of political action committees (PACs) formed specifically to back left-wing DA candidates. In total, Soros cash has generously supported over 20 individual candidates, many of whom won their elections and remain in office today.

The Soros District Attorneys

In most states, the chief prosecutor in a state jurisdiction is called a district attorney, but some states use other titles. For example, in Virginia, the position is called commonwealth attorney. In St. Louis, the term is circuit attorney. In general, we will refer to all of them as district attorneys.

Below is a list by state and jurisdiction of every DA that CRC has discovered receiving Soros funding, and some notable details about each. This section is long because the consequences from these DA's are a matter of life and death to law abiding citizens and they need to know who is responsible for their safety and well-being.

Diana Becton—Contra Costa County, California. Backed by $275,000 from Soros in 2018, Becton became the first woman and first African American elected to serve as DA for Contra Costa County. She is also one of the first in the position to have zero prior experience as a prosecutor. During Becton's first years in office four Contra Costa cities made the list of the top 100 most dangerous cities in California in 2018, and both violent crime and property crime increased by several percent during 2019.

George Gascon—Los Angeles County, California. Soros has spent a combined $6 million on California DA races, much of it wasted on failed candidates, but almost half was spent on the successful campaign of George Gascon for Los Angles DA. Soros was the largest spender in the race, and Gascon won easily.

Since the election, his implementation of left-wing policies led to a crime wave that has become the stuff of legend. Homicide rates soared, organized shoplifting sprees ravaged the city, trains were stopped and ransacked by mobs of looters. Under Gascon's watch the city of Los Angles has rapidly become a national disgrace.

Monique Worrell—Ninth Judicial Circuit (Orange and Osceola Counties), Florida. Monique Worrell is the second Soros candidate to become state attorney for Orange and Osceola Counties. Her predecessor, Aramis Ayala, was a "long-shot candidate" elected in 2016 with the help of more than $1.3 million in spending by the Florida Safety and Justice PAC. Ayala immediately earned a reputation for her activist approach, which led to her removal from multiple high-profile murder cases by two different Republican governors. During Ayala's tenure, violent crime increased dramatically, with murders increasing by 26 percent during 2020.

After Ayala left office to run for Congress, Worrell filled her shoes, with $1 million from Soros's Democracy PAC surging into the race at the last minute to help her claim victory against her moderate opponent in 2020.

Darius Pattillo—Henry County, Georgia. Receiving just under $150,000 from Soros through the Georgia Safety and Justice PAC, Patello was elected in 2016 and has remained the most unremarkable Soros-backed DA elected to date. In fact, Soros's funding of Patello nearly went unreported, possibly because Patello does not seem to share the radical views of his fellow Soros DAs.

Kim Foxx—Cook County (Chicago), Illinois. Probably the most famous Soros-backed DA, Foxx was boosted into office with the help of $2 million in Soros cash. Foxx has most recently been in the news for potential ethics violations in her 2019 decision to drop charges against Jussie Smollet for his infamous hate crime hoax. (Smollett was recently convicted on the same charges.) Foxx has also made headlines for presiding over Chicago's largest spike in homicides in more than 30 years while her office dropped charges against 30 percent of felony defendants during 2020.

James Stewart—Caddo Parish, Louisiana. Probably the least well-known and least radical Soros-funded DA, James Stewart was elected as the DA of Caddo Parish, Louisiana, in 2015 with the help of more than $930,000 in funding from Soros. Stewart has enacted few radical reforms since his election, potentially a disappointing result for Soros. His opponents at the time worried that his progressive views on criminal justice would be "detrimental to the safety of Caddo Parish."

Scott Colom—Circuit Court District Sixteen, Mississippi. Another of the lesser-known Soros-funded Das, Colom quietly received over $926,000 in funding from Soros to help unseat a long-time incumbent in 2015. Colom oversees District 16 in Mississippi, which includes Lowndes, Oktibbeha, Clay, and Noxubee Counties. Colom was recently recommended by Rep. Bernie Thompson (D-MS) for a position as a judge for the U.S. District Court of the Northern District of Mississippi. Meanwhile, violent crime, specifically gun violence, remains a serious and growing problem for cities and counties in the 16th Circuit, a problem that Colom has been accused of doing little to combat.

Jody Owens—Hinds County, Mississippi. Aided by a $500,000 contribution from Soros's Mississippi Justice and Public Safety PAC, Owens was elected in 2019 after running on a platform that promised reform and "alternatives to incarceration." Owens brought controversy with him to the DA's office. In 2019, Owens was accused of sexually harassing his female colleagues while working at the Southern Poverty Law Center, an organization with a well-documented proclivity for enabling and ignoring sexual harassment in the workplace.

Owens has also recently brought highly questionable murder charges against two police officers. The charges were dismissed with prejudice for lack of evidence that officers "caused any injury" to the alleged victim. Under Owens, Jackson has become one of the deadliest cities in the nation, and in 2021 the city saw over 150 homicides (98 murders per 100,000 residents), an all-time high.

Kim Gardner—St. Louis, Missouri. One of the most famous and polarizing Soros-backed DAs, Kim Gardner has served as the circuit attorney of crime-ridden St. Louis since 2017 and has repeatedly used her office to prosecute conservatives while allowing criminals to walk free.

In 2018, Gardner launched a bogus criminal investigation against Missouri's Republican governor, which led to a special investigation into her office that found probable cause that Gardner engaged in professional misconduct by hiring a private investigator who has since been charged with perjury and evidence tampering. Gardner was also the lead attorney in the absurd prosecution of Mark McCloskey, but was removed from the case by a judge who wrote "the Circuit Attorney's conduct raises the appearance that she initiated a criminal prosecution for political purposes."

Gardner was caught lying about police officers who pulled her over for driving without headlights at night, has admitted to campaign finance violations, and has badly mishandled murder cases. The year after Gardner's election, St. Louis became the murder capital of the nation, but this did not stop Soros from contributing $116,000 to aid her reelection in 2020. In early 2021, St. Louis became one of the deadliest cities in the world.

Raul Torrez—Bernalillo County (Albuquerque), New Mexico. Although his ties to Soros are less well known and his ideas are slightly less radical, Albuquerque's DA also got his start from $107,000 in Soros cash that boosted his unopposed campaign in 2016. As of mid-November, Albuquerque had experienced 102 homicides in 2021, the highest number ever recorded, compared to the 67 reported at the same time last year. Meanwhile, Torrez is busy campaigning for New Mexico Attorney General. Soros's money is likely to make an appearance in that upcoming race as well.

Alvin Bragg—Manhattan, New York. One of Soros's newest DA's, Bragg was elected in 2021 as the DA of Manhattan, largely thanks to approximately $1.1 million given by Soros that year to groups supporting Bragg. Even though Bragg has barely been in office, his tenure is already shaping up as a disaster. After Bragg released a memo stating that his office would not be seeking prison sentences for crimes such as armed robbery, drug dealing, and burglary, more than nine prosecutors in Manhattan quit. Interestingly, one area where Bragg is not expected to be overly lenient is an investigation into President Donald Trump's business practices, which Bragg conveniently took over after assuming office.

David Clegg—Ulster County, New York. Soros cash to the tune of at least $184,000 was used to push Ulster County DA David Clegg across the finish line in his 2019 election, but it was also the source of a major controversy at the time. In an embarrassing guffaw, the New York Justice and

Public Safety PAC paid for mailers that featured Clegg shaking hands with a prominent criminal and left-wing activist. Under Clegg, gun crimes and shootings have surged dramatically, and high profile cases have been badly mishandled, including a murder case in which the suspect was released because Clegg's office failed to file an indictment on time.

Larry Krasner—Philadelphia, Pennsylvania. Among the most famous Soros-backed DAs, Krasner has been supported by more than $2 million from Soros funneled through the Pennsylvania Justice and Public Safety PAC and the Philadelphia Justice and Public Safety PAC. Krasner was reelected in 2021 with the help of a $259,000 contribution from Soros. Under Krasner's watch, crime rates have soared, and in 2021, Philadelphia became the murder capital of the United States with the highest per capita homicide rate of the country's 10 largest cities.

Jack Stollsteimer—Delaware County, Pennsylvania. Lesser known but also well financed by Soros, Stollsteimer was the first Democratic DA ever elected in Delaware County, boosted by roughly $100,000 in ads paid for by Soros during 2019. While still undoubtedly a progressive, Stollsteimer is much less radical than Krasner and has not been openly hostile to police. He did, however, recently feud with police over the graphic details of a report on a rape in broad daylight on a train with many witnesses, none of whom tried to intervene. During Stollsteimer's first year in office, homicides in Delaware County increased 127 percent, though many attribute this to the county's proximity to Philadelphia.

Joe Gonzalez—Bexar County (San Antonio), Texas. George Soros has even dared to mess with Texas. Joe Gonzalez is one of Soros's favorite DAs, receiving nearly $1 million in backing from the billionaire during his 2018 campaign, upsetting incumbent Democrat Nico LaHood in the primary. Just as in Dallas, violent crime reportedly increased by 15 percent in San Antonio under Gonzalez, while convictions dropped by 17 percent.

John Creuzot—Dallas County, Texas. Backed by an estimated $236,000 from Soros, Creuzot became the DA of Dallas County in 2018 and immediately moved forward with a plethora of radical reform policies, including decriminalizing theft under $750, criminal trespass, and drug possession. During his first year in office crime reportedly increased by 15 percent while total convictions dropped by 30 percent. Most recently, Creuzot failed to get a conviction in straightforward case against Billy Chemirmir, a Kenyan immigrant charged with murdering and robbing 18 elderly women in assisted living facilities. He was found with his alleged victims' personal papers and jewelry in his possession at the time of his arrest.

Brian Middleton—Fort Bend County, Texas. Although it went unnoticed and unreported by the media, Soros played a major role in the 2019 campaign of Fort Bend County DA Brian Middleton, spending nearly $200,000 on advertising in support of his campaign. Middleton has been extremely moderate as far as Soros-backed candidates go, and as a result Fort Bend County has not seen a dramatic spike in crime.

Kim Ogg—Harris County (Houston), Texas. In 2016, Kim Ogg became the state's first Soros-backed DA after Soros spent more than $600,000 on the race. As one of the first reform DA's backed by Soros, Ogg is also one of the most moderate. She has stopped prosecuting marijuana offenses, but often seeks high cash bail, causing her to be ostracized by many progressives and apparently Soros.

José Garza—Travis County (Austin), Texas. In 2020, Garza was elected as Austin's DA with the aid of more than $400,000 in ads paid for by the Texas Justice and Public Safety PAC, one of Soros's private PACs that has received roughly $3.6 million from the billionaire since its creation in 2018. Since assuming office, Garza has developed a reputation for letting violent offenders go free on little to no bail.

In 2020, Garza released hundreds of inmates from jail over COVID-19 protocols, even though only six people in Austin at the time were known to have COVID-19. In 2021, Garza released a man with eight prior felony convictions after he was caught toting a gun in a meth-fueled car chase with police. After his release with an ankle monitor, the man allegedly went on a crime spree committing 10 armed robberies. Since Garza was elected, police budgets have been slashed, and Austin has experienced skyrocketing crime rates and a record number of homicides.

Parisa Dehghani-Tafti—Arlington County and City of Falls Church, Virginia. Backed by over $600,000 from the Justice and Public Safety PAC, one of George Soros's many personal PACs, Dehghani-Tafti won her 2019 election by toppling a moderate Democratic incumbent and has been a center of controversy ever since. Dehghani-Tafti, along with several other Soros-backed DAs in Virginia, is facing a recall petition after crimes like felony aggravated assault rose 40 percent during her first year in office.

Steve Descano—Fairfax County, Virginia. Steve Descano, who is also facing a recall petition, was elected in 2019 and has endorsed a progressive platform typical of the left-wing DA faction. Descano has made it his office's official policy not to prosecute more than 20 different crimes including shoplifting for goods under $1,000, prostitution, and indecent exposure. Descano's initial campaign benefitted from approximately $600,000 from Soros.

Buta Biberaj—Loudoun County, Virginia. As Loudoun County District Attorney, Buta Biberaj has championed an anti-incarceration approach to the job, but made headlines for personally seeking jail time for Scott Smith, a father who was arrested for misdemeanor disorderly conduct at a Loudoun County School Board meeting while protesting the School Board's cover-up of his 14-year-old daughter's rape by a transgender boy in a school bathroom. Smith's defense attorneys reported that it was "completely unheard of" for a DA to personally handle a misdemeanor, much less to pursue jail time, court-ordered anger management, and a hefty fine. Biberaj's campaign in 2019 was boosted by over $650,000 in Soros cash, and she is now facing a recall petition.

Ramin Fatehi—Norfolk County, Virginia. One of the latest additions to Soros's collection of rogue prosecutors, Ramin Fatehi was one of very few Democrats to win a Virginia election in 2021, largely thanks to about $220,000 in funding from Soros. Fatehi has yet to make a name for himself as DA, but he ran on the typical progressive platform of promising to abolish cash bail and decriminalize marijuana possession.

A Trail of Destruction

The patterns within the list are clear: skyrocketing violent crime, countless murders, little to no accountability, limited prosecutorial experience, a proclivity for scandal, and a tendency to unfairly prosecute political adversaries. George Soros certainly has a type.

Now more than ever, it is vital that communities maintain or regain control of their own criminal justice systems and reject the false promises of the progressive district attorney movement. These "woke" criminal justice policies have universally led to disaster, and our poorest communities, not Soros, are left holding the body bags.

Check the Appendix for the George Soros Donations to Democratic Candidates and Super PACS list from Open Secrets.

BLM Is a Moral, Political, and Policy Disaster

Credit: Erin Scott/Reuters - Another BLM protest.

Per the Rich Lowry National review February 2022 article "BLM Is a Moral, Political, and Policy Disaster": The Democratic Party is finally realizing its vulnerability on culture issues, and perhaps no group better exemplifies the problem than Black Lives Matter.

The group's eponymous slogan swept all before it in recent years. It was repeated by Democrats around the country. Corporate leaders paid obeisance to it. Sports leagues displayed it. Such was its totemic power that a more inclusive version of the three words—all lives matter—was considered a dangerous heresy.

The BLM agenda on criminal justice—based on the idea that fewer criminals should be arrested and held in jail—took hold in blue jurisdictions, and the slogan "defund the police" got traction despite its utter impracticality and obvious political destructiveness.

Now, it's obvious how shortsighted and foolhardy all this was. The rise in violent crime is a clear and present danger to the Democratic majorities in the House and Senate, and progressive prosecutors allied with BLM who have pursued soft-on-crime policies in the midst of a crime wave are under fire, facing either recall or heavy criticism.

BLM the group is continuing to find ways to underline its own extremism as it withers under scrutiny for its dodgy finances.

In the wake of George Floyd's death, BLM's radicalism was very good business. The group's co-founder, Patrisse Cullors, said the other day that the money raised itself, as practically every entity in America that wanted to bolster its "social justice" credentials tried to buy its way into BLM's good graces. "People have to know we didn't go out and solicit the money," Cullors explained. "This is money that came from white guilt, white corporation guilt, and they just poured money in."

If that sounds a tad defensive, it's because BLM raised $90 million in 2020, and it's unclear who has stewardship of the funds or how they're being spent. BLM has gone from a sainted group to one that's on the run. California and Washington have ordered BLM to stop fundraising in those states, and in a telling symbolic blow, impeccably woke Amazon has kicked BLM off its charity platform, AmazonSmile.

Cullors has the explanation that you'd expect for the new focus on BLM's lack of financial controls—"anti-black racism." Yes, good accounting is racist now.

What's Next for Antifa?

From the Jacob Zenn *City Journal* November 2020 article "What's Next for Antifa?":

Antifa differs from other far left-wing groups, including the Democratic Socialists of America, in that it explicitly endorses "physical confrontation" in order to deny freedom of speech and assembly to its opponents. Antifa was relatively unknown in the U.S. until Trump's 2016 presidential victory.

In the past, left-wing activism took the form of the anti-World Trade Organization, anti-Iraq War, and Occupy Wall Street movements. Antifa's main cause now is Black Lives Matter—effectively aligning it with the Democratic Party and, ironically, BLM's corporate sponsors. Sympathetic city officials in Berkeley, Charlottesville, and Portland have often avoided prosecuting Antifa members arrested for acts of vandalism and violence. Typically, Antifa activists who commit violence or destroy property are bailed out by groups like the Minnesota Freedom Fund, a bail fund that Kamala Harris urged her followers to support after George Floyd's death.

Reducing Antifa to an "idea," as Joe Biden did during the first presidential debate, was an expedient move for Democrats during the election season. Throughout the summer and fall, Antifa members have filled out BLM street rallies (while transitioning to black-bloc garb by night), denied public spaces to Trump supporters, and rioted in order to portray "Trump's America" as divisive and dangerous.

Antifa's political demands include no U.S. foreign intervention, no national borders, and no jails or police, among other policies that don't align with a center-Left agenda. Many Antifa adherents recall Harris's "pro-incarceration" record as California's attorney general. They won't hesitate to label Biden a "fascist" if he deviates from their demands or those of BLM. The far-Left and center-Left were united against Trump for four years; now we'll see if Antifa moves the goalposts for "fascism" to include some of its more centrist former allies.

Neighborhood Scout Ranking of the Most Crime-Ridden Cities and Their Mayors

From *Crime Rate Madness*, NeighborhoodScout.com puts out a yearly report of the 100 most dangerous cities in America with populations of 25,000 or more, based on the number of violent crimes per 1,000 residents. Violent crimes include murder, rape, armed robbery, and aggravated assault. The data used for this research are the number of violent crimes reported to have occurred in each city, and the population of each city.

See the complete dangerous U.S. cities list in the Appendix link. For the 20 most crime-ridden cities and their mayors the list (mostly Democrat) is below from worst to least-worst:

1. Detroit: Violent crime rate (per 1,000 residents): 20.0 Odds of being a victim: 1 in 50 Mayor: Michael Edward Duggan, Democrat.

2. Memphis, Tennessee: Violent crime rate (per 1,000 residents): 19.5 Odds of being a victim: 1 in 51 Mayor: Jim Strickland, Democrat.

3. Birmingham, Alabama: Violent crime rate (per 1,000 residents): 19.3 Odds of being a victim: 1 in 52 Mayor: Randall Woodfin, Democrat.

4. Baltimore: Violent crime rate (per 1,000 residents): 18.5 Odds of being a victim: 1 in 54 Mayor: Jack Young, Democrat.

5. Flint, Michigan: Violent crime rate (per 1,000 residents): 18.3 Odds of being a victim: 1 in 55 Mayor: Sheldon Neely, Democrat.

6. St. Louis: Violent crime rate (per 1,000 residents): 18.2 Odds of being a victim: 1 in 55 Mayor: Lyda Krewson, Democrat.

7. Danville, Illinois: Violent crime rate (per 1,000 residents): 18.0 Odds of being a victim: 1 in 55 Mayor: Ricky Williams Jr. (nonpartisan election).

8. Saginaw, Michigan: Violent crime rate (per 1,000 residents): 16.7 Odds of being a victim: 1 in 60 Mayor: Floyd Kloc (nonpartisan election).

9. Wilmington, Delaware: Violent crime rate (per 1,000 residents): 16.3 Odds of being a victim: 1 in 61 Mayor: Mike Purzycki, Democrat.

10. Camden, New Jersey: Violent crime rate (per 1,000 residents): 16.2 Odds of being a victim: 1 in 62 Mayor: Francisco Moran, Democrat.

11. Pine Bluff, Arkansas: Violent crime rate (per 1,000 residents): 16.0 Odds of being a victim: 1 in 62 Mayor: Shirley Washington, Democrat.

12. Kansas City, Missouri: Violent crime rate (per 1,000 residents): 15.9 Odds of being a victim: 1 in 63 Mayor: Quinton Lucas, Democrat.

13. San Bernardino, California: Violent crime rate (per 1,000 residents): 15.3 Odds of being a victim: 1 in 65 Mayor: John Valdivia, Democrat.

14. Alexandria, Louisiana: Violent crime rate (per 1,000 residents): 14.6 Odds of being a victim: 1 in 68 Mayor: Jeffrey Hall, Democrat.

15. Little Rock, Arkansas: Violent crime rate (per 1,000 residents): 14.6 Odds of being a victim: 1 in 68 Mayor: Frank Scott Jr., Democrat.

16. Cleveland: Violent crime rate (per 1,000 residents): 14.5 Odds of being a victim: 1 in 69 Mayor: Frank Jackson, Democrat.

17. Milwaukee: Violent crime rate (per 1,000 residents): 14.3 Odds of being a victim: 1 in 70 Mayor: Tom Barrett, Democrat.

18. Stockton, California: Violent crime rate (per 1,000 residents): 14.2 Odds of being a victim: 1 in 70 Mayor: Michael Tubbs, Democrat.

19. Monroe, Louisiana: Violent crime rate (per 1,000 residents): 14.1 Odds of being a victim: 1 in 71 Mayor: James Earl Mayo, Democrat.

20. Chester, Pennsylvania: Violent crime rate (per 1,000 residents): 14.0 Odds of being a victim: 1 in 71 Mayor: Thaddeus Kirkland, Democrat.

America's Ten Worst Sanctuary Communities

From *Crime Rate Madness,* calling attention to a grave threat to our country, the Immigration Reform Law Institute (IRLI) has released its list of America's Ten Worst Sanctuary Communities. Home cities of Reps. Pelosi, AOC, and Omar rank 1-2-3 on "List of Shame." Per the September 2019 report authored by Brian Lonergan:

Sanctuary policies often prohibit local law enforcement personnel from cooperating with requests from ICE to hold illegal aliens in police custody for possible deportation. These policies release dangerous foreign nationals into communities, often resulting in violence and even death.

"Sanctuary policies are absolute poison for America," said Dale L. Wilcox, executive director, and general counsel of IRLI. "They are unconstitutional—a violation of the Supremacy Clause—and threaten the integrity of our republic. More importantly, sanctuary policies bring violent crime and murder that is entirely preventable.

"Political leaders who advocate for and defend sanctuary policies are directly responsible for the lawlessness and human suffering they have inflicted on their communities. The law-abiding, legal residents of these communities need to know that their leaders have prioritized the interests of often violent illegal aliens over them."

"This is a list of shame," he added (and it's mostly Democrat), and is shown below:

1 – San Francisco, California: Mayor: London Breed (Democrat)

2 – New York City, New York: Mayor: Bill de Blasio (Democrat)

3 – Minneapolis, Minnesota: Mayor: Jacob Frey (Democrat)

4 – Philadelphia, Pennsylvania: Mayor: Jim Kenney (Democrat)

5 – Seattle, Washington: Mayor: Jenny Durkan (Democrat)

6 – Chicago, Illinois: Mayor: Lori Lightfoot (Democrat)

7 – TIE: Montgomery County, Maryland and Fairfax County, Virginia:

Montgomery County, Maryland: County Executive: Marc Elrich

Fairfax County, Virginia: County Chair: Sharon Bulova; County Executive: Bryan Hill

8 – Prince George's County, Maryland: County Executive: Angela Alsobrooks

9 – Boston, Massachusetts: Mayor: Marty Walsh (Democrat)

10 – Santa Clara County, California: Board of Supervisors

As Biden's America Becomes Less Safe, the Violence and Crime Could Cost Democrats

Per the Armstrong Williams *The Hill* July 2021 article "As Biden's America Becomes Less Safe, the Violence and Crime Could Cost Democrats":

Under the Biden administration, violent crime continues to rise across the country, particularly in cities controlled by Democrats. Regardless of this alarming trend, neither President Biden nor the leaders of his Democratic Party have taken significant steps to combat increasing crime, or even shown serious concern about the uptick.

Following the May 2020 death of George Floyd at the hands of Minneapolis police, and the subsequent ludicrous push to defund police departments, violent crime hasn't let up.

Some mayors are struggling to walk the line of supporting police officers while also caving to the pressures of vocal progressives who push to defund and reform police agencies. Some cities have reversed the decision to lower funding to police. And in many cities, morale among officers has plunged so low that a June survey of nearly 200 police departments by the Police Executive Research Forum (PERF) shows a 45 percent increase in retirement rates and nearly a 20 percent increase in resignations.

President Biden's lack of commitment to America's law enforcement community—which he relies upon—is causing officers to quit because, understandably, many no longer want to do the job. The result may be that neighborhoods are more unsafe, and Americans are more likely to become crime victims. In many ways, America is effectively less safe than it was five years ago, and the group to blame for this unfolding tragedy is Democrats who have advocated for severely limiting police budgets, effectively taking away resources or officers to combat violent criminals.

As the saying goes, elections have consequences, and the consequences this time mean a less-safe America. Our homes or those of our neighbors may be burglarized; a couple walking home from a date night may be robbed at gunpoint; diners enjoying a meal in Baltimore's historic Fells

Point may be privy to the pop, pop, pop of gunfire. It's an America where even young city kids walking to or from school can be fatally shot because of turf wars or gang violence.

The question that Americans should ask themselves—particularly with the 2022 midterms approaching and the balance of power in the House at stake—is a simple one: Do they feel safer in Biden's America? I think many Americans will acknowledge that they do not feel safe and, if that is their answer, they should return power to Republicans who could serve as a check on Biden and Democratic congressional leaders to help restore law and order to America's streets.

Are all police officers good? No, but this isn't unique to police forces; you can find bad people among all sectors of the workforce. Yes, we should work to rid police forces of bad apples, but we also should support and elevate officers who work hard and put their lives on the line to keep us all safe. We should think about increasing the salary for police positions so that we attract good candidates for the job. We should increase—not decrease—police budgets so that officers get the continuous training they may need and desire.

If Democrats can't understand why it's important to support good police officers, they effectively give a green light to criminals to do what they want, where and when they want. But the blame for high crime will fall squarely on President Biden and his party.

Americans yearn for safety because safety is tied to wellness, wholeness, success and longevity. It's what everyone wants—regardless of race, ethnicity or religious affiliation—yet the Biden administration seems unaware and ill-equipped to provide what Americans seek. This could cost the Democrats when midterm elections arrive, but that's the price of playing politics with people's safety.

8 – Election Integrity: Gaming Elections, Voting Irregularities & Big Tech Collusion on Hunter's Laptop

Credit: Raphaël Vicenzi - Hunter Biden's laptop story.

From *Voting Madness*, the general consensus in mainstream media, big tech, and many Democrats regarding 2020 election and voting fraud claims: There's no evidence of widespread fraud in the 2020 election and voting officials from both political parties have stated publicly that the election went well, and international observers confirmed there were no serious irregularities. Any claims otherwise are considered "false" or "fake news" or "conspiracy theories" and it's time to move on.

Voter fraud has become an increasingly partisan issue in recent years and came to the forefront of the 2020 election. Republicans have warned that mail-in ballots, same-day registration and lack of voter ID laws create ripe opportunities for liberal mischief. Democrats counter that efforts to curb those things are part of a larger plot by the GOP to suppress voting from poor and minority communities, core Democratic constituencies.

The Democratic Party line treats voter fraud as little more than a Republican Party (GOP) fever dream—and if it is conspiracy theory labeled with false accusations—why did President Joe Biden spent decades of his career sounding the alarm about it. Biden, the Democratic standard bearer, consistently shared GOP concerns about voter fraud during his 36 years as a United States senator from Delaware per the September 2020 article in *New York Post* by Jon Levine titled "Joe Biden spent decades warning of voter fraud—now called a myth by Dems."

Throughout the 1980s and 1990s, Biden worked closely with now-Senate Minority Leader Mitch McConnell to stiffen penalties for voter fraud. "Should Voters Be Allowed To Register On Election Day? No," Biden wrote in an op-ed to a now-defunct Wilmington, Delaware newspaper in 1977. He even chided President Carter at the time for proposing it.

A "reservation I have and one that is apparently shared by some of the top officials within the Department of Justice is that the president's proposal could lead to a serious increase in vote fraud," Biden wrote.

In 1988 Biden introduced the "Anti-Corruption Act," which McConnell co-sponsored. The bill would have enacted penalties for anyone who deprived anyone of "a fair and impartially conducted election process through the use of fraudulent ballots or voter registration forms or the filing of fraudulent campaign reports."

Biden and McConnell tried again in 1989 and Sen. Strom Thurmond was also a co-sponsor of the bill. "Current law does not permit prosecution of election fraud … This bill makes it a federal offense to corrupt any state or local election process," Biden argued on the Senate floor. McConnell noted in his own floor assessment that it would "raise the maximum penalty for both election fraud and public corruption to 10 years in federal prison and a $10,000 fine." Unfortunately for all voting Americans and safe elections, the bill failed.

Voter & Election Fraud Convictions Are a Fact and So Is the Data

From *Voting Madness*, The Heritage Foundation has so far documented 1,371 proven cases of voter fraud since America's founding, 1,179 criminal convictions, and 48 civil penalties. Nonetheless, these numbers are miniscule compared to the millions of legal votes cast. Even if they likely represent the tip of an iceberg of voter fraud—there are not enough "proven" cases in the 2020 election to alter the seven million plus Joe Biden election victory margin. Or are there?

Is there some truth to Donald Trump's claims of a "stolen election" and "massive voter fraud" to justify his 2020 election loss when you analyze huge pro-Biden vote dumps after election night in key battleground states? If we replace the phrases of "stolen election" and "massive voter fraud" with "gamed" election and massive voter "irregularities"—does he have a case?

Furthermore, if we quantify these 2020 election gaming and irregularities by including the effect from election law changes enacted during the pandemic; combined with the subliminal leftist influence of big tech; a tsunami of fake news and false narratives, or voter fraud news suppression by mainstream media; and record setting funding by left leaning groups—yes, Trump has a case!

As covered in *Voting Madness: A SAPIENT Being's Guide to Election Irregularities, Voter Fraud, Mail-In Ballots, HR1 and More (Summer 2021)*, the combined impacts of "gaming" and "irregularities" and perhaps outright voter "manipulation"—could have influenced millions— perhaps tens of millions of American votes—mostly Millennials—to the overwhelming benefit of Biden and Democratic candidates.

Trump's legal team submitted more than 800 sworn eyewitness statements across six states consisting of affidavits, whistleblower accounts, witnesses, expert testimony, video and photographic evidence, statistical anomalies, and mathematical analyses to provide respective state and federal courts with innumerable demonstrations of mismanaged ballots, voting machine irregularities, due process transgressions, equal protection violations, actual fraud, and more.

However, the vast majority have been dismissed due to improper legal procedures, lack of evidence or legal precedent, and some have been debunked and withdrawn. Yet others cannot be explained away—and until they are/or not—ongoing election integrity will be in doubt.

The 5 Biggest Myths Regarding Voter Fraud, Suppression & Election Integrity

From *Voting Madness*, many readers of *Democratic Party Madness* may not be aware of how prevalent and widespread the five common myths related to voter and election fraud are. That's why in this section we'll look at the hard facts, unbiased statistics, and overwhelming evidence—and let readers come to their own conclusions about each prevailing myth.

One of the refrains from those who oppose election reforms designed to protect the security and integrity of the voting process is that serious vote fraud is a myth. Downplaying the risks and vulnerabilities for election fraud in the current system exacerbates existing problems and compromises the most sacred right a free people have. One person—one vote.

The threat of vote fraud is real—and it could make a difference in a close election. Dirty voter rolls, mail-in voting, and ballot harvesting are three areas ripe for abuse. Strict voter-ID laws have long been denounced as voter suppression—but the overwhelming evidence shows it's not true. And do illegal aliens and non-citizens vote and affect outcomes? Yes, sometimes.

Democrats take great pains to perpetuate these five common myths of:

1) There is no voter and election fraud in American elections.

2) Requiring voter ID leads to or is a form of voter suppression.

3) Cleaning up voter rolls is a right-wing conspiracy.

4) The 2016 election Russian interference and Trump.

5) There is no voting by illegal aliens and non-citizens.

The Right to Vote Defines the Essence of American Citizenship & Exceptionalism

An independent, nationwide analysis of voter rolls in 42 states has identified thousands of probable deceased and duplicate registrants, as well as cases of individuals credited for voting more than once. The Public Interest Legal Foundation (PILF) has launched the Safeguarding America's Votes and Elections (SAVE) Database as an analysis tool to track voter roll deficiencies and potential problem areas across America. Per PILF, the groundbreaking findings in their national report indicates that the SAVE Database raises serious concerns over the integrity of states' voter files.

After PILF collected data from 42 states and put it into a format where it could be critically studied, it was rigorously compared to commercial and government databases to increase confidence in the conclusions with particular emphasis on validating identities matched across state lines. Their September 2020 report, which is covered in this section, is titled "Critical Condition: American Voter Rolls Filled with Errors, Dead Voters, and Duplicate Registrations."

Also included with the data were voter history fields, namely, data about when each registrant voted. The combination of state election data, commercial data, and federal sources such as the Social Security Death Index, provides researchers with perhaps the best platform ever constructed to analyze the health of the voter rolls and catalogue potential vulnerabilities.

The findings are a helpful starting point for state election officials to review the findings and make final determinations and take appropriate actions.

Notable Safeguarding America's Votes and Elections (SAVE) Database Findings:

- 349,773: total number of potentially deceased registrants across 41 states.

- Michigan, Florida, New York, Texas, and California account for roughly 51% of national dead registrants.

- In 2016, 7,890 registrants were apparently credited for voting after death.

- In 2018, 6,718 registrants were credited for voting after death.

- North Carolina leads the U.S. in dead registrants credited for voting after death.

- 43,760 likely duplicate registrants appear to have cast second votes in 2016 from the same address.

- 37,889 likely duplicate registrants appear to have cast second votes in 2018 from the same address.

- Thousands of these apparent double votes were exclusively mail ballots.

- 8,360 – Number of registrants apparently registered in 2 states and credited for voting in both states in 2018.

- 5,500 – Number of apparently duplicate registrants credited for voting twice in the same state from 2 different addresses in 2018.

- 34,000 – Number of registrants credited for voting from apparently non-residential addresses in 2018.

2000 Mules: They Thought We'd Never Find Out. They Were Wrong

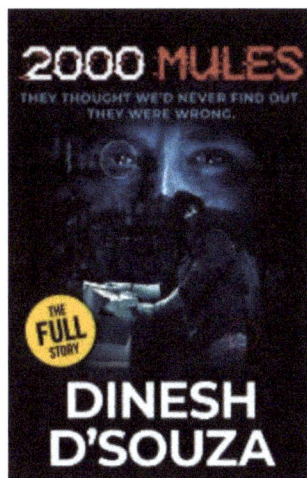

Credit: Salem Media Group.

A year and a half after the 2020 presidential election, documentary filmmaker and bestselling author of *America, Death of a Nation*, and *United States of Socialism*, Dinesh D'Souza exposes a colossal voting racketeering operation that you were told didn't exist.

D'Souza makes a powerful argument that the 2020 presidential election was stolen as asserted by ex-president Trump. More importantly, D'Souza proves it by drawing on research presented by the election integrity group True the Vote, who presents two types of evidence: video surveillance and geotracking.

The video surveillance captures a massive network of fraudulent voters who stuffed ballot boxes which ultimately skewed the overall results by changing the outcome of key battleground states. This is a baseline claim, in some form or another, it has been a focal point for many Americans, besides Trump, ever since the November 2020 election.

The geotracking evidence, based on a database of 10 trillion cell phone pings, unveils an elaborate network of paid professional operatives called *mules*, who deliver fraudulent and illegal votes to mail in drop boxes in the five key battleground states of Arizona, Georgia, Michigan, Pennsylvania and Wisconsin.

In this #1 bestselling film on Amazon, you will find the receipts—the transcripts and confirmatory details—for the facts establishing 2020 election fraud presented in D'Souza's major motion picture documentary, "2000 Mules," with a 6.2 IMDb rating. Check out the Appendix for the "2000 Mules" IMDb review and trailer

Fact or fiction, watch the movie premier from the link provided in the Appendix, and you be the judge and follow the other link for the companion book on Amazon, that responds to debunked claims by so-called fact checkers, to be published on August 30. 2022.

It Took Only 537 Votes To Decide the 2000 Presidential Election

From *Voting Madness*, finally and most graphically, it took only 537 verified and certified votes out of almost six million cast in Florida in the 2000 presidential election to give George W. Bush the edge over Al Gore nationally with 271 to 266 electoral votes.

Yes, 537 votes decided the 2020 president election! Please let that sink in whenever you hear "a few votes cannot make a difference!" Oh yes they can!

After an intense recount process and the United States Supreme Court's decision in *Bush v. Gore*, Bush won Florida's electoral votes by a margin of only 537 votes out of almost six million cast (9/1000 of 1%) and, as a result, became the president-elect winning the electoral vote 271 to 266. Let this historical voting lesson sink in.

Contrary to the claims of many prominent Democrats, voter fraud is a very real problem as shown by The Heritage Foundation. As the Supreme Court noted when it upheld Indiana's voter ID law, flagrant examples of voter fraud have been documented throughout this nation's history.

The National Commission on Federal Election Reform has said that in many close elections, fraud can absolutely change the outcome. Cases of local elections getting overturned because of fraud have occurred in New Jersey, Indiana, and other states.

Although hundreds of people have been convicted in recent years, voter fraud often goes undetected. And even when it's discovered, overburdened prosecutors rarely prioritize these cases. Fraudsters can steal votes and change election outcomes in several ways, including:

- Voting in someone else's name.

- Registering in multiple locations to vote multiple times in the same election.

- Voting even though they're not eligible because they're felons or noncitizens.

- Or paying or intimidating people to vote for certain candidates.

Why Safeguarding Our Elections Matters and the Risks That Threaten Them

From *Voting Madness*, the Hans von Spakovsky's November 2020 "Why Safeguarding Our Elections Matters" article in The Daily Signal states that the survival of our democratic republic depends on Americans' belief that their vote counts and their continued faith in the fairness and security of our electoral process.

Per von Spakovsky, steps must be taken to combat fraud and other weaknesses in our electoral system that could result in stolen votes and elections. Failure to do so—is un-American!

Nobody knows for sure how much election fraud actually is committed. But it is beyond dispute that American elections are vulnerable to fraud and administrative errors that could make the difference in a close election—especially in state and local elections, and even federal elections.

Example: the 9th Congressional District race in North Carolina that was overturned in 2018 due to absentee ballot fraud and illegal vote harvesting.

Despite the threat that fraud poses to our democratic republic, the Democrats consistently deny the existence of election fraud. Even after being presented with case after case after case of evidence and irrefutable statistics, those on the left often dismiss the problem as "not widespread" enough to warrant action.

The Heritage Foundation's Election Fraud Database demonstrates that there are many ways to engage in election fraud, and that it occurs often enough that we should be concerned about it and should try to address it. Liberal media and fake news attacks on the database have not been able to find a single instance of an error. See the Appendix for the link to the database and judge for yourself. See the Appendix for the link to the dtabase.

A 2005 report by the Commission on Federal Election Reform, a bipartisan commission led by former President Jimmy Carter and Secretary of State James Baker, was clear that election fraud does exist, that it must be deterred to preserve election integrity, that it could make the difference in a close election, and that absentee ballots "remain the largest source of potential voter fraud." We have an obligation to secure our elections against these vulnerabilities.

The Vote Fraud That Democrats Refuse to Acknowledge

From *Voting Madness*, the *New York Post* article "The vote fraud that Democrats refuse to see" by Deroy Murdock in July 2017 explains:

Not since the outcome of the Carter-Baker Commission on Election Reform in 2005 has this topic been a national priority—until then President Trump in 2017 addressed vote fraud seriously enough to appoint a bipartisan panel, the Presidential Advisory Commission on Election Integrity, to get to the bottom of it, after his 2016 election win.

Never mind, leading Democrats insisted the issue is bogus, and the commission is evil. Election fraud denial is a serious threat. An example of the Democrats new math of election fraud denial could be: 265 + 742 + 765 + 953 + 7,474 = 0.

The facts below are more concrete proof that vote fraud exists but when Democrats add up the values below (bolded)—they still arrive at the same sum of zero as if they don't exist:

- In May 2016, CBS2 Los Angeles identified **265** dead voters in southern California. Many cast ballots "year after year."

- The Heritage Foundation's non-exhaustive survey confirms, since 2000, at least **742** criminal vote-fraud convictions.

- North Carolina announced in April 2014 that 13,416 dead voters were registered, and 81 of them recently had voted. Among 35,750 North Carolinians also registered in other states, **765** voted in November 2012, both inside and outside the Tarheel State.

- South Carolina's attorney general concluded in January 2012 that **953** people "were deceased at the time of their participation in recent elections."

- The Public Interest Legal Foundation recently discovered that Virginia removed 5,556 non-citizens from its voter rolls between 2011 and last May. Among these non-Americans, 1,852 had cast a total of **7,474** illegal ballots across multiple elections.

Craftier liberals have inched away from the baseless "Vote fraud = Loch Ness Monster" argument. Now, some claim, vote fraud is not "widespread."

Why Do Democrats Pretend Voter Fraud Doesn't Exist?

From the November 2018 *Investor's Business Daily* article "Why Do Democrats Pretend Voter Fraud Doesn't Exist?" they point out how Texas State Attorney General Ken Paxton decided to crack down on voter fraud before the 2018 midterm elections. So far, he's prosecuted 33 people for 97 counts of voter fraud that year alone. Among the discoveries was a voter fraud ring that had received financial support from the former head of the Texas Democratic Party.

Yet there are those—mostly Democrats and mainstream journalists—who continue to insist that voter fraud is a myth. *The New York Times'* Glenn Thrush once declared, for example, that "there is essentially no voter fraud in this country."

When shown concrete examples, the response is usually "well, it's not widespread."

But that reflects a fundamental misunderstanding of elections. You don't need "widespread" voter fraud to change election outcomes, just small-scale efforts targeted on tight or consequential elections.

The fact is that committing voter fraud isn't all that difficult, but minimizing it is easy. Cleaning up registration rolls, enacting voter ID requirements, using paper ballots, and implementing better controls on early and absentee voting would make non-citizen voting and other forms of fraud virtually impossible.

Critics of such efforts say that they will only serve to suppress the vote of minorities and the poor—that is, voters who tend to vote Democratic. They want to make it easier and easier to register and vote.

But there's no evidence that voter ID laws suppress turnout. In fact, of 11 states that adopted strict voter ID laws, nine either saw increased turnout in 2016, or had turnout rates higher than the national average, the Heritage Foundation notes. The data are not on their side. Consider the latest from the Pew Research Center: In 2018, voter participation surged, and "last year's midterm voters [were] the most racially and ethnically diverse ever."

Nor does cleaning up registration rolls, aggressively pursuing voter fraud cases, using paper ballots, or other measures to ensure the integrity of the ballot suppress legitimate voters.

Those who say voter fraud is no big deal should realize something. Every single vote cast fraudulently cancels out one legitimate vote. They need to ask themselves how they'd feel if it was their vote being canceled.

Big Lie About Georgia Voting Has Been Shredded

This section is from the Rich Lowry *National Review* May 2022 report "Big Lie About Georgia Voting Has Been Shredded":

The surge in the early vote in Georgia shows that all the smears about the state's new voting law, repeated by everyone from the president of the United States on down, were complete nonsense—a fevered fantasy that the credulous and fanatical believed because they didn't know better, and the cynical and opportunistic believed because it served their purposes.

On the Republican side, according to the secretary of state's office, there were 453,929 early votes and 29,220 absentee votes so far this primary season (the absentee votes will keep coming in through Election Day). This is compared with just 153,264 early votes and 14,795 absentee voters during the last, pre-pandemic midterm, in 2018.

The Democrats have seen a similar surge. In 2022, there were 337,245 early votes and 31,704 absentee votes so far, compared with only 134,542 early votes and 13,051 absentee votes in 2018.

Early Vote Among Minorities in Particular is Up Markedly

As Jim Geraghty has pointed out, the early vote among minorities in particular is up markedly. It never made sense that the Georgia law was going to stop anyone from voting.

The provisions that the Left complained about were clearly innocuous.

The rule against third parties providing food and drink to voters standing in lines at the polls was merely meant to stop electioneering at polling places (and the law attempts to address long lines, typically a problem of large, Democratic-run jurisdictions). The law limited drop boxes, but they hadn't existed prior to 2020. It moved from signature match on mail-in ballots to the more reliable driver's license or state-ID number—not a sea change. And it expanded hours available for early voting.

Now that a tsunami of early voting has shown that, indeed, there's no voter suppression in Georgia, the disinformation scolds are nowhere to be seen; the fact-checkers aren't swinging into action; the major newspapers aren't preparing tick-tocks on how the president was led down the path of promoting misinformation about the legitimacy of our electoral system; shows didn't do long segments devoted to the theme of how democracy in Georgia, once claimed to be hanging by a thread, has remarkably revived—praise God, and hallelujah.

Nina Jankowicz hasn't celebrated the triumph of truth over a baldly misleading viral narrative in prose, verse, or song—and presumably she never will. As with the Russian hoax, having promoted the Georgia voting hoax means never having to admit error, let alone apologize.

There wasn't a cottage industry, as the cliché has it, devoted to warning of the dire effects of the Georgia voting law; there was a veritable pollution-belching smoke-stack industry.

The widely quoted Brennan Center, whose job is to seed the media with left-wing arguments masquerading as neutral analysis, went into overdrive. It claimed that, as one headline had it,

"Voter Suppression Efforts in Georgia Are Escalating," and in another piece, titled simply, "Georgia's Voter Suppression Law," that "Gov. Brian Kemp signed a wide-ranging bill that targets Black voters with uncanny accuracy."

The progressive commentariat wrote as if the 1950s were upon us once again. Charles Blow of the *New York Times* was on the case. He wrote columns headlined "Voter Suppression Must Be the Central Issue" and "Voter Suppression Is Grand Larceny." Like much of the Left, he believed that President Biden was a near-quisling for not fighting the scourge of disenfranchisement on the landing grounds and the beaches—"Mr. President, You're Just Plain Wrong on Voter Suppression" read another headline. According to Blow, "Biden wants to make history with his agenda, but history is already being made by Republicans with this extraordinary voter suppression push."

Question: "If It's Not Jim Crow, What Is It?" Answer: Another False Democrat Narrative

Newsrooms took up the same themes and false narratives. A headline in a news story in the *New York Times* read, "Georgia G.O.P. Passes Major Law to Limit Voting Amid Nationwide Push." Another headline on a *Times* story ran, "Why the Georgia G.O.P.'s Voting Rollbacks Will Hit Black People Hard."

That report claimed that "the Republican legislation will undermine pillars of voting access by limiting drop boxes for mail ballots, introducing more rigid voter identification requirements for absentee balloting and making it a crime to provide food or water to people waiting in line to vote."

Of course, civil-rights activists and politicos didn't hold back. "Our democracy stands in its final hour," NAACP president Derrick Johnson said, in urging to Joe Biden to do even more after his speech attacking the Georgia law last January.

In Georgia, Bishop Reginald T. Jackson, a leader of the state's African Methodist Episcopal churches, related to reporters after a meeting with the lieutenant governor: "I told him exactly how I felt: that these bills were not only voter suppression, but they were in fact racist, and they are an attempt to turn back time to Jim Crow."

State senator Jen Jordan, a Democrat from outside Atlanta, called the bill "a Christmas tree of goodies for voter suppression."

Stacey Abrams, the original fount of much of the misinformation about voting in Georgia, explained the alleged Republican approach: "Instead of winning new voters, you rig the system against their participation, and you steal the right to vote."

And then, at Atlanta University in January, Biden came in with his disgraceful speech condemning the Georgia law. "Every Democrat, independent, and Republican will have to declare where they stand," he said, adding, "History has never been kind to those who side with voter suppression over voting rights."

"Do you want to be on the side of Dr. King or George Wallace?" he asked. "The side of John Lewis or Bull Connor? The side of Abraham Lincoln or Jefferson Davis?"

Well, It's Election Season in Georgia and Bull Connor and Jeff Davis Haven't Shown Up

The journalistic reaction has been, shall we say, muted. Despite its dire previous coverage, the *New York Times* didn't see fit to mention the false warnings about the Georgia law in its report on the early vote.

The AP had run a story in which Georgia featured prominently, headlined "As America embraces early voting, GOP hurries to restrict it." But a report on what's happened so far in the primaries notes, without mentioning the erroneous prior warnings, that Georgia voters "are turning to early, in-person voting, which is setting records. About 305,000 ballots have been cast at early voting locations across the state, or three times as many who did so for the same period during the 2018 primary, according to state officials."

To its credit, the *Washington Post* didn't memory-hole the long freak-out about Georgia, running a story headlined "Voting is surging in Georgia despite controversial new election law." A better headline would have been "Voting is surging in Georgia despite allegations about new election law."

Key Things You Need to Know About HR 1, the For the People Act of 2021

Per the Masooma Haq *Epoch Times* March 2021 article "Key Things You Need to Know About HR 1, the For the People Act of 2021":

On March 3, 2021, the Democrat-led House passed H.R. 1, the For the People Act of 2021, which was introduced by Rep. John Sarbanes (D-Md.). The election reform package, if passed by the Senate, would transfer authority over how elections are administered from states to the federal government and make permanent many voting rules that opponents say lead to voter fraud.

The sweeping election reform package is divided into three major sections; the second section is the main body of the legislation, with three subsections: a) voting, b) campaign finance, and c) ethics. Section three is the "Findings of General Constitutional Authority," and section four is the "Standards for Judicial Review."

Here are some of the key changes to election laws made by H.R. 1 that should concern all Americans who believe in election integrity:

1. Gives the federal government authority to administer elections: Although the U.S. Constitution gives states the authority to run their elections as they see fit, Democrats have interpreted the Constitution in their favor, stating in H.R. 1 that "Congress finds that it has broad authority to regulate the time, place, and manner of congressional elections under the Elections Clause of the Constitution, Article I, section 4."

2. Limits a plaintiff's access to federal courts when challenging H.R. 1: The bill mandates that any lawsuits challenging the constitutionality of H.R. 1 could only be filed in the District

Court for the District of Columbia and all plaintiffs would be required "to file joint papers or to be represented by a single attorney at oral argument."

3. Mandates automatic voter registration (AVR) in all 50 states (19 states currently have AVR): In what proponents call "modernizing" elections, any person who gives their information to designated government agencies, such as the Department of Motor Vehicles, a public university, or a social service agency, would be registered to vote. The bill mandates same-day and online registration.

4. Mandates no-fault absentee ballots: This provision does away with witness signature or notarization requirements for absentee ballots. Additionally, it would force states to accept absentee ballots received up to 10 days after Election Day.

5. Prevents election officials from removing ineligible voters from registries or confirming the eligibility and qualifications of voters: The bill would make it illegal to verify the address of registered voters, cross-checking voter registration lists to find individuals registered in multiple states, or ever removing registrants, no matter how much time has elapsed.

6. Restores the Voting Rights Act: This provision requires states to obtain approval from the federal government before implementing any changes to voting rules. There is also a provision that criminalizes the "hindering, interfering, or preventing" of anyone from registering or voting.

7. Bans state voter ID laws: States would no longer be allowed to require ID for voting and would be forced to accept signed statements from individuals claiming to verify who they say they are.

8. Ensures illegal immigrants can vote: The bill shields non-citizens from prosecution if they are registered to vote automatically. Agencies wouldn't be required to keep records of those who decline to affirm their citizenship.

9. Allows same-day voter registration: States would be required to permit same-day registration, including for early voting, at polling stations. The section includes a clause that requires same-day voter registration to be implemented in time for the upcoming elections in 2022.

10. Allows 16-year-olds to register to vote: From Jan. 1, 2022, states wouldn't be allowed to refuse a voting application from anyone aged 16 or older. Additionally, states would be required "to carry out a plan to increase the involvement of individuals under 18 years of age in public election activities."

11. Prohibits the publication of "misleading information" about elections: The bill makes it a federal crime to "communicate or cause to be communicated" information that is knowingly false and designed to discourage voting, carrying a sentence of up to five years. Opponents say the provision raises First Amendment concerns.

12. Allows felons to vote: Under the Democracy Restoration Act, federal dollars for prisons would be restricted in states that don't allow ex-convicts to vote. The bill says that all felons can vote unless they are "serving a felony sentence in a correctional institution or facility at the time of the election."

13. Mandates early voting: States would be required to allow anyone to cast a ballot during an early voting period prior to the date of the election.

14. Legalizes nationwide mail-in voting, without photo ID: Absentee voting by mail would be allowed in all federal elections and "may not require an individual to provide any form of identification as a condition of obtaining an absentee ballot." A witness signature wouldn't be required.

15. Promotes ballot harvesting: Any designated person would be allowed to return absentee ballots to any ballot drop-off location or election office, so long as the person doesn't receive compensation based on the number of ballots he or she collected. Additionally, there would be no limit on the number of absentee ballots any designated person could return.

16. Requires states to accept ballots 10 days after Election Day: States would be required to accept any mailed ballots postmarked before or on Election Day that arrive within 10 days of the election. The bill allows states to expand that deadline.

17. Prohibits state election officials from campaigning in federal elections: State election officials would be banned from participating in political management or campaigns for any election in which the officials have supervisory authority. This would most affect states like Georgia, whose secretaries of state have been notably involved in elections.

18. Requires colleges and universities to hire "campus vote coordinators": The bill requires institutions of higher learning to employ an official who would be responsible for informing students about elections and encouraging them to register to vote. It would incentivize voter registration by giving grants to institutions that have a high registration rate.

19. Mandates that states make absentee voter boxes available for 45 days within an election: Drop boxes would be made available for individuals to drop off absentee ballots for federal elections at any time, 24 hours a day, during the voting period.

20. Requires states to allow curbside voting: States may not "prohibit any jurisdiction administering an election for Federal office in the State from utilizing curbside voting as a method by which individuals may cast ballots in the election."

21. Urges statehood for the District of Columbia and representation for territories: The bill points to the fact that the District of Columbia is not yet a state, adding, "The United States is the only democratic country that denies both voting representation in the national legislature and local self-government to the residents of its Nation's capital." It appoints a commission that would advocate for congressional representation and presidential votes.

22. Requires states to redraw congressional districts through "independent" commissions: Taking power away from state legislatures, the bill would require redistricting to occur through commissions that are also required to show "racial, ethnic, economic, and gender" diversity.

23. Creates a national commission to "protect United States democratic institutions": A national commission would study elections and produce a report after 18 months with recommendations for improving elections. It would comprise 10 members, only four of whom would be selected by the minority party, giving control to the majority party (at this time, Democrats).

24. Mandates new disclosure for corporations: The bill codifies the Democrats' DISCLOSE Act, to restrict corporate participation in elections. Democrats say this provision will shed light on dark money, while Republicans counter that the legislation's transparency requirements would violate free speech rights.

25. Oversight of online political advertising: A provision called the Stand By Every Ad Act would stop campaign dollars from covering any form of advertising over the internet. Opponents say this would increase the cost of campaigning.

26. Weakens the Supreme Court's 2010 decision in the case Citizens United v. Federal Elections Commission (FEC): The bill states that "the Supreme Court's misinterpretation of the Constitution to empower monied interests at the expense of the American people in elections has seriously eroded over 100 years of congressional action to promote fairness and protect elections from the toxic influence of money." It also suggests that the Constitution should be amended "so that Congress and the States may regulate and set limits on the raising and spending of money."

27. Allows politicians to use campaign funds for personal use: Under a provision called the Help America Run Act, the bill legalizes the use of campaign donations for personal expenses such as child care.

28. Changes the composition of the FEC: The bill decreases the number of members on the FEC from six to five. Four members can be associated with a particular political party, making the fifth member "independent" but nominated by a president associated with a party. Former FEC members have written to Congress, warning about this change and other related provisions.

29. Changes rules around conflicts of interest for the president and vice president: It would require the president or vice president to divest all financial interests that could pose a conflict of interest for them, their families, or anyone with whom they are negotiating or who is seeking employment in their administration.

30. Changes FEC rules to require presidential candidates to provide their tax returns: Within 15 days of becoming a "covered candidate," the individual would be required to submit copies of his or her tax returns, going back 10 years, to the FEC.

9 – The January 6th Show Trial Commission vs. Summer 2020 Riots Highlight Prime Time Illiberalism

Credit: Greg Groesch/The Washington Times.

One year after the Jan. 6 Capitol riot, President Joe Biden gravely informed the nation that the incident, during which exactly one person, an unarmed female pro-Trump protester, was killed—shot to death at close range, without warning, by a Capitol Hill policeman—was "the most significant test of our democracy since the Civil War."

Biden delivered this extraordinary assessment immediately after Vice President Kamala Harris solemnly equated the out-of-control D.C. protest to both the Dec. 7, 1941 attack on Pearl Harbor that killed 2,403 Americans and injured 1,178, and the Sept. 11, 2001 terror attacks that killed 2,977 Americans and injured over 6,000. The Civil War killed an estimated 750,000 Americans.

Insurrection? Sedition? Incitement? A Legal Guide to the Capitol Riot

This section Is from the analysis by Peter Blumberg Bloomberg June 2022 in his "Insurrection? Sedition? Incitement? A Legal Guide to the Capitol Riot" article:

By comparison, more than 850 people have been criminally charged in connection with the riot at the US Capitol on Jan. 6, 2021 by a mob of then-President Donald Trump's supporters. Most are accused of conventional offenses such as trespassing and assault, while 16 members of two right-wing groups are facing a more exotic charge: seditious conspiracy. Just before he left office, Trump was impeached by the House of Representatives for incitement of insurrection but was acquitted of the charge by the Senate. The legal terminology around the unprecedented events that shocked Americans and the rest of the world requires some unpacking.

1. What is insurrection?

The term broadly means a revolt against an established government, usually employing violence. However, the federal statute against it—which is rooted in the American Civil War of the 1860s and provides up to 10 years' imprisonment for inciting, assisting or engaging in insurrection—doesn't define the term, so the parameters of the law are unclear. It's been prosecuted rarely.

2. What is seditious conspiracy?

It's the name given in federal law to the crime of sedition, which generally means the organized encouragement of rebellion or civil disorder against the authority of the state. In this case, the statute, also a reaction to the Civil War, spells out acts that constitute violations; that is, two or more people conspiring to overthrow the US government or to forcibly oppose its authority, interfere with the execution of any law, or seize any property of the US. The crime carries a maximum prison term of 20 years.

3. What charges are rioters facing?

The Justice Department has charged people from all 50 states for storming the Capitol, where lawmakers were counting electoral votes from the November 2020 presidential race to certify Joe Biden as the winner. The crowd overran the Capitol police, injured an estimated 140 officers, and temporarily halted the vote count.

- Seventeen months after the attack, about 246 rioters have pleaded guilty to misdemeanor charges such as illegal parading, while another 59 have admitted to felonies. About 70—fewer than 10% of the total charged—have been sentenced to time behind bars for assaulting law enforcement officers and other crimes. Among those who've already been sentenced, Jacob Chansley—the self-proclaimed "QAnon Shaman" who wore a coyote-skin headdress into the Senate chamber while carrying an American flag—was ordered to serve 41 months in prison after pleading guilty to obstructing an official proceeding. Chansley vowed to appeal the sentence.

- In January 2021, three members of the far-right group Oath Keepers became the first to be charged with conspiring to forcibly storm the Capitol in order to prevent ratification of the election results. About four dozen more people have since been charged with conspiring to obstruct a congressional proceeding, obstruct law enforcement or injure officers, or some combination of those.

- On January, 2022, 11 leaders of the Oath Keepers were charged with seditious conspiracy, the most serious charges yet filed. In early June, the government added seditious conspiracy charges to cases already pending against five members of the Proud Boys, another extremist group.

4. What would prosecutors have to prove in the sedition cases?

Intent is important. It's not enough for prosecutors to demonstrate that the accused advocated violence. Investigators have to show evidence of a deliberate conspiracy to use force to prevent the certification of Biden's election. The indictment announced Jan. 13 describes how the Oath

Keepers allegedly set up staging areas for equipment in Washington's suburbs and organized training sessions to teach paramilitary combat tactics.

The charging document also includes details of extensive electronic communications between the alleged co-conspirators and others before the assault, as well as excerpts of some of their encrypted messages during the riot. Oath Keepers founder Elmer Stewart Rhodes, referring to Biden as a "usurper," at one point said there would be a "bloody and desperate fight," according to the filing. Rhodes has publicly stated that he wasn't present at the Capitol during the riot and that Oath Keepers who made trouble went rogue.

5. What is incitement?

Legally, incitement is the act of urging others to commit a crime. The article of impeachment against Trump adopted by the House cited his comments before a crowd of supporters Jan. 6, when he urged them to march to the Capitol while saying, fallaciously, that he had won the presidential election and that "if you don't fight like hell you're not going to have a country anymore."

At the conclusion of Trump's impeachment trial, which occurred after he'd already left office, the Senate voted 57–43 to convict him of inciting insurrection, falling 10 votes short of the two-thirds majority required by the Constitution, and Trump was therefore acquitted.

6. Could Trump face criminal charges?

Inciting an insurrection or riot is a federal crime, but the Justice Department would have to charge him separately. That's unlikely, according to Frederick Lawrence, a lecturer at the Georgetown University Law Center. Not only would prosecutors have to prove Trump intentionally whipped up his supporters, Lawrence said, but also that he intended for them to break into the Capitol, loot and cause bodily harm.

A further complication is a 1969 Supreme Court precedent that shields inflammatory speech under the First Amendment unless it's aimed at "imminent" lawless behavior. Apart from what Trump said in his speech, prosecutors could take an alternative path if they uncover evidence that the former president or his advisers were involved in planning the riot. Whether such conspiracy charges are viable would depend on the nature of the plotting and how close Trump and his inner circle was to it. "It would all turn on who was in the room and what they are prepared to testify to," Lawrence said.

The January 6 Committee's Futile Prime-Time Political Ad

Per the Andrew C. McCarthy *National Review* June 2022 article "The January 6 Committee's Futile Prime-Time Political Ad":

The *New York Times* could not have been more unseemly in its table-setting piece about the January 6 committee's extravaganza scheduled to begin tonight: The Gray Lady has her pom-poms out because the Democrat-dominated panel is producing a prime-time television special that will masquerade as a bipartisan congressional hearing.

The hearings could better be understood as a 90-minute political ad, slickly produced by a former top ABC executive. Their objective is unabashedly partisan: Break the spell of soaring prices and woke-progressive failure that has Democrats careening into a midterm rout that would cost them control of Congress by refocusing voters on Donald Trump and the Capitol riot.

Good luck with that. Trump derangement still seizes the media–Democrat complex and some Republican pockets, but the vast majority of Americans have moved on from Trump and the events of January 6. That includes Republicans who approved of much of what Trump did— those many of us who appreciate that the Trump administration was far better for the country than the train wreck that is the Biden administration, but who have no use for Trump the man and no interest in a reprise of Trump the president.

No one approves of rioting—not the five-hour riot by Trump fanatics at the seat of our government, but also not the months of lethal rioting, looting, and arson perpetrated by the radical Left after George Floyd's death in police custody.

The problem for Biden and the Democrats is that no one is fooled by their claptrap about how the Insurrection™ was different because it was an attack on democracy itself. Not when they are no longer content just to avert their eyes from the jack-booted neo-Marxists on their own side, but now go the extra mile to coddle violent radical lawyers who firebomb police cars.

Down here on Earth, where all political violence is to be condemned regardless of what "ism" ignites it, we're not very interested in further hysteria about the Capitol riot. Not from people who go out of their way not to notice that our streets have been torched. Not when our cities are engulfed by crime because those people won't enforce the laws against anyone other than Trump and his myrmidons.

The January 6 committee apparently intends to do a big song-and-dance about Trump's attempt to use the Justice Department to coerce state officials, such as those who ran Georgia's GOP-controlled government, into reversing Biden's victory in their popular elections. But even the committee's portrayal of it as an attempt is extravagant. It never had a prayer of working. After Attorney General Robert Barr, just before leaving his post, made the obvious explicit by declaring the lack of material election fraud, his successors in DOJ leadership told Trump to pound sand. And Trump fecklessly retreated.

That didn't happen because there was no existential threat to our democracy. The riot, if we were to dignify it as a strategy rather than a petulant outburst, was ineffectual. It probably wouldn't have happened, and would certainly have been rapidly contained, if the security forces had been adequate and competent—or President Trump had condemned the rioters as they stormed the Capitol and demanded they leave peacefully.

But neither happened!

'Sprint Through the Finish': Why the Jan. 6 Committee Isn't Nearly Done

From the Kyle Cheney and Nicholas Wu Politico July 2022 update titled "'Sprint Through the Finish': Why the Jan. 6 Committee Isn't Nearly Done":

The Jan. 6 select committee once envisioned a single month packed with hearings. Then a fire hose of evidence came its way—and now its members have no interest in shutting or even slowing the spigot.

As its summer hearings show some signs of chipping at Donald Trump's electoral appeal, select panel members describe this hearing as only the last in a series. Committee members, aides and allies are emboldened by the public reaction to the information they're unearthing about the former president's actions and say their full sprint will continue, even past November.

The only hard deadline, they say, is Jan. 3, 2023, when Republicans likely take over the House.

Thursday's hearing will focus on Trump's hours of inaction on Jan. 6, 2021, while a mob ransacked the Capitol and supporters, aides and family members begged him to speak out. But beyond that, the committee is pursuing multiple new avenues of inquiry created by its investigation of Trump's scheme to seize a second term he didn't win, from questions about the Secret Service's internal communications as well as leads provided by high-level witnesses from his White House.

"It's been amazing to see, kind of, the flurry of people coming forward," said Rep. Adam Kinzinger (R-Ill.), one of the panel's two Republican members. "So it's not the time to wind it down."

The new open-ended timeline is a marked shift in the public posture of a committee that once eyed a conclusion as early as springtime, then looked to a September wrap-up. A confluence of forces, led by a series of recent breakthroughs, has led to its new posture.

A major reason to continue, for many select panel members, is the public discussion they've driven about what they see as an ongoing threat to democracy posed by Trump and his allies. With every new hearing, particularly as White House aide Cassidy Hutchinson described an enraged Trump directing armed supporters to the Capitol and trying to join them there, the panel has seemed to get further under the skin of the former president as he contemplates a third bid for the White House.

New Insights About the Trump-Driven Push to Unravel His Loss

Each hearing has offered new insights about the Trump-driven push to unravel his loss based on false fraud claims—and as a result has motivated new witnesses to come forward. Aides and members say, featuring witnesses including former Trump White House press aide Sarah Matthews and former deputy national security adviser Matthew Pottinger, will be no different.

"We're going to sprint through the finish," select panel member Rep. Pete Aguilar (D-Calif.) said in a brief interview. "The peak investigative time was probably February, March, or April," he said. "It's fewer interviews right now, but I don't think that means we're letting up. We're doing some re-interviews of folks, but it's important."

The panel has spent recent weeks highlighting several facets of Trump's election subversion effort: his bid to deploy the Justice Department to help sow doubts about the election, his pressure on state legislatures to defy the will of voters by appointing alternate electors, his push for then-Vice President Mike Pence to single-handedly reverse the outcome, and the way his rhetoric activated domestic extremists and conspiracy theorists to march on the Capitol.

As Aguilar observed, the rhythm of witness interviews has remained steady, far from an indication of a wind-down. Former Overstock.com CEO Patrick Byrne participated in a lengthy interview to discuss his participation in a Dec. 18, 2020, Oval Office meeting in which Trump and outside advisers discussed the prospect of martial law and seizing voting machines.

Steve Bannon, the erstwhile Trump ally whose criminal trial for defying a select committee subpoena began with jury selection, has also indicated in recent days that he would cooperate with the select committee after months of defiance. But Bannon hasn't made good on that yet, and the panel has indicated it wants to receive subpoenaed documents from him before agreeing to a belated deposition.

Several critical Jan. 6-related lawsuits are also still underway, with key inflection points arriving next month. Those include the select panel's separate fights to secure documents and testimony from former White House chief of staff Mark Meadows and the Republican National Committee.

The committee is also pursuing leads revealed by Hutchinson, who testified last month that Trump was aware of armed elements in the crowd that he directed to march on the Capitol—and that he sought to join them there before staff and Secret Service officials stopped him.

Two Secret Service officials whom Hutchinson referenced—former White House deputy chief of staff Tony Ornato and Robert Engel, the head of Trump's Secret Service detail—have indicated they may return to the committee to respond to some of Hutchinson's testimony under oath. Despite interest among Trump allies in an attempt by either man to discredit Hutchinson's version of events, neither have appeared yet.

A third official, the as-yet-unidentified driver of Trump's SUV on Jan. 6, is also engaging with the committee about testimony.

The panel subpoenaed the Secret Service, through its outgoing director James Murray, for internal reports related to Jan. 6, as well as reams of text messages sent by agents that day. The agency has said many of those messages were erased as part of a staff-wide phone upgrade that commenced last year; some may come into the select committee's possession this week.

The select committee is also still weighing how hard to fight for the testimony of Virginia Thomas, known as Ginni, the longtime conservative activist and wife of Supreme Court Justice Clarence Thomas. She had become part of the select panel's investigation after revelations she had texted Meadows, then White House chief of staff, and others about contesting Trump's loss.

Ginni Thomas had also invited John Eastman, an architect of Trump's post-election legal efforts, to speak to a conservative group known as the Frontliners about election litigation. Her attorney pushed back on the panel's request for a voluntary interview last month.

The Committee is Unlikely to Wrap Up imminently

Another significant indicator that the committee is unlikely to wrap up imminently: its staff has mostly stayed intact.

Typically, when congressional inquiries reach their codas, top investigators depart. So far, the Jan. 6 panel's main teams remain fully staffed, with the only notable exits coming from former Rep. Denver Riggleman and senior investigative counsel John Wood, who left to run for Senate as an independent in Missouri.

Despite the newly open-ended timeline, the committee is still likely to produce a comprehensive report this fall. Its chair, Rep. Bennie Thompson (D-Miss.), has emphasized that the panel intends to spend much of the August lull compiling and distilling its 1,000 witness interviews and tens of thousands of documents into a cogent narrative.

But in recent days, Thompson also floated the prospect of issuing an "addendum" to the report based on any findings the select panel makes later in the year.

"I would say we would be open for any information until we more or less finish," Thompson told reporters.

The committee's prime-time hearing was initially viewed as framing its most explosive evidence yet: the story of Trump's inaction while thousands of rioters battered Capitol Police, forcing Congress, Mike Pence and a building full of aides to flee on the day lawmakers were required to count electoral votes showing Joe Biden defeated Trump.

As new material pours in and a potential second round of hearings gets slated for the fall, though, this week looks more like a season finale than a series ender.

58 Percent Say Jan. 6 House Committee is Biased: Poll

Per the Julia Manchester *The Hill* August 2021 article "58 Percent Say Jan. 6 House Committee is Biased: Poll": A majority of voters say they believe the House select committee investigating the Jan. 6 attack on the Capitol is biased, according to a new Harvard CAPS-Harris Poll survey.

Fifty-eight percent of voters polled said they believed the committee set up by Speaker Nancy Pelosi (D-Calif.) was biased, while 42 percent said they thought it was fair.

"Americans want an examination of the riots over the summer and the origins of the virus over investigating Jan. 6th," said Mark Penn, the co-director of the Harvard CAPS-Harris Poll survey. "The voters reject the Pelosi move to toss Republicans off of the committee and see it now as just a partisan exercise."

Furthermore, from the Editors at Real Clear Investigations per their September 2022 report "Introducing Real Clear Investigations' Jan. 6-BLM Riots Dataset":

Republicans, Trump supporters, and others see a double standard at play in Democrats' emphasis on Jan. 6. They note that many Democrats cheered nationwide protests, and some even put up bail after the May 2020 murder of George Floyd, a black man, by a white police officer—prolonged unrest that generated far more death and destruction. They argue that groups associated with the summer's violence, such as Black Lives Matter and Antifa, themselves aim to subvert democracy, and acted accordingly in targeting cops, public offices, and private businesses.

The electorate itself is divided, but doesn't necessarily view this issue as an either/or choice. Polling shows that a large majority of Americans support the idea of examining the causes of both the 2020 summer riots in America's cities and the Jan. 6 riot at the Capitol.

It is clear, then, that many Americans see two sides to this story. In keeping with its mission to fill gaps in press coverage, RealClearInvestigations is launching a running compendium of data, with hyperlinked sourcing, comparing the damage done on Jan. 6, and the subsequent treatment of those accused of perpetrating it, with two other recent events: the summer 2020 riots and—in some ways a closer analogy—the all-but-forgotten riot in Washington on Inauguration Day 2017, as protesters challenged Donald Trump's election and legitimacy much as Jan. 6 rioters challenged Joe Biden's.

RealClearInvestigations has found that:

The summer 2020 riots resulted in some 15 times more injured police officers, 30 times as many arrests, and estimated damages in dollar terms up to 1,300 times more costly than those of the Capitol riot. George Floyd rioters were found to have used more sophisticated and dangerous tactics than did the Capitol rioters, and in some cases weapons of greater lethality.

Authorities have pursued the largely Trump-supporting Capitol rioters with substantially more vigor than suspected wrongdoers in the earlier two cases. Many accused Capitol rioters, unlike accused participants in the other riots, have been held in pretrial detention for months—with one defendant serving more time than the maximum sentence for the charge to which he pleaded guilty. Some allegedly endured solitary confinement and other mistreatment.

With authorities applying lenient prosecutorial standards in many major cities torn by the summer riots, the vast majority of charges last year were dismissed, as were charges in the Inauguration 2017 unrest. Charges have to date been dropped in only a single Capitol riot case.

You can access the database at the bottom of the Introducing Real Clear Investigations' Jan. 6-BLM Riots Dataset in the Appendix.

Where are the Congressional Hearings for the George Floyd Riots?

From the Jim Patrick Law Enforcement Today July 2021 report titled "Thousands of Cops Were Injured, Over $2 billion in Damage During Floyd Riots. Where are the "Congressional Hearings"?":

A Rasmussen/National Police Association poll released on July 21, 2021, shows more voters favor a Congressional investigation into the violent Black Lives Matter/Antifa riots last summer than the so-called January 6 "insurrection." With that in mind, we thought it would be interesting to compare and contrast the two.

As we have seen since January 6, Democrats have seized on the incident to commission a January 6 inquiry, no doubt reminiscent of a Spanish inquisition, ostensibly to look into what led up to the siege at the US Capitol. Unfortunately, this inquisition committee will be nothing more than a politically charged witch hunt with the intention of laying the entire blame for the incident on former President Trump and his supporters.

That became quite clear when House Speaker Nancy Pelosi (D-CA) Pelosi, tapped Rep. Adam Kinzinger (Ill.) to serve alongside fellow GOP Trump critic Rep. Liz Cheney (Wyo.) on the committee after she blocked pro-Trump Reps. Jim Jordan (R-Ohio) and Jim Banks (R-Ind.) from serving on the panel. Jordan and Banks both voted to overturn the 2020 presidential election results hours after a pro-Trump mob violently breached the Capitol during the election certification process.

Pelosi was apparently afraid of what they might seek to gain information on, such as why repeated requests from former Capitol Police Chief Steven Sund for national guard troops were summarily rejected. That of course falls on Pelosi, who is in charge of Capitol security.

Meanwhile, Biden, the Justice Department and the rest of the Democrats totally ignored the violence across the country that started last year and continues in some cases unabated today. The organized riots of last summer have given way to skyrocketing violent crime this summer.

According to the Armed Conflict Location and Event Data Project (ACLED), 95 percent of the riots that took place last summer were linked to Black Lives Matter. Six percent of the protests which occurred between May 26 and Sept. 5 involved rioting, looting and similar violence, including 47 fatalities, The Frontier Post reported.

Of the 633 incidents coded as riots, 88 percent were coded as involving Black Lives Matter activists. All told, there were 12,045 incidents.

The rioting wasn't only concentrated in large metropolitan areas, but also found its way into smaller cities such as Fort Collins, Colorado, Cottonwood Heights, Utah; Gilbert, Arizona; and Davenport Iowa. The riots spread across 47 states.

The 2020 Riots Caused an Estimated $2 billion in Damages Across the Country

The riots that took place last year caused an estimated $2 billion in damages across the country, overtaking the 1992 Los Angeles riots that took place in the wake of the initial Rodney King verdict, which caused $775 million in damage. According to Axios, adjusted for inflation, those costs would amount to $1.42 billion.

The damage estimate, provided by Property Claim Services only accounted for damages caused between May 26 to June 8, 2020 according to *The Sun*.

Loretta L Worters of the Insurance Information Institute told *The Sun* that since the damages were from "all over the country" and not in just one state, which could account for the large sum. She also said, "And this is still happening so the losses could be significantly more." And it is.

No specific estimate is available for all the damage caused by riots that continued throughout last summer and into the fall, but it would be easy to assume you can multiply that $2 billion by a factor of four or five. In Portland, Oregon alone, the riots continued for over 100 consecutive nights, including the siege of a federal courthouse.

The Foundation for Economic Education (FEE) explained the losses above do not account for damages that were not insured. According to FEE, 75 percent of US businesses are underinsured and about 40 percent of small businesses have no insurance at all. Those numbers do not factor into the $2 billion figure.

It also doesn't account for lost business or personal pain and suffering, upon which you cannot put a price tag. This also doesn't consider people who lost their means of income due to businesses damaged.

That figure also doesn't consider the long-term economic impact that riots have on communities. For example, a study of the 1992 Los Angeles riots concluded that above and beyond the damages that were done, it led to an economic decline of $3.8 million in sales activity and $125 million in lost tax revenue.

The most ludicrous thing about these riots is the disproportionate impact they have on the black community. A 2005 study that examined similar riots from the 1960s discovered "negative, persistent and economically significant effects of riots on the value of black-owned housing," leading to a "10 percent decline in the total value of black-owned property in cities."

Newsweek reported that in Minneapolis alone, over 1,500 businesses were damaged in the riots, with many expected to take years to rebuild.

And what of the personal cost the riots wrought? According to The Guardian, 25 Americans were killed in George Floyd-related riots between the end of May and the end of October last year. Eleven were killed directly participating in riots, while 14 died in incidents linked to the political turmoil.

To make matters worse, a number of deadly crimes occurred in the vicinity of protests which have not been tied directly into the riots.

And what of police officers? According to the Major Cities Chiefs Association (MCCA) as cited in American Military News, over 2,000 police officers sustained injuries in just the first few weeks of the Floyd riots in the time period between May 25 through July 31, a total of 2,037 injured officers. The report only covered MCCA-affiliated cities. At the White House, some 60 U.S. Secret Service Agents were injured, some seriously as real insurrectionists attempted to breach the White House fence, American Military News reported.

Meanwhile in 2021, the number of officers feloniously killed in the line of duty has soared 40%, with officers being rammed by vehicles, killed by gunfire or stabbed to death, the *Washington*

Examiner reported. In addition, ambush assaults of officers is up by 91% over last year, Fox News reported.

Let's Contrast the Billions of Dollars of Damage During the George Floyd Riots With the Capitol "Insurrection" on January 6

According to *The Hill*, the worst "insurrection" in world history on January 6 caused an estimated $1.5 million in damage, according to a plea document entered for one of those arrested in connection with the incident. Defense attorneys told The *Washington Post* that prosecutors in the U.S. Attorney's Office were seeking $2,000 in restitution for every felony case, $500 for each misdemeanor case.

In other words, the Department of Justice has dispatched hundreds of FBI agents nationwide, posted pictures on social media of the bandidos who trespassed at the US Capitol and jailed some of those arrested in solitary confinement for over six months for $1.5 million in damage.

What about injuries? Well the *New York Times*, which virtually ignored the riots last summer in Minneapolis, Portland, and so on called Jan. 6 "one of the worst days of injuries for law enforcement in the United States since the Sept. 11, 2001 terrorist attacks.

One-hundred forty police officers were injured—73 from the Capitol Police and 65 from DC Metro, obviously a disturbing number. The contrast between how the two incidents were reported is what is infuriating. The Times seemed far-less concerned about police officers having commercial-grade fireworks shot at their heads, being shot and stabbed than they were about the officers on Jan. 6.

The fact that the *Times* let politics skew its reporting about Jan. 6 vs the summer of riots would almost be laughable if it weren't so sad. As to the comparison, 140 officers pales in comparison to the thousands (more likely tens of thousands) of officers injured during the Floyd riots all last summer across the country.

How many people died at the US Capitol on January 6? Well, despite leftists breathlessly referring to it as a "deadly" insurrection, only one person died that day as a "direct" result of the incident—Air Force veteran and Trump supporter Ashli Babbitt, an unarmed woman shot to death ostensibly by a plain-clothes, US Capitol police officer.

How "damaged" was the Capitol? In other words, how long was it that our "Democracy" was shut down for? Mere hours. How many members of Congress were injured or directly threatened? None. How many protesters were arrested in connection with the siege? Over 500. And as stated, many of them are in solitary confinement, held without bail, and if some reports are correct being subjected to physical and psychological torture. In the United States of America.

A tale of two "riots." One gets a special, albeit politically tainted "special commission." The other gets ignored.

10 – Economics Madness: Budgets, Spending Proposals, Inflation, Taxes, Debt and the Next Recession

UNSUSTAINABLE BUDGET DEFICITS

DEFICITS AS PERCENTAGE OF GDP

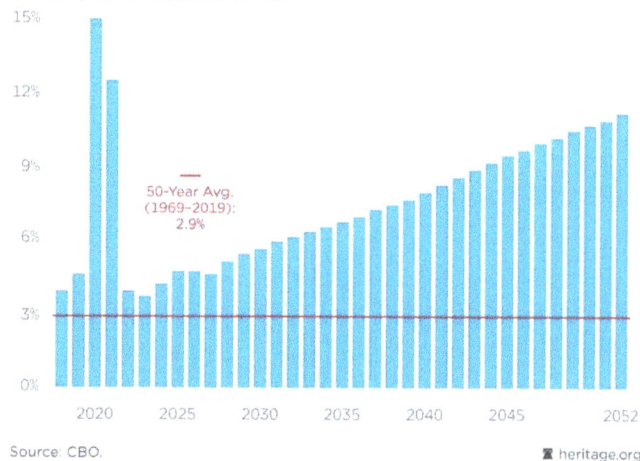

50-Year Avg.
(1969-2019):
2.9%

Source: CBO.

heritage.org

Per the Marc A. Thiessen *The Washington Post* June 2021 article "Biden's Budget Is a Lie":

President Biden's initial $6 trillion budget is both staggering in its scope and dishonest in its design. The *New York Times* reports that Biden's plan "would take the United States to its highest sustained levels of federal spending since World War II" while collecting "more tax revenue as a share of the economy than at almost any point in the last century."

That's bad enough, but here is what Biden is not telling you: either he has abandoned major campaign promises just months into his administration, or he actually plans to tax and spend a whole lot more.

For example, a centerpiece of Biden's campaign—his plan to create a "public option" for health care and lower the age at which Americans can receive Medicare—is nowhere to be found in this budget.

According to Manhattan Institute budget expert Brian Riedl, Biden's missing health proposals will cost $1.45 trillion. That's a huge omission. So, I asked Riedl what else is missing from Biden's budget? A lot, it turns out. He points out that Biden also did not include a host of other spending plans he proposed during the 2020 campaign—such as his plan to expand Social Security and Supplemental Security Income (SSI), as well as much of the K-12 spending and higher education spending that he promised.

In addition, Biden's budget assumes that items he did include—such the child tax credit expansion in his American Family Plan and long-term care for seniors—will expire before Biden's 10-year budget window closes, when, in fact, the president has no intention of allowing those programs to expire.

According to Riedl, when you add up the costs of all the missing items—plus the hundreds of billions in interest costs from these new initiatives—it comes to a whopping $5.8 trillion in additional spending. That means Biden's actual spending plans are nearly double those outlined in his first budget—which is already the highest level of proposed spending since the Second World War.

A Lower- and Middle-Income Tax Increase Gotcha!

And there is something that Biden's budget does include which he did not propose on the campaign trail—a lower- and middle-income tax increase.

When he ran for president, Biden declared, "Under my plan, if you make less than $400,000, you won't pay a single penny, more in taxes. You have my word on it." But in this budget, Biden breaks his word. The White House budget assumes that Biden will allow the Trump tax cuts for low- and middle-income Americans to expire as scheduled in 2025. Letting tax cuts expire is a tax increase.

Who would be affected by those tax hikes? The nonpartisan Tax Policy Center estimates that 65 percent of Americans saw their taxes go down under Trump's tax reform—which means that under Biden's budget 65 percent of Americans will see their taxes go up. Even the Institute on Taxation and Economic Policy—a left-wing group which opposed the Trump tax cuts—acknowledged that every income group in every state would pay less on average thanks to those cuts—which means that every income group in every state will pay more if Biden lets their tax cuts expire.

Biden did not campaign on a pledge to raise taxes on the majority of Americans, comprising every income group. And yet, he is baking in a massive lower- and middle-income tax increase into his budget plans. Why is Biden counting revenue he promised not to collect from working-class Americans in his budget? Because, according to Riedl, "the president has already used up nearly everything from his campaign tax hikes in his current proposals."

Even with a lower- and middle-income tax increase, he is still short of revenue to pay for all the $6 trillion in spending he admits to in his budget—leaving him with no way to pay the additional $5.8 trillion in spending he has pledged. That means, despite already proposing the highest levels of taxation in a century, he will have to raise taxes even more.

In other words, from spending to taxes, Biden's budget is a lie. He plans to tax you more, and spend far more of your money, than even his record-breaking budget plan admits.

New Charts Reveal Harms of Biden's Budget-Busting Binge

Per the David Ditch The Heritage Foundation June 2022 report titled "New Charts Reveal Harms of Biden's Budget-Busting Binge":

The harmful effects of excessive government spending have become the most pressing issue for Americans due to the worst inflation surge in decades. Washington's reckless choice to pump trillions of dollars into the economy is the reason we face more inflation than other top economies around the world. Yet, incredibly, Congress is still planning an onslaught of additional inflationary spending bills with seemingly no end in sight.

A recent report from the nonpartisan Congressional Budget Office helps to underscore the severity of the fiscal problems facing the nation and the urgent need for a new approach.

Biden's Budget Bust

President Joe Biden has been engaging in extra-strength political spin by repeatedly taking credit for a reduction in the budget deficit. Yet this happened despite Biden's policies, not because of them: Record-setting deficits during the COVID-19 pandemic were already expected to come back down to earth as the worst of the pandemic seemed to wane.

A more accurate way to see whether Biden has been good for the nation's financial health is to compare where things stood when he took office with where they stand today. The comparison in the chart below makes it clear: Biden has repeatedly chosen to make things worse.

Compared to projections from February 2021, when Biden had just taken office, the latest analysis shows a combined $2.77 trillion in additional deficits over the 2021-2031 period. The largest factor for this increase was the wasteful and opportunistic $1.9 trillion COVID-19 package that passed with exclusively Democratic support in March 2021. The shoddy $1.2 trillion infrastructure bill that Biden championed added even more red ink.

Incredibly, things could have been even worse if any version of Biden's disastrous Build Back Better multitrillion-dollar debacle had become law. Despite the false spin from leading Democrats, it would have led to significantly higher deficits over the first several years (at minimum), pouring more gasoline on the inflationary fire.

Biden's budget plan is similarly bankrupt, with more inflationary spending; anti-growth tax hikes; and radical, left-wing policy goals. It's clear that the administration isn't even considering the idea that now is the time to rein in out-of-control spending.

Spending Binge and Hangover

While the activist left claims that deficits are the result of taxes being too low, the reality is that the IRS has been raking in record hauls after the passage of the 2017 tax cuts.

In addition, the CBO's long-term projection makes it clear that we're on the wrong path due to ever-increasing spending, not because Uncle Sam is taking it easy on taxpayers.

The Grand Canyon-sized gulf between federal spending and revenues in the below chart means that the record-setting deficits seen at the height of the COVID-19 pandemic will eventually return simply by continuing with the government we have today.

GROWING SPENDING IS THE PROBLEM

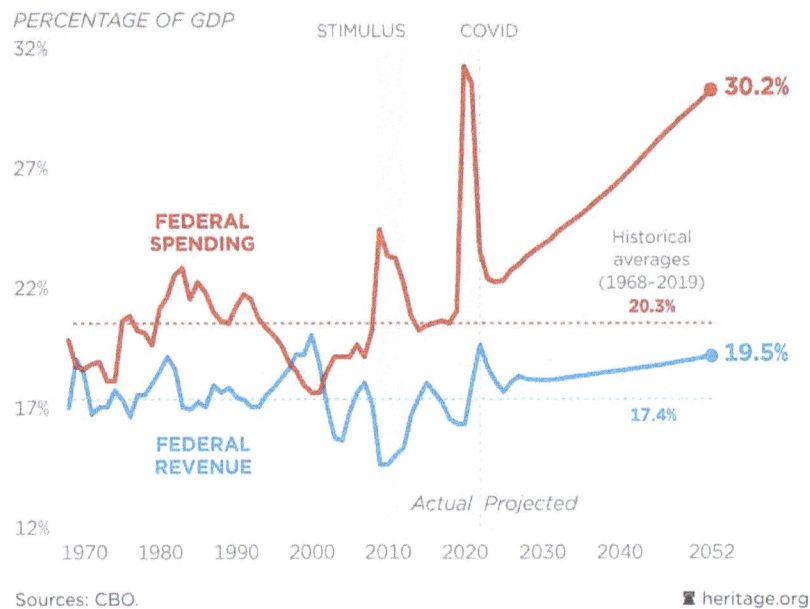

PERCENTAGE OF GDP

STIMULUS   COVID

**FEDERAL
SPENDING**

Historical
averages
(1968-2019)
20.3%

30.2%

19.5%

17.4%

**FEDERAL
REVENUE**

Actual Projected

32%

27%

22%

17%

12%

1970   1980   1990   2000   2010   2020   2030   2040   2052

Sources: CBO.   heritage.org

The mounting deficits seen in the chart above would have a twofold effect. First, they would mean that inflation would become a much more enduring threat than the Biden administration would have you believe, since large federal deficits financed by the Federal Reserve are inherently inflationary.

Second, as the national debt continues to grow, the cost of just paying the ever-increasing interest on that debt threatens to become another anchor around our necks. The chart below illustrates one of the country's biggest threats:

No Way to Run a Country

Even if we set aside those 30-year projections, our current situation is unacceptable, as the chart below makes clear: The break-neck speed at which Washington's spending has added to the national debt can't be sustained. Washington's short-sighted attitude about mounting debt has pushed America to a lopsided position.

Washington has proven over and over that it will choose the political expediency of debt and deficits rather than the sober work of serious budgeting.

The irresponsible way that Congress and the Biden administration treat the nation's finances is nothing new, and it's abundantly clear that the left views government spending as the answer to seemingly every problem under the sun.

The only solution is for Americans to make their voices heard and hold officials accountable. The Tea Party movement and the 1994 Republican "revolution" both led to improvements for a few years, but this was followed by backsliding when budgeting fell out of the headlines and the American people weren't putting constant pressure on their representatives to exercise the kind of fiscal restraint they had to exercise at home.

Only sustained pressure can change Washington's broken and dysfunctional internal culture. Our future depends on it.

Biden's Busted Budget

From the Tom Cole Congressman 4th District Oklahoma April 2022 Weekly Column "Biden's Busted Budget":

In April 2022, President Joe Biden submitted to Congress his second budget proposal for fiscal year (FY) 2023 that plainly states his funding priorities and goals. Like all presidential budgets, it is simply a request and is not enforceable by law. In fact, several policies recommended in this budget stand no chance of passing both chambers and being signed into law.

Unfortunately, the wish list reveals President Biden's desire to double down on his out-of-touch policies and out-of-control spending from his failed budget proposal from the previous fiscal year and the wildly unpopular Build Back Better bill. Clearly, in ignoring the actual priorities of the American people in his dead-on-arrival budget, the president has learned nothing from his first year.

With a price tag of $5.8 trillion, President Biden's proposed budget would spend $73 trillion over the next 10 years, a 66 percent increase from the previous 10 years. This would be the highest sustained level of government spending in American history and would also lead to the highest level of deficits ever.

Although President Biden claims that this budget plan would reduce our national debt, it would lead to the accumulation of $16 trillion in new public debt and $1.1 trillion in yearly debt interest payments by 2032.

At a time when inflation is costing the average household nearly $3,500 extra a year, President Biden's budget outlined that he wants to collect $58 trillion in taxes on hardworking Americans, families and businesses over the next 10 years—the highest sustained tax burden in American history. This would only further strap their wallets, lessen their purchasing power and further fuel the inflationary crisis.

Furthermore, after Democrats were forced to restore longstanding pro-life protections in the FY 2022 omnibus funding package recently signed into law, President Biden chose to pick the same losing fight against those protections in his FY 2023 budget. For example, he removed the longstanding Hyde Amendment which rightly prevents taxpayer dollars from funding abortions and protects the conscience rights of all Americans. Additionally, his budget proposal calls for a $400 million increase for Title X funding to go toward Planned Parenthood and other entities that perform abortions.

Finally, while Americans struggle to afford to fill their gas tanks and power their homes because of high energy costs, President Biden wants to push our country further away from energy independence with more anti-American energy policies.

After shutting down the North American Keystone XL pipeline and preventing energy leasing on federal lands and waters on day one of his presidency, gas prices have reached the highest level ever. During the Trump Administration, America produced more at home and bought more from our allies and neighbors such as Canada. Now, as revealed in his budget, President Biden wants to increase this burden by adding $45 billion in new taxes on domestic energy production.

President Biden has delivered another busted budget that would continue to bankrupt our nation, make inflation worse for middle class Americans, leave us with a weak national defense and keep us at the mercy of tyrants and state sponsors of terrorism for our energy needs. President Biden introduced a similar budget last year. It did not work then, and it will not work now.

Furthermore, Democrats propose using budget reconciliation which was created in the 1974 Congressional Budget and Impoundment Control Act, and the process allows the House and Senate to pass a budget, and then a bill implementing it, with majority votes, tight rules on allowable amendments, and limited time for debate. The process was first used in the last year of the Carter presidency to assemble unrelated budget cuts from several congressional committees into one omnibus bill. President Carter signed the Omnibus Reconciliation Act into law in December 1980.

In 1985, reconciliation was modified in the Senate by then-Senator Robert Byrd. He had become concerned that the process was being used to bypass the Senate's tradition of unlimited debate (i.e., filibusters). He pushed, successfully, to amend the Senate's rules to limit reconciliation bills to matters directly affecting taxes or government spending. The Byrd rule, as it is now known, and its enforcement, has been an important Senate-focused reconciliation ritual ever since.

Tracking the Trillions

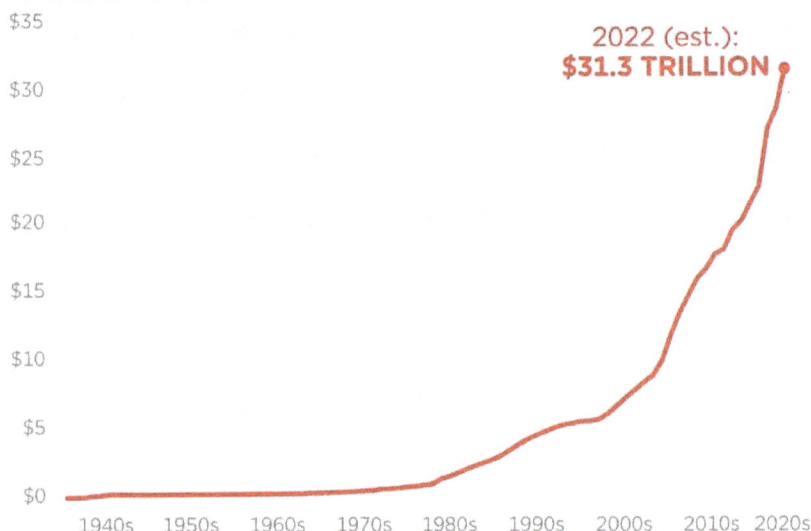

DEBT LIMIT SURPASSES $30 TRILLION

IN TRILLIONS OF CURRENT DOLLARS

2022 (est.):
$31.3 TRILLION

Source: Whitehouse.gov.   ♖ heritage.org

Per the James C. Capretta The Dispatch April 2021 article "Tracking the Trillions": Biden promises to pay for his ambitious plans with tax hikes. What about the stuff we're already supposed to be paying for?

Losing track of the trillions? It is easy to do in the spending frenzy now underway in Washington. Even budget veterans are finding it hard to keep up, and it appears most in Congress stopped counting some time ago. But obliviousness is no excuse for steering into a budgetary dead end. Before going any further, the nation's leaders need to take stock of the fiscal implications of recent decisions and their planned initiatives to ensure future taxpayers are not overwhelmed by debt.

For two decades, Democrats and Republicans have prioritized ideological ambitions over fiscal prudence. But the confluence of the pandemic response and Democratic control of government has created an environment that might supercharge the deterioration.

President Biden's win for that deterioration was the $1.9 trillion COVID response plan, passed by Congress with no offsetting spending cuts or tax hikes. It is stacked on top of $4 trillion in emergency legislation approved in 2020 during the Trump administration.

All of this is occurring after four years of deficit neglect by President Trump. He cut taxes by $1.5 trillion over a decade and downplayed spending restraint. To get approval for increases for national defense, he agreed to multiple deals providing equivalent add-ons to domestic accounts. Even before the pandemic hit, he presided over a deteriorating fiscal outlook, with the annual budget deficit widening from 3.1 percent of GDP in 2016 to 4.6 percent in 2019.

The Biden administration argues its agenda will not make the outlook worse because it is offset with tax hikes on big companies and high-income households, and with higher economic growth.

The case is unpersuasive

While some infrastructure investment might push productivity up, a big spending plan will displace some commitments that would have occurred anyway, especially by state and local governments. One element of the Biden plan is $100 billion for building new public schools, and $213 billion for home construction. These are domains that traditionally have been the responsibilities of other levels of government, and the private sector.

More important, the tax hikes will close off options. If new revenue is raised to pay for new spending, and not to cover previous commitments, then there will be less room to raise taxes to prevent the debt spiral CBO is projecting. The Biden administration may claim that the rich can be tapped again, to close the fiscal gap it inherited. But that assumes there is no political ceiling on how high tax rates can go.

The alternative to more revenue is structural reform of the major entitlement programs. The probability of this occurring with Democrats fully in charge of the government is even lower than piling on yet higher tax rates on the rich.

Biden officials believe the pandemic has created an opportunity to expand the federal government's role in American life. They are ignoring the trillions of dollars in previously enacted commitments that have yet to be tied to reliable revenue sources. Raising taxes for new initiatives will only make it harder to pay for obligations entered into years, and sometimes decades, ago.

The president did not cause the nation's fiscal problems, but that does not matter. He is now responsible for minimizing the possibility that excessive debt will emerge as a crippling economic challenge. He can still advance his agenda, but he must do so while first ensuring the government he inherited, and bequeaths, is solvent and sustainable.

US Deficit: $3,100,000,000,000—The Gov't Will Borrow in 2020

Per The Concord Coalition 2020 report "US Deficit: $3,100,000,000,000—The Gov't Will Borrow in 2020":

The federal budget is an expression of our country's values. What we choose to spend money on and how much we spend, who we tax and how we collect, and the borrowing we engage in to make up the difference between the two, all reflect the basic math of national priorities. Take the fiscal year 2019 below as an example:

Government Spending = $4.45 trillion in Fiscal Year 2019

The federal budget consists of two types of spending. "Discretionary spending" (national defense, education, transportation) is determined through the annual appropriations process in Congress. "Mandatory spending," the largest programs of which are Social Security and Medicare, essentially run on autopilot under formulas set in law. Interest payments on the national debt are also considered mandatory. Discretionary spending has been steadily shrinking as a share of the budget and now makes up less than a third of all federal spending.

Minus Government Revenue = $3.45 trillion in Fiscal Year 2019

The other piece of the federal budget is its revenue. Most of the government's revenue comes from the taxes that Americans pay on their income. The individual income tax and payroll taxes (including Social Security, Medicare Hospital Insurance, and Unemployment Insurance) are the largest sources of government revenue. Corporate income taxes are a distant third revenue source.

Equals = Annual Budget Deficit of $984 billion in Fiscal Year 2019

When the government spends more than it takes in, it has to borrow money to make up the difference. In any given year this mismatch equals the budget deficit. Cumulatively, year after year, our nation's debt stands at an outstanding 26.5 trillion. If you add up all of the borrowing the U.S, government has done over time you get the national debt, technically called the "gross debt."

U.S. National Debt = $26,505,315,299,968

Good decision-making in government depends upon an informed electorate, so the most important thing we can do to help guide the budget process towards a more sustainable fiscal future is to educate ourselves about the hard budget decisions that we face as a nation. Take steps to stay informed about the past, present, and future of the federal budget, and then get involved with the effort to inform others and make your voices heard by your elected officials.

Downsides to the Democratic Spending Plan

From the Chris Edwards Cato Institute October 2021 article "Downsides to the Democratic Spending Plan":

When President Biden released a framework for his Build Back Better plan in 2021, The plan included spending increases of $1.85 trillion over 10 years, but that figure relies on gimmicky accounting and the actual cost would be higher.

The plan includes new and expanded subsidies for housing, preschool, renewable energy, health care, elderly care, electric cars, child care, school meals, higher education, farming, refundable tax credits, and other activities. The aim is to pass the plan as a reconciliation bill, which requires 51 votes in the Senate.

The spending would be funded by a $2 trillion tax increase, thus likely damaging investment, hiring, and growth. A rule of thumb is that each dollar of an income tax increase causes about 50 cents of deadweight losses or economic damage. Thus, a $2 trillion tax increase would damage the private sector by about $3 trillion.

But the spending itself would be harmful even without a tax increase. Let's look at 10 downsides to the Democratic spending plan.

> **1) States Can Do It.** Much of the proposed spending is for activities that states can fund themselves. Expanding subsidy programs is a bad idea, but such programs are even more inefficient when imposed top-down by Washington. If West Virginia or Arizona want to subsidize housing, preschool, or renewable energy, they can do so with their own state revenues. There is no need for aid from the federal government, especially when it is running large budget deficits while West Virginia, Arizona, and other states have large surpluses. State and local tax revenues are currently up 11 percent over pre-pandemic levels.

> **2) Private Sector Can Do It.** Some proposed spending is for activities that the private sector is already doing, so there is no need for new subsidies. The plan would increase subsidies for electric vehicles even though EV sales are already booming. In other cases, the plan would subsidize activities that the private sector would address by itself if governments got out of the way. The plan, for example, includes $150 billion in housing subsidies, but governments are causing the affordable housing problem by restricting supply with excessively tight zoning and building regulations.

> **3) Fix Existing Policies.** The plan includes $555 billion in subsidies to address climate change, but the government itself imposes policies that exacerbate the harms from climate-related

disasters such as hurricanes, droughts, and fires. Furthermore, the green way to fund infrastructure is through user charges that restrain resource use, but the Democrats plan to subsidize infrastructure, which is not green or efficient. Rather than creating new subsidies to address climate change, the government should fix its current anti-green policies.

4) Federal Overload. Policymakers do a poor job of managing and overseeing the vast array of current federal programs, and new programs would further overload them. The federal budget at $6.8 trillion is 150 times larger than the average state government budget of $45 billion. Most federal politicians have probably never even heard of hundreds of the government's 2,300 or so programs, let alone actively oversee them.

5) Democracy. The spending plan would reduce democratic control of government. When the federal government funds state and local activities, decisionmaking moves from elected state and local officials to unelected and unknown officials in far-away Washington. The Democratic plan would move control over activities such as preschool and child care to federal bureaucrats. In an April speech, President Biden lauded "democracy" 16 times, but his spending plan would result in more top-down mandates on state and local activities.

6) Diversity. Residents of each state have varying preferences for spending programs and taxes. State governments can maximize value by tailoring policies to those preferences. But the Democratic proposals would undermine such beneficial diversity by imposing one-size-fits-all rules for energy, preschool, child care, and other activities. Biden promised that he would bring the nation together, but trying to force conformity on Americans with top-down programs would increase anger and division.

7) Corporate Welfare. Democratic leaders often rail against corporate subsidies, yet their spending plan includes subsidies for industries such as housing, automobiles, and energy. The subsidies would increase the feeding frenzy of corporate lobbying in Washington.

8) Costly Regulations. Federal subsidies come tied to regulations that raise costs for the states, cities, businesses, and organizations that receive funding. Federal infrastructure subsidies, for example, come tied to labor and environmental rules that raise costs and delay projects. The Democratic spending plan would probably lead to costly new rules imposed on education, energy, housing, preschool, child care, and other activities.

9) Fraud and Waste. Federal subsidy programs suffer from waste and fraud because state and local administrators have little incentive to restrain costs when the funds come "free" from Washington. Programs such as Medicaid and school lunches have long had high fraud rates, and we have seen massive fraud in recent pandemic aid to the states. Meanwhile, federally funded projects, such as light-rail systems, often suffer from large cost overruns. The new hand-out programs would likely suffer these same problems.

10) Programs With Poor Records. The Biden administration promised that it would follow "evidence-based policymaking," but Biden's plan would expand programs that have poor track records. For example, the plan would expand workforce training subsidies, but such efforts have never worked very well. And the plan would expand the earned income tax credit, but the program has an error and fraud rate of about 20 percent, and it creates work disincentives as income rises and the credit is phased out.

Five Takeaways From the Stunning Inflation Numbers

Per the Tobias Burns *The Hill* July 2022 analysis "Five Takeaways From the Stunning Inflation Numbers":

Consumer inflation is still shooting upward despite interest rate hikes from the Federal Reserve and a host of policy responses from lawmakers over the past several months aimed at fixing supply chains.

The Labor Department reported in July 2022 that the consumer price index (CPI) increased 1.3 percent from May to June and was up 9.1 percent over June of last year, the highest rise since 1981. Inflation briefly dipped this year from April to May, but otherwise has been steadily rising since May of 2020.

There's already been an outcry from lawmakers about the latest numbers.

"Today's consumer price inflation reading of 9.1 percent is a painful reminder that Americans' paychecks continue to be strained by the high inflation that was fueled by Democrats' untargeted and partisan spending spree. As the economy faces runaway inflation and rising odds of a recession and stagflation, raising taxes, killing jobs, smothering wages and imposing price controls makes no sense," leading Senate Finance Committee Republican Mike Crapo (Idaho) said in a statement.

The chances of a recession are growing.

Due to high inflation and rising interest rates to slow it down, Deutsche Bank researchers launched a new research series devoted to the likelihood of a recession, writing in a note last week that "recession [fears] are boiling to a fever pitch."

"In the US, jobless claims continued to tick higher, which our US economists have shown are one of the best leading indicators of recession risk," Deutsche Bank strategist Tim Wessel and his co-authors wrote in a note to investors.

Since the Fed started raising interest rates in March 2022, the S&P 500 stock index is down almost 9 percent. The Dow Jones Industrial Average is down more than 6.5 percent during the same period and is down almost 16 percent since the beginning of the year.

The 'Putin's Price Hike' Inflation Canard

Per the David Harsanyi *National Review* April 2022 article "The 'Putin's Price Hike' Canard":

In March 2022, inflation jumped 8.5 percent, the biggest spike since 1981. Economic growth is expected to slow. Voters are expected to be angry. Yesterday, Jen Psaki warned, "We expect March CPI headline inflation to be extraordinarily elevated due to Putin's price hike."

Her future employer, NBC, reported: "Inflation hits 40-year high of 8.5 percent due to war in Ukraine, rent hikes." The *Washington Post* says much the same. Biden's senior adviser for communications at the National Economic Council, Jesse Lee, went even farther, accusing those who blame Joe Biden for inflation woes of being "fully in lockstep" with Vladimir Putin.

The Biden administration, in fact, spent a year downplaying inflation fears despite the warning signs, contending that inflation was only "transitory," claiming that "nobody" was "suggesting there's unchecked inflation on the way—no serious economist," dismissing price spikes as a "high-class" problem, and arguing that higher prices might actually be a good thing. (Let's just say Jen Psaki isn't cracking jokes about "the tragedy of the treadmill that's delayed" anymore.)

Like most presidents, Biden wants credit for every decimal point of positive economic news but blame for nothing. Considering that we are seeing the return of jobs initially decimated by state-imposed Covid lockdowns, the president's boasting is even more misleading than usual.

Inflation is a complex, multifaceted problem, that, of course, isn't entirely any one person's or event's fault. Yet easy monetary policy and lots of federal spending during a recovering economy were probably bad ideas, as it turns out. Democrats threw $2 trillion into an overheating economy, on top of the $3 trillion bipartisan Covid-relief bill that preceded that bill. With an assist from some Republicans, Democrats okayed another trillion-plus-dollar infrastructure bill. The Biden administration wanted to pass another $5 trillion in social spending, despite inflationary concerns.

It should not be left unsaid that Democrats want to artificially drive up the price of fossil fuels—which account for 80 percent of our energy—as a means of constricting usage. This is the intent of almost every climate-agenda proposal.

On Inauguration Day 2021, the average price of gas in the U.S. was $2.37 a gallon. Between that day and Putin's invasion of Ukraine, Biden signed an executive order pausing all new government leases on public lands, shut down the Keystone XL Pipeline, and stopped pursuing drilling in the Gulf of Mexico over concocted "social cost of carbon" externalities. Russia provided less than 8 percent of all oil imported into the U.S. World communities are fungible, but Democrats want to prepare for the next gas-price shock by ignoring the abundant availability of reliable energy and retrofitting the entire economy to the tune of tens of trillions of dollars.

You might also recall that before "Putin's price hike" became the go-to talking point, Democrats spent months trying to convince us that, after 30 years of low inflation, corporations had suddenly conspired to stop competing and began reckless gouging. These ham-fisted efforts to deflect anger over the mismanagement of the recovery are unlikely to work with anyone whose memory goes back even a couple of months.

11 – Biden's Border Crisis: Mayorkas, Enforcement, Asylum, Sanctuary Cities, Drugs, Crime, DHS & ICE

Border encounters with single adults, families and unaccompanied children all increased in 2021

Migrant encounters at U.S.-Mexico border, by demographic type and fiscal year

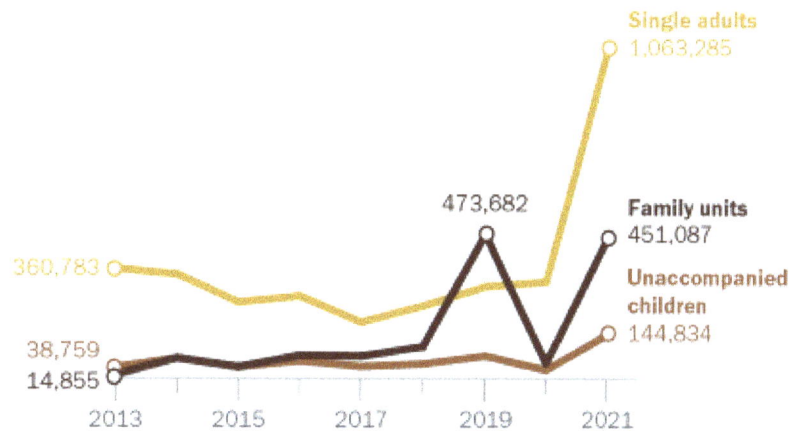

Single adults
1,063,285

473,682

Family units
451,087

Unaccompanied children
144,834

360,783

38,759
14,855

2013   2015   2017   2019   2021

Note: Beginning in fiscal 2020, annual totals combine expulsions and apprehensions into a new category known as encounters. Annual totals before fiscal 2020 include apprehensions only.
Source: U.S. Customs and Border Protection.

PEW RESEARCH CENTER

President Joe Biden has let more illegal migrants into the United States than there are people in his home state of Delaware—a shocking 1.049 million, per the administration's own disclosures. And that's just the adults they caught and released; if you add in got aways and unaccompanied minors, that figure approaches 2 million (closer to a West Virginia or an Idaho).

From the *New York Post* Editorial Board July 2022 update "Biden's Immigration Insanity is Breaking the Nation":

Never mind the horror stories like the one about the 53 migrants who died in a truck in San Antonio, Texas, in June 2022; a population increase of that size will have an enormous impact on the US itself. Especially so given the more than 11 million people here illegally at the start of

2022, according to estimates from the Center for Immigration Studies—a massive uptick over the previous year's figure, courtesy of Let-'Em-In Joe.

Every month, in the first half of 2022, the number of migrants encountered by US Customs and Border Protection keeps rising. May's was the highest ever, breaking the record set in April. There won't be any letup until the White House stops its wink-and-nod routine that heartlessly encourages illegal migration.

Don't think the nation can absorb this massive influx without major changes—and pain. Just look at the town of Eagle Pass in Texas. Video taken there showed hundreds of suspected illegal migrants gathered by a roadside, in a town of 30,000 that's seen 1,000 illegal migrants apprehended and processed there *per day*.

The town's mayor, Rolando Salinas Jr. (a Democrat), says his police and fire services are stretched thin and expresses deep frustration: The US needs to let the world know "there are rules, there's laws you have to follow. If you come to the US, you're not going to get all these resources because that's what they think."

Yet that's just what the Biden administration has encouraged them to. Indeed, human traffickers allegedly call his policy "La Invitación" and it's destroying small border towns like Eagle Pass and beyond. And it has huge implications for politics, budgets and crime around the country: These numbers are like adding whole new states.

Don't believe anyone who says we can't do anything about it. These numbers were nowhere near as bad during the Trump administration. Then, the US posture was clear—i.e., that immigrants must pursue legal pathways—and included elements like the Remain in Mexico policy, which Biden is ending, and the Title 42 expulsion rule, which he's vowed to end.

Illegal Immigration Soars Under Biden to Third-Highest in 97 Years

This section is from the Anna Giaritelli *Washington Examiner* October 2021 article "Illegal Immigration Soars Under Biden to Third-Highest in 97 Years": Nearly 2 million people were encountered by federal law enforcement while attempting to enter the United States illegally over the past year.

Data released by U.S. Customs and Border Protection shows that federal law enforcement officials stopped 1,956,519 noncitizens who tried to gain entry to the U.S. by walking across from Canada or Mexico, entering by way of the Atlantic or Pacific coasts, or passing through an air, land, or sea port.

The large majority of the 1.9 million, 1.66 million, were stopped by the Border Patrol, whose officers work in the land between ports of entry. That is close to the highest number seen over the past century and is indicative of the border disaster President Joe Biden has overseen and that has dragged down his approval ratings.

In fiscal year 2020, border officials encountered 646,822 people nationwide, federal data show. In 2019, a year in which both Democrats and Republicans declared a "crisis" at the southern border, 1,148,024 people were taken into custody. CBP would not provide data from before 2017, when 526,901 encounters were made.

Illegal immigration to the U.S., the extent of which cannot be fully known because of how many evade federal police and get away, has risen at a faster rate in the first nine months of President Joe Biden's tenure than any time in the Border Patrol's 97-year history.

The 1.66 million unlawful crossings that Border Patrol thwarted nationwide over the past 12 months is the third-highest in U.S. history, coming in close to 1,692,544 in 1986 and 1,676,438 in 2000.

The Large Majority of the Border Patrol's Encounters Took Place at the Mexican Border

Over the past decade, roughly 30,000 to 50,000 people have been encountered illegally crossing the southern border each month. That number dropped to below 20,000 at the start of the coronavirus pandemic, partly as the result of a Trump administration order that any child, adult, or family who illegally crossed be sent back to their home country rather than taken into custody.

But illegal crossings from Mexico began to rise through the summer and fall last year as the Border Patrol was only able to turn away migrants but did not refer them for prosecution, essentially giving people unlimited tries to get into the U.S. without getting caught. The 20,000 figure rose each month and hit 71,000 people in December 2020, weeks before Biden took office.

After taking office on Jan. 20, the Biden administration told migrants not to go to the border. However, it stopped turning away children who showed up alone at the border, and in the months that followed, more children showed up at the southern border than at any time in U.S. history.

Alejandro Mayorkas, the secretary of homeland security, said in an ABC News interview in March 2021 that 'now is not the time to come,' but that the U.S. was 'building safe, orderly and humane ways to address the needs of vulnerable children.'

In total, 146,925 unaccompanied children were encountered at the southern border, between the ports, and at the ports of entry. It nearly doubled the record set in 2019, when 80,000 children came to the border.

As more children streamed to the border from Central and South America, more adults and families also began arriving.

Border Patrol surpassed 169,000 encounters in March and 173,000 in April as Biden eased border policies, including ending the Migrant Protection Protocols implemented under Trump that had forced migrants to live in Mexico while asylum cases made it through the courts.

The change meant people fleeing their homes or coming to America for economic reasons would overwhelmingly be apprehended at the border but quickly released into the U.S., oftentimes not being given court dates but told to self-report to Immigration and Customs Enforcement in whichever city they ended up. If they showed up to ICE, they would be given documents that allow them to work in the U.S. legally, and only then would they be put into the immigration court system, which has 1.4 million cases before approximately 500 federal immigration judges.

Biden's Immigration Insanity is Breaking the Nation

Mayorkas falsely stated in September 2021 that migrants were put in court proceedings when released from the border. However, the majority of migrants released from Border Patrol custody are not put in court proceedings. Because asylum-seekers cannot seek protection until appearing before a judge, the Biden administration's releasing people without first giving them court dates makes seeking asylum a challenge for migrants.

Border officials continued to make more than 170,000 encounters in each of May and June then the number jumped to more than 200,000 in July and 195,000 in August. In September, the final month of fiscal year 2021, 192,000 migrants were stopped at the southern border.

More than 479,700 people arrived as part of a family, 2,100 were accompanied minors, and the remaining 1,105,925 were single adults. Of the 1,734,686 who came to the southern border, 1.04 million were immediately turned away under the coronavirus health policy known as Title 42, and 618,000 were taken into custody. CBP does not disclose how many were released into the country or where they are residing.

Border Patrol Chief Raul Ortiz told reporters at a press conference in August 2021 that South Texas saw 60% of known illegal crossings, though all nine of the regions that the Border Patrol divides the southern border by have been dramatically affected by illegal immigration over the past 12 months.

Biden initially explained the uptick in illegal migration this spring as "seasonal." But the numbers have continued to spike through the summer months when fewer migrants have historically been apprehended at the border because the hot temperatures act as a deterrent.

House Republican Leader Kevin McCarthy of California criticized Biden following the release of the numbers. "Despite the flashing red warning signs, President Biden and his appointed border czar, Vice President Harris, continue to think they can wish the situation away and pretend that they are powerless in the very crisis they created," he said in a statement.

Last spring, Homeland Security Secretary Alejandro Mayorkas rolled out the Biden administration's four-prong plan to stem the flow of migrants illegally entering the country. This included addressing the root causes that lead people to leave their home countries, rebuilding the asylum process, improving border security management, and taking down smugglers. To date, the Biden administration has not made substantive progress in any of the four areas.

Effective Immigration Enforcement Can't Rely on Honor System

This section is from the Tom Homan The Heritage Foundation March 2022 article "Effective Immigration Enforcement Can't Rely on Honor System":

Despite President Joe Biden's State of the Union call March 1, 2022, to secure our border, his administration continues to keep our border open and further neuter immigration enforcement. It's become increasingly clear that the Biden administration has a globalist view and is not interested in protecting this country's borders—or its citizens.

Now, it appears the president wants to fulfill the activist left-wing goal of dismantling the agency of U.S. Immigration and Customs Enforcement, making it impossible to fulfill its mission of enforcing our country's immigration laws.

Americans should ignore Biden's words and focus on his administration's actions. With 12 consecutive months of shockingly high numbers of illegal alien encounters on our southern border, the Biden administration has simultaneously drastically decreased both detentions and deportations. And fewer detentions of course means fewer deportations.

The Department of Homeland Security's own data shows that when individuals were only briefly detained, they were more likely to disappear into the interior of the country—3% of those people were actually repatriated, while 12% were granted relief.

Cases involving the rest—a whopping 85%—were left unresolved. Those seeking to end ICE's ability to detain know that it significantly lowers the chances of deportation, a goal of open-borders advocates.

As part of the Biden administration's new vision for ICE enforcement—one that aligns with the goals of open-borders activists—DHS is not only avoiding detention, but also gutting effective alternative programs, and turning to "community" outreach programs that amount to "catch and release."

In a recently issued federal request for proposal, the government announced it was seeking contractors to run a new alternative to detention program—one that would ban the use of monitoring and diminish compliance requirements for 18- and 19-year-olds who are in ICE custody.

All of This Comes While Record Numbers of Migrants Are Being Released Into the U.S.

This troublesome development signals that the Biden administration may be looking to replace existing programs that have been successfully implemented for nearly two decades with community support services that would require little more than a phone call every three months to monitor migrants' whereabouts after illegally crossing the border.

The current program, called the Intensive Supervision Appearance Program, utilizes a blend of technology solutions and case-management protocols to help ensure compliance with court dates and hearings. It has a pretty good record of ensuring that migrants appear throughout their immigration proceedings.

However, the most effective way of ensuring an alien is removed after receiving a final order of removal is detention. Since detention funds have a limit, the use of programs such as Intensive Supervision are a necessary element to use along with detention.

The Intensive Supervision Appearance Program already covers the population covered by the new request for proposal, so this new case-management program appears to be a redundant waste of taxpayer money that will eliminate any possibility of ensuring individuals actually adhere to the requirements of their immigration proceedings.

Put another way, the administration seems to be launching a program to "catch and release." Further, it's reasonable to wonder whether this program is designed to benefit Biden administration cronies through sweetheart deals, as seen last year in the case of the contractor Family Endeavors.

Why is this administration ignoring the jaw-dropping increase of illegal aliens crossing the southern border, while refocusing ICE programs that will result in high rates of absconding?

In December 2021 and January 2022 alone, there were more than 330,000 encounters at the southern border. House Democrats, led by Rep. Alexandria Ocasio-Cortez, D-N.Y., and others in the left wing of the party, are pressing Biden to dismantle ICE and replace its protocols with a catch-and-release programs that rely on illegal migrants to adhere to little more than an honor system.

U.S. Customs and Border Protection data from a year ago shows the agency arrested more than 10,000 illegal immigrants with criminal convictions in fiscal year 2021, a 341% increase over the prior year.

And let's not forget that every day thousands of unlawful border crossers, known as "got-aways," successfully sneak into the country. It's no wonder 13 U.S. senators have written to the homeland security secretary questioning "the mass release of criminal immigrants into our communities under the cover of darkness."

This administration is taking steps to gut ICE's effective enforcement tools and replace them with weak alternatives. In his zeal to undo the policies of the Trump administration, Biden has allowed upheaval to fester at the border and indirectly encouraged thousands to risk their lives trying to reach the U.S., knowing there is a good chance they will be allowed to disappear into the interior of the country, even if they are arrested.

If Biden really means what he said in his State of the Union address, he needs to direct DHS to stop dismantling ICE enforcement. Enforcing our immigration laws is a necessary element to securing our border.

Sadly, it seems the president's words were meant only to affect voting in this year's midterm elections. That is no way to protect our borders or our citizens.

Mayorkas' "6 Pillars" Border Security Plan Is Delusional

This section is from the Simon Hankinson The Heritage Foundation May 2022 article Mayorkas' "6 Pillars" Border Security Plan Is Delusional":

As May 23, 2022 neared, when border agents' Title 42 public health authority to quickly expel illegal aliens was due to expire, U.S. Customs and Border Protection already had seen predicted increased numbers of illegal aliens. Even the Biden administration admitted that "migration levels will increase."

Homeland Security Secretary Alejandro Mayorkas issued a 20-page memo April 26 detailing his agency's plan for coping with the expected surge of illegal immigration after the lifting of Title 42. Title 42 authority has been used more than 2 million times since March 2020 to expel illegal entrants at the border, in a process much quicker than the normal Title 8 process.

The termination of Title 42 was set to go into effect on May 23, but a federal court in Louisiana blocked the Biden administration from doing so. As of the time of publication, Title 42 remains in effect following that court order.

Mayorkas' six-pillar "Plan for Southwest Border Security and Preparedness" is a continuation of the Biden administration's approach to those illegally crossing the border; namely, quickly process them into the U.S., release them under parole, and grant them asylum.

The plan is lightly sweetened with optimistic, underfunded measures to mitigate the collateral damage on local communities. For example, DHS' Southwest Border Coordination Center and Customs and Border Protection leaders would engage in regular coordination, which "includes a focus on noncitizen transport and capacity planning, resolving logistical challenges, and addressing community concerns through shared solutions."

In the very first lines of his plan, Mayorkas gaslights Americans by blaming the previous administration for handing DHS "a broken and dismantled immigration system," but still claims credit for managing "an unprecedented number of [illegal aliens] seeking to enter the United States" and higher numbers of drug and smuggling interdictions.

Rather than admit the powerful pull factor of the Biden administration's lax policies generally, and proposing to end Title 42 specifically, for the expected surge in illegal entries, Mayorkas blames larger global trends, such as violence, hunger, severe poverty, corruption, climate change, the COVID-19 pandemic, and dire economic conditions.

None of those is grounds for asylum, yet the administration's plan is for all those illegally crossing our border to be able to seek asylum, in most cases under fraudulent pretexts, then expecting to be released into the interior.

Pillar 1 of the plan is a small increase in Customs and Border Protection staff and enlarged or new facilities to increase its capacity to hold aliens up to 18,000 at a time, from 13,000 currently. DHS has also doubled its ability to transport illegal aliens, mostly by bus, away from processing centers once they have been given paperwork to pursue asylum.

This is the essence of the plan: Get the illegal entrants out of detention and into the asylum pipeline as fast as possible, all to avoid media scrutiny and political outrage.

Pillar 2 describes a pilot program using "Enhanced Central Processing Centers," combining Customs and Border Protection, Immigration and Customs Enforcement, unspecified nongovernmental organizations, and "possibly other entities" to more efficiently get illegal aliens out of custody.

The first joint center was scheduled to go online April 29 in Laredo, Texas, and more are planned. Nongovernmental organizations will be present to provide legal orientation services and "onward transportation" for the vast majority of the illegal aliens who will be released into the country.

Pillar 3 is where Mayorkas disingenuously promises "consequences for unlawful entry, including removal, detention, and prosecution," and that "[c]ore to this plan is our commitment to continue to strictly enforce our immigration laws."

In reality, he has already issued multiple memos to prohibit most ICE arrests, detentions, and prosecutions. Mayorkas is also well aware that immigration court cases take years due to the 1.7 million-case backlog and an abusive number of continuances, motions, and appeals—all of which buy illegal aliens more time in the U.S. and make their ultimate removal increasingly unlikely.

When immigration judges do issue final orders of removal, Mayorkas has prohibited ICE from detaining and removing such aliens, so they will remain in the U.S.

Pillar 4 reveals the growing administration reliance on nongovernmental organizations to perform government functions and provides a mere glimpse into the money going to these groups.

Mayorkas' plan states that these groups will "receive" illegal aliens, who will be released directly into the community and provide them with "onward travel" out of sight and mind. The DHS offers $150 million in taxpayer-funded Federal Emergency Management Agency grants to nongovernmental organizations "to help alleviate" the population and fiscal "pressures" that communities experience from "increased migration levels."

States should note this admission when they sue the Biden administration for the expenses they incur due to its refusal to secure the border or enforce immigration laws.

DHS is exploring additional ways to give money to communities to resettle illegal alien populations and will do so by giving more taxpayer money to community organizations. The Biden administration is thus both rewarding its ideologically aligned nongovernmental organizations and attempting to buy off community leaders to accept the illegal aliens the administration is encouraging and processing into this country.

Pillar 5 targets "transnational criminal organizations and smugglers who take advantage of and profit from vulnerable migrants and who seek to traffic drugs into our country."

The Biden administration's open-border policies have caused the smuggling of humans and drugs to thrive, and yet Mayorkas has the audacity to pat himself on the back for increased drug and smuggling arrests.

What would really disrupt the cartels would be preventing illegal immigration in the first place and cutting off their revenue source. This plan will only further enrich the cartels and smugglers, kill more Americans with more drugs and crime, and endanger more migrants.

Pillar 6 is a pie-in-the-sky search for a magical deal with Latin American countries that will somehow stem flows of illegal migration with causes far beyond the control of foreign governments.

It contains the forlorn hope that sending a counter-message through media and diplomacy that "the termination of the Title 42 public health order does not mean that the U.S. border is open" will fool anyone.

Mayorkas touts recently struck deals with Panama and Costa Rica, but the deals have few practical applications yet.

He boasts of "close cooperation with Mexico," but the illegal immigration numbers are increasing, not decreasing. As the memo states, "In the past three weeks, [Customs and Border Protection] has encountered an average of over 7,800 migrants per day across the Southwest Border … compared to a historical average of 1,600 per day in the pre-pandemic years (2014-2019)."

In short, Mayorkas' "Plan for Southwest Border Security and Preparedness" is a 20-page, six-pillar delusion. There's nothing safe, orderly, or humane about the border currently. As a result, neither our national security nor our public safety is protected.

Mayorkas concludes that DHS has been "able to manage increased encounters because of prudent planning and execution." Yet, privately, he has told his agents that the border numbers are unsustainable.

The bottom line is this: Mayorkas' public statements cannot be taken seriously, and his policies have put Americans in daily danger.

Mayorkas' New Policies Effectively Abolish ICE

Per the Preston Huennekens ImmigratoinReform.com October 2021 post "Mayorkas' New Policies Effectively Abolish ICE":

During the Trump administration, progressive politicians and activists made abolishing Immigration and Customs Enforcement (ICE) a top campaign issue. Representatives Alexandria Ocasio-Cortez (D-N.Y.), Mark Pocan (D-Wis.), Pramila Jayapal (D-Wash.) and Senators Elizabeth Warren (D-Mass.), Bernie Sanders (I-Vt.), and Kirsten Gillibrand (D-N.Y.) all called on Congress to support legislation abolishing or otherwise reorganizing the responsibilities of ICE.

That was all before Joe Biden became president in January 2021. It turns out that the progressives did not need Congress to act at all. Through the use of two memoranda, Department of Homeland Security (DHS) Secretary Alejandro Mayorkas used his power to abolish ICE.

The memos do not abolish ICE in the literal sense—the agency is still an existing component of DHS. But the memos are a broadside against ICE's purpose, and mark a total abandonment of immigration enforcement.

Mayorkas released the first memorandum on September 30. Titled "Guidelines for the Enforcement of Civil Immigration Law," the document outlines new guidance to ICE officers for the apprehension and removal of illegal aliens. Relying on the doctrine of prosecutorial discretion, Mayorkas lays out the case for refusing to prosecute and remove most illegal aliens present in the United States.

Mayorkas writes that "We do not have the resources to apprehend and seek the removal of every one of these noncitizens… In exercising our discretion, we are guided by the fact that the majority of undocumented noncitizens who could be subject to removal have been contributing members of our communities for years."

Mayorkas declares that ICE will prioritize for removal only aliens who are a threat to national security, public safety, and border security. Threats to national security include those suspected of terrorism and espionage. The second category addresses threats to public safety, but includes exceptions if these violent criminals are of "advanced or tender age," have lived in the United States for a "lengthy" period of time, have a mental illness that led to their criminal conduct, or whose removal would leave dependents behind.

This is remarkable. This policy will shield criminal aliens if they are elderly, have lived here for a long time, or who have children. Anyone who can claim some form of mental illness can remain, regardless of the lives their crimes shattered. Ignoring any sense that criminal aliens pose threats to U.S. citizens, Mayorkas ends by defending his actions by saying that: "The gravity of an apprehension and removal on a noncitizen's life, and potentially the life of family members and the community, warrants the dedication of investigative and evaluative effort."

Secretary Mayorkas is Very Concerned About the Well-Being of Criminal Aliens and Their Families

The final catch-all, "threats to border security," include any illegal aliens apprehended in the U.S. who entered after November 1, 2020. This renders safe any illegal alien who happened to arrive before November 1, 2020. This is the equivalent of Mayorkas ordering DHS and its immigration enforcement components to throw in the towel. It is difficult to prove time-of-entry and the Biden administration already made it clear they intend to remove as few illegal aliens as possible. This third point is nothing more than a paper tiger.

Mayorkas released the second memorandum on October 12. The document, "Worksite Enforcement: The Strategy to Protect the American Labor Market, the Conditions of the American Worksite, and the Dignity of the Individual" bars ICE from conducting worksite enforcement. This is a crucial aspect of ICE's work, and reverses gains made under the Trump administration.

Worksite enforcement is a crucial tool that ICE used to detain large numbers of illegal aliens at once while also holding accountable the unscrupulous employers who choose to hire them instead of Americans. Illegal aliens come to the U.S. for one reason—to work and make money. In an ideal world, worksite enforcement would be the preferred way to identify and remove illegal aliens while cracking down on the employers who hire them.

Addressing the memorandum, FAIR's president Dan Stein stated that:

The 1986 Immigration Reform and Control Act (IRCA), which then-Senator Joe Biden voted for, explicitly prohibits the employment of illegal aliens. The stated intent of the law was to cut off the magnet of jobs that draws illegal aliens to the U.S., and protect the jobs and wages of American workers. As president, Joe Biden's policy is precisely the opposite: to draw as many illegal aliens as possible to the United States, no matter the cost to national security, public health, burdens to taxpayers, or the jobs and wages of American workers.

This policy does just that. It encourages additional illegal immigration by promising that ICE will not investigate or prosecute the employment of illegal aliens. Instead of allowing ICE to do its job and prosecute employers and illegal aliens, this memo empowers employers who run afoul of existing law and shields illegal aliens from deportation.

Taken together, these two memos destroy ICE's capability to enforce our immigration laws in the interior of the country. Ask yourself—what can ICE do with these policies in place? They cannot prosecute employers who hire illegal aliens. They cannot conduct worksite enforcement investigations to detain illegal aliens working in the U.S. without authorization. They can detain only the most extreme of criminal aliens, and even then there are carve-outs. Are there any illegal aliens in the United States not shielded by these two policies, aside from terrorists?

With the stroke of a pen, President Biden's DHS secretary—Alejandro Mayorkas—all but abolished the effectiveness of ICE.

Biden Encourages Massive Illegal Immigration and Tries to Hide It With Secret Flights

From the Lora Ries and Mark Morgan *New York Post* January 2022 news report "Biden Encourages Massive Illegal Immigration and Tries to Hide It With Secret Flights":

The Biden administration doesn't want media attention on illegal immigration, its open border policies, or the results of those policies. How do we know? A security officer just said so, in an explosive video of secretive, dark-of-night flights transporting illegal immigrants to various points throughout the US.

This video merits coast-to-coast media coverage, not just to expose the administration's stealth operations that flout the laws, but to encourage Americans and leaders at all levels of government to demand that the administration start protecting our border, our country, and our citizens.

The list of lies administration officials have told regarding their handling of illegal immigration is extensive and still growing. How many times have they refused to call the historic numbers of illegal immigrants crossing the southern border a "crisis" or implausibly claimed the border is "closed"?

Department of Homeland Security Secretary Alejandro Mayorkas grossly pushed the false racist narrative that Border Patrol agents on horseback mistreated migrants attempting to illegally enter during the Del Rio International Bridge episode. Biden's Federal Aviation Administration made up a ridiculous drone ban, prohibiting Fox News from showing any more footage of the thousands of mostly Haitian illegal immigrants amassing under that bridge. (The FAA rescinded the ban after reporter Bill Melugin continued filming the Del Rio crisis from a Texas Department of Public Safety helicopter.)

The Administration Refuses to Use the Term "Crisis" to Describe the Southern Border

In 2021, night flights of illegal migrants have been periodically reported in places such as Florida, New York, Pennsylvania and Tennessee. In each instance, state and local officials received no notice they were coming, let alone given an option to refuse them admission. The administration has no apparent concern with how these "air lifts" may burden local officials with additional costs and facilities capacity in areas such as education, housing, healthcare and law enforcement.

Footage shows planes full of undocumented immigrants being unloaded at Westchester County airport during the middle of the night on August 13, 2021. Check the Appendix for the revealing video footage at: 'Betraying the American people': Leaked video reveals Joe Biden's 'hush hush' migrant invasion.

When asked why the administration was flying illegal immigrants in the middle of the night, Press Secretary Jen Psaki belittled the reporter and then lied. She claimed that the flights were resettling unaccompanied children. Yet videos of these surreptitious flights clearly show full grown adults emerging from the planes. At best, this is lying by omission.

Videos posted in January 2022 reveal more lies by the Administration. They show streams of adult males being released in Brownsville and San Antonio, Texas. This reportedly has been occurring since last spring of 2021. Some are known to have criminal records, including drunk driving, assault, and drug possession. Yet Biden officials have stated that only family units and unaccompanied alien children are being release, not single adults.

By law, Mexican males are usually subject to Expedited Removal to quickly return them over the border. If they are from a non-contiguous country, Immigration and Customs Enforcement usually detains them because they are not subject to the arbitrary 20-day Flores detention rule applied to families and unaccompanied children.

Releasing single adult males is a game ender for trying to enforce immigration law. Releasing this population means all demographics of illegal immigrants are now being released—whether single or a family, young or old. By failing to detain or remove single adult males, the Administration has removed the last disincentive to illegal immigration. Smugglers will market this and enrich themselves even beyond the billions they've already made since Biden took office.

Judge Blocks Biden Administration From Lifting Title 42 Border Policy

From the Myah Ward and Jonathan Lemire Politico May 2022 update "Judge Blocks Biden Administration From Lifting Title 42 Border Policy":

The pandemic-related health order, which was implemented in March 2020 to control the spread of Covid, was set to expire on May 23, 2022. However, a federal judge blocked the Biden administration's move to lift Title 42, a Trump-era policy used to expel more than one million migrants at the southern border.

The measure gave the U.S. the authority to immediately expel asylum seekers without a legal process, and the recent ruling means an even longer waiting time for migrants seeking refuge in the United States.

Louisiana U.S. District Judge Robert R. Summerhays, an appointee of former President Donald Trump, ruled that the restrictions must stay in place until a lawsuit by 24 states, led by Arizona, Louisiana and Missouri, is resolved in the courts. In the April 3 lawsuit, filed after the Centers for Disease Control and Prevention announced plans to lift the public health order, the states argued the policy needed to remain to avoid "wave of illegal migration and drug trafficking."

White House press secretary Karine Jean-Pierre said in a statement, adding that the White House disagrees with the decision. "As the appeal proceeds, the Department of Homeland Security will continue planning for the eventual lifting of Title 42 in light of CDC's public health judgment, at which point anyone who attempts to enter the country unlawfully will be subject to Title 8 Expedited Removal proceedings, if they do not have grounds to remain in the United States," Jean-Pierre said.

Texas Seized Enough Fentanyl to Kill 200 Million People This Year Alone, Officials Say

Per the Timothy H.J. Nerozzi Fox News December 2021 news story "Texas Seized Enough Fentanyl to Kill 200 Million People This Year Alone, Officials Say":

The Texas Department of Public Safety (DPS) announced that in this year alone they have seized enough fentanyl crossing the border to kill 200 million people. The drug seizures are part of Operation Lone Star—a Texas initiative to curb entry of human traffickers and drug runners into the state.

According to new data provided by the Texas DPS, Operation Lone Star has seized 160 pounds of fentanyl within its targeted area. Other drugs seized within that area include marijuana (13,494 pounds), cocaine (2,430 pounds), meth (1,647 pounds), and heroin (37 pounds).

Combining activity inside and outside of Operation Lone Star's area of interest, the Texas DPS has seized 886 pounds of fentanyl—approximately 200,790,522 lethal doses, according to data provided by the DPS in a slide presentation.

"They try and sell it as 'synthetic heroin' in order to increase their profits," DPS seized drug system trainer Jennifer Hatch said. "But what ends up happening with a lot of these is they end up leading to death because people don't know these are in the drugs they're ingesting."

"Most recently it's been found in ecstasy tablets," she later added.

A spokesperson also presented data showing Operation Lone Star has resulted in at least 165,497 migrant apprehensions and referrals. Operation Lone Star reported the additional seizure of 477 firearms, as well as over 10,000 criminal arrests.

Operation Lone Star was formed in March of this year under Republican Texas Gov. Greg Abbott.

"The crisis at our southern border continues to escalate because of Biden administration policies that refuse to secure the border and invite illegal immigration," Abbott said at the time of the operation's launch.

"Texas supports legal immigration but will not be an accomplice to the open border policies that cause, rather than prevent, a humanitarian crisis in our state and endanger the lives of Texans. We will surge the resources and law enforcement personnel needed to confront this crisis."

The U.S. recorded its highest number of drug-overdose deaths in a 12-month period, eclipsing 100,000 for the first time, according to the Centers for Disease Control and Prevention.

There were an estimated 100,306 drug deaths in the 12 months running through April, the latest CDC data show. This marks a nearly 29% rise from the deaths recorded in the same period a year earlier, indicating the U.S. is heading for another full-year record after drug deaths soared during the COVID-19 pandemic.

12 – Education Madness: Masks, CRT, Marxists, Wokeness, Teacher's Unions vs. School Choice

Credit: Daniel A. Varela/Miami Herald via AP - Florida Gov. Ron DeSantis signing of HB7, "individual freedom," also dubbed the "stop woke" bill on April 22, 2022.

Across America, states have gone on the offensive, targeting the radical sex and "gender" curriculums in grade schools. These proposals follow increasing calls from parents to reject sexually explicit content unearthed in public school classrooms.

Per the John Schoof The Heritage Foundation April 2022 article "Parents Are Going on Offensive to Fight Indoctrination in Education":

The Parental Rights in Education law, recently signed by Florida Gov. Ron DeSantis, sparked heated conversations throughout the nation regarding sex education and "gender ideology." The Florida law addresses teacher conduct and material allowed in classrooms. It also postpones any teaching of sexual orientation and "gender identity" until after third grade.

Thus far, schools and school boards have been the primary target of parental push back against radical gender ideology. However, the issue goes beyond one's local public school district. The organizations that supply the curriculum and teacher training materials are just as important to examine.

One such organization is the Sexuality Information and Education Council of the United States. This organization is a nonprofit devoted to sexual education advocacy.

Along with tracking current and future legislation nationwide, the group publishes guidelines for grade school children and young adults. It partners with groups such as the American Civil Liberties Union, Advocates for Youth, and Planned Parenthood Federation of America to promote model legislation on "comprehensive sex education."

Since its beginning in 1964, the Sexuality Information and Education Council of the United States and its partners have been successful advocates for their cause. Through activism and political pressure, they have gained heavy influence in curriculum and government. They have advocated "gender-affirming" programs. They have also pushed opt-out bills as opposed to opt-in bills. That means parents must take their children out of a controversial class rather than place them in it.

Parents are worried that this agenda not only exposes children to inappropriate content at early ages, but it also promotes lifestyles that are contrary to many parents' values. But these activist groups have no intention of losing the ground that they have gained.

The Controversial Sexuality Information and Education Council of the United States

And in the 2022 Legislative Look-Ahead, the Sexuality Information and Education Council of the United States condemns parental rights bills as "insidious," promising to increase efforts to fight such proposals.

Parents have been primarily taking on the public school system. However, to address the radical sexual orientation and gender identity agenda and other unsettling content, parents and concerned citizens should push for parental bills of rights.

In a recent report, Heritage Foundation experts Jonathan Butcher and Lindsey Burke lay out what an ideal proposal would look like. They begin with changing the way schools view students in their care. According to the report, a parent bill of rights must affirm parents as the child's primary caregivers.

Parents are the ones "primarily responsible for their children's education and health, as well as their moral and religious upbringing." Students must also be protected from compelled speech and parents must have the final say regarding health and counseling services that are provided to their child.

To directly address the curriculum developers, lawmakers and parents should push for transparency in the classroom. This transparency should not only include specifics about the curriculum, but who is providing the school with it

Parents have a right to know what is being taught to their children, and should have easy access to class syllabi, textbooks, homework, and reading materials. A school should make this easily accessible on its website and learning management system.

Another avenue is supporting grassroots organizations like Parents Defending Education who are "fighting indoctrination in the classroom." Many such groups diligently file Freedom of Information Act requests to expose explicit content and litigate on behalf of families.

In addition to transparency, parents should enjoy far more school choice. This would give parents exit options when they don't like what their children's schools are teaching.

This year alone, 27 states have put forward proposals for new school choice programs or the expansion of existing ones. Parents should have the choice to send their child—and their money—to the school that they believe aligns with their values.

Change in the Air in San Francisco

Per the Erica Sandberg *City Journal* February 2022 article "Change in the Air in San Francisco":

The recall of three school board members is a win for good sense over radical-left politics when San Francisco held its first recall election in nearly four decades. Residents voted to oust three of the seven members of the San Francisco Unified School District's Board of Education: its president Gabriela López, Alison Collins, and Faauuga Moliga.

The board members found themselves on the recall ballot for egregious incompetence. San Francisco was among the last major cities in the U.S. to reopen its public schools after the worst of the pandemic.

While keeping the schools closed, the board seized the opportunity to fulfill a radical political agenda. They attempted to rename 44 schools based on historical misinformation and personal opinion, including those named after Abraham Lincoln, George Washington, Thomas Jefferson, Robert Louis Stevenson, and even Dianne Feinstein.

The board also purged the merit-based admissions process for Lowell High School, on the justification that the school lacked diversity (Asians comprised the majority of the student body). This beloved, academically rigorous institution obviated the need for low-income families to pay for expensive private education elsewhere. When an angry parent challenged the board's decision on Twitter, López responded with a middle-finger emoji.

Many of the board's resolutions concerned racial equity, even as a 2016 tweet from Alison Collins resurfaced in which she referred to Asians as "house n****s." The statement led the board to strip Collins of her vice president status. Collins then filed an $87 million lawsuit against the board itself, claiming her colleagues and the school district had violated her free speech rights. She eventually dropped the lawsuit.

For San Francisco, change is in the air. For most people here, it feels marvelous. The recall was essential, and not just to improve a damaged public school system that now runs a deficit so large that teachers' jobs are at risk. Had this recall effort failed, it might have deflated enthusiasm for the next one in June for Chesa Boudin, San Francisco's calamitous district attorney.

"The DA should be very nervous," says Stephen Martin-Pinto. "People have confidence now that recalls can succeed. I think the momentum to recall Boudin will only grow from now on."

There's much more for residents to do in this crisis-ridden city. Crime, chaos, and squalor are the next targets. Many San Franciscans are suddenly more optimistic that they have the power to change their community for the better.

Nearly Three-Quarters of Americans Support School Choice

From the Alexandra DeSanctis *National Review* March 2022 report "Nearly Three-Quarters of Americans Support School Choice":

According to a new poll from RealClear Opinion Research, nearly three-quarters of Americans now say they support school choice, a marked increase from two years ago. Seventy-two percent of registered voters said they back school choice, while only 18 percent said they don't. The poll was conducted between February 5 and February 9 in 2022 and surveyed 2,000 registered voters.

That support for school choice held across the ideological spectrum: Eighty-two percent of Republicans, 68 percent of Democrats, and 67 percent of Independents said they like the idea of funding students instead of the public-school system.

Perhaps most interesting, support for school choice remained strong across all the demographic groups surveyed. Hispanic Americans were most supportive of school choice (77 percent), followed closely by white respondents (72 percent), black respondents (70 percent), and Asian respondents (66 percent). School choice is, in other words, a significant wedge issue for the Democratic Party.

This support for school choice has risen steeply across all these demographics since the start of the pandemic. As of April 2020, 64 percent of Americans supported school choice, along with 75 percent of republicans, 59 percent of Democrats, and 60 percent of Independents. Evidently, one major result of the Covid-19 pandemic has been to focus Americans' attention on education, and many parents appear not to like what they see.

Parents Wanted School Choice—and They Voted

Per the Corey DeAngelis, Ph.D. and Jason Bedrick The Heritage Foundation June 2022 update "Parents Wanted School Choice—and They Voted":

In November 2021, Glenn Youngkin won Virginia's gubernatorial election by riding a wave of parental discontent over district schools that were failing to open for in-person instruction, be transparent about radical curricular materials, or even keep kids safe. Youngkin promised to make schools more accountable to parents and to enact policies that give parents more choices among schooling options.

Governor Youngkin's victory owed much to the playbook used by Ron DeSantis in the 2018 race for governor of Florida. DeSantis made school choice a centerpiece of his campaign, and voters rewarded him. In a race decided by fewer than 40,000 votes, his unusually high level of support among black women (18 percent, or about 100,000 votes), who chose him over an anti–school choice black Democrat, Andrew Gillum, proved decisive.

The source of this support was likely related to the state's tax-credit scholarship policy, which empowers more than 100,000 low- and middle-income students to attend the schools their families choose. Gillum backed a lawsuit that threatened to eliminate it. DeSantis promised to defend and expand it. The rest is history.

In the wake of these victories, Republicans began wrapping themselves in the mantle of parental rights and school choice, but the fulfillment of their promises has been mixed. States such as West Virginia and New Hampshire enacted bold new education-choice policies in 2021, while Florida, Indiana, and more than a dozen other states expanded existing choice policies.

Nevertheless, choice initiatives stalled this year in Georgia, Idaho, Iowa, Oklahoma, and Utah, with some Republicans casting the deciding votes. Voters have started to take notice.

Teachers Unions Are More Powerful Than You Realize—But That May Be Changing

This section is from the Kerry McDonald Cato Institute August 2020 report "Teachers Unions Are More Powerful Than You Realize—but That May Be Changing":

School reopenings are closely linked to the power and influence of teachers unions in a given location—not to virus-related safety concerns. Teachers unions throughout the US claim to be looking out for the best interests of teachers and students, but they are deeply political organizations with significant influence over what, how, where, and with whom most children learn.

While the nation's largest teachers' unions have long been deeply connected to the Democratic Party and left-wing ideology, this political affiliation has become increasingly apparent in recent months. From hinging their support for reopening schools on outrageous policy demands to launching court battles, threatening strikes, and openly supporting disturbing actions during recent protests, today's teachers unions are more powerful and dangerous than many parents may realize.

Public sector unions by their nature are problematic because they are funded by taxpayers under a threat of force and often have monopoly power. Unlike private sector unions where consumers have more choice, no taxpayer can opt out of paying their portion of public sector union dues (which come from government employee salaries), including what those dues fund.

School reopenings are closely linked to the power and influence of teachers unions in a given location—not to virus-related safety concerns.

In July, the Los Angeles teachers union released a report detailing the conditions they identified for a safe reopening of schools. This document went far beyond requesting social distancing plans and personal protective equipment to an agenda that eclipsed both COVID-19 and educational matters. Specifically, it laid out policy requirements for school reopening, including passing Medicare for All at the federal level, raising state taxes, defunding the police, and imposing a moratorium on charter schools.

In Florida, the teachers union waged a court battle against the state's school reopening plans this fall. In New York City, the teachers union is threatening to strike this week over in-person school reopening plans. And in Massachusetts, teachers unions recently succeeded in delaying the school start date to later in September, ensuring no funding cuts, and pushing for remote-only learning in many districts.

As Corey DeAngelis of the Reason Foundation observed, school reopenings are closely linked to the power and influence of teachers unions in a given location—not to virus-related safety concerns. Citing mounting data on school reopening plans across the country, DeAngelis reports that the "relationship between unionization and reopening decisions remains substantively and statistically significant even after controlling for school district size and coronavirus deaths and cases per capita in the county during the month of July."

Shining an Illuminating Spotlight on Teachers Unions and Their Established Political Affiliations

Contentious back-to-school plans, a heated presidential election cycle, and mounting civil strife are shining an illuminating spotlight on teachers unions and their established political affiliations. While we may think of public schools across the country as reflecting the political and ideological diversity of their local communities, the reality is that the teachers unions and their members swing hard left.

According to EducationNext, the nation's two top teachers unions have been among the leading financial contributors to national elections since 1990: "They have forged an alliance with the Democratic Party, which receives the vast majority of their hard-money campaign contributions as well as in-kind contributions for get-out-the-vote operations." Teachers union members comprise 10 percent of the delegates at the Democratic National Convention, where they represent "the single largest organizational bloc of Democratic Party activists."

Fortunately, the 2018 US Supreme Court's Janus decision freed non-members of public sector unions from being forced to contribute union dues, allowing government employees to avoid supporting political organizations and platforms with which they may disagree. Despite this win, the influence of teachers unions on progressive policy across the country continues unabated. In fact, the National Education Association (NEA), the nation's largest public sector union and the largest teachers union, reported that both dues and membership increased a year after the Janus decision.

At their July convention, the American Federation of Teachers (AFT), the nation's second-largest teachers union, voted almost unanimously to endorse Joe Biden's presidential bid. In her convention speech, AFT president Randi Weingarten made no secret of the far-left policies and politics her union and its members endorse. She said:

Imagine a world with: universal pre-K; debt forgiveness for educators; triple Title I funding; expanded community schools; supports for kids with special needs; high-stakes testing thrown out the window; charter school accountability; public colleges and universities tuition-free for families who earn less than $125,000

That's not from an AFT resolution. That's straight from the Democratic Party platform, born out of the Biden-Sanders Unity Task Force recommendations we helped draft.

Additionally, the AFT endorsed other progressive policies at their convention that are unrelated to education, such as the Green New Deal, affordable housing, and universal healthcare. For many of the parents of the nearly 50 million K-12 public school students in the US, these policies likely go against their personal and political beliefs, and they should be concerned that this leftist ideology is creeping into their child's classroom.

California State lawmakers Paved the Way for the Country's First Mandatory Ethnic Studies Graduation Requirement

This seems to already be occurring in California. State lawmakers have paved the way for the country's first mandatory ethnic studies graduation requirement, a move that is actively embraced by the California Teachers Union (CTU). The *Wall Street Journal* editorial board wrote about California's planned curriculum mandate: "This is ugly stuff, a force-feeding to teenagers of the anti-liberal theories that have been percolating in campus critical studies departments for decades. Enforced identity politics and 'intersectionality' are on their way to replacing civic nationalism as America's creed."

Parents and taxpayers should also be concerned if teachers unions had overwhelmingly right-wing ideas and influence as well, which is why limiting the overall power of public sector unions is so crucial.

While COVID-19 has caused major disruptions in how we live and learn, it has also empowered parents to look more closely at their children's education. As more families choose independent homeschooling and learning pods this fall, education is becoming more decentralized and family-centered. A recent *Wall Street Journal* op-ed speculated that this education trend is likely to strike teachers unions hard: "What happens when they refuse to do their jobs and it turns out home-schoolers are better at it anyway?"

Education choice and innovation during the pandemic will loosen the clutch of the powerful teachers unions and their progressive agenda. Despite some schools and teachers trying to push parents away from observing their child's instruction, more parents are waking up to what their children are learning in school and realizing that, in many cases, it may run counter to their own values. A vocally progressive agenda and broad Democratic Party allegiance by powerful teachers unions, combined with the proliferation of more schooling alternatives resulting from the pandemic, may prompt more parents to opt out of their local district school for other options.

The pandemic is set to weaken the long-held grip of teachers unions on US education and social policy, and strengthen educational diversity and choice for more families. It may also prompt a closer look at the outsized influence of public sector unions more generally. Taxpayers should know what they are paying for.

Student Loan Forgiveness Scam is Already Biden Policy

Per the Virginia Foxx Fox News June 2022 interview "Student Loan Forgiveness Scam is Already Biden Policy":

Republican Virginia Foxx represents North Carolina's 5th District in the U.S. House of Representatives. She is the ranking member of the House Education and Labor Committee and is a member of the House Oversight and Reform Committee.

Biden expected to cancel $6 billion in student loan debt and wants to make ordinary Americans pay billions more in college debt for white-collar Democrats.

Policymakers and millions of Americans are rightfully worried about the headlines that President Joe Biden is seriously considering mass student loan forgiveness for 44 million borrowers. The ramifications of such a policy for taxpayers, students, and our society cannot be overstated. Blanket student loan forgiveness will lead to more inflation-filled deficit spending and the removal of any incentive for schools and students to practice financial responsibility.

Yet, while members of Congress and talking heads are distracted by what Biden might do on student loans, they're missing the widespread debt cancellation happening right before their eyes—and that's exactly what the president wants.

Take the Department of Education's recent announcement providing loan forgiveness waivers for borrowers with longer term repayment plans. The department notes that this action will lead to the automatic cancellation of student loan debt for 40,000 borrowers, who were supposedly promised forgiveness and harmed by the broken system Democrats created. Yet, when you look below the surface and into the details of this action, you'll find the Biden administration may have canceled as much as $211 billion in outstanding student loan debt for over 4 million borrowers—many who were never eligible for forgiveness.

Moreover, when combined with the windfall provided through the repayment pause and his re-write of Public Service Loan Forgiveness, Biden is writing off as much as $400 billion with the stroke of a pen; that is true harm.

However, that's just an estimate. The department is refusing to provide a cost analysis for the student loan pause or the series of waivers and "fresh starts" that impact over 40 million borrowers and the country's 150 million taxpayers. Clearly the administration is doing this behind closed doors because it knows this is not sound fiscal policy or even remotely justified as "targeted relief," but rather a blatant political ploy. It's not a stretch to assume they are doing as much as they can to bow to progressives before November.

Biden knows this radical policy is unpopular among millions of Americans. But, by characterizing his administration's actions like the waiver for government and nonprofit employees as making a broken program "live up to its promise" for public servants, it's easy to convince taxpayers that providing $100,000 in tax-free student loan forgiveness to doctors and Georgetown law students is a noble act.

Democrats are right, the program is broken. But Biden didn't fix it; he instead eliminated the income test and expanded it to ineligible borrowers and high-level Democrat campaign staff and left the single mother of three working the night shift and paying $5 a gallon at the pump to foot the bill.

Democrats Can't Keep Dismissing Complaints About 'Critical Race Theory'

Per the Natalie Wexler *Forbes* November 2021 article "Democrats Can't Keep Dismissing Complaints About 'Critical Race Theory'":

The Virginia gubernatorial race shows that if Democrats want to win elections—and allow kids to get a meaningful education—they should stop dismissing parents' complaints about "critical race theory" as nonsensical fabrications.

Governor-elect Glenn Youngkin found an apparently winning campaign formula after noticing that promises to ban critical race theory from the school curriculum drew cheers, he expanded his message into a vow to enable parents to control their children's education. Then, a few weeks before the election, his Democratic opponent Terry McAuliffe handed him a gift he wasted no time exploiting.

"I don't think parents should be telling schools what they should teach," McAuliffe said during a gubernatorial debate. That statement became fodder for what the *Washington Post* termed a "massive" advertising campaign, which "likely cost McAuliffe the governorship," according to political scientist Stephen Farnsworth.

Exit polls in Virginia showed that about 25% of voters named education as "the single most important issue in deciding their vote," and about 50% said parents should have "a lot" of say over what their child's school teaches. Only 10% said parents should have little or no say.

No doubt there were other factors in Youngkin's win, including others related to education—like slow school reopening during the pandemic, which some voters attributed to the Democrats' cozy relationship with teachers unions. But McAuliffe's remark clearly sparked a strong negative reaction—and not just with conservative white voters.

"What really motivated me was the statement that parents should not have a say in their children's education," one Black parent told a reporter. Reactions like that have helped convince the GOP that parental control of education is now their issue.

More problematic, though, is the standard response to complaints about critical race theory from Democrats like McAuliffe, along with left-of-center commentators and the mainstream media: that it's an academic framework taught at the college or graduate level and not in K-12 schools. If Democrats want to win over parents—and win back some moderate and left-leaning parents of all races—they're going to have to do better than that.

It's unclear how widely these developments have spread. Overwhelming majorities of teachers say they don't teach "critical race theory," but given the vagueness of the concept, that doesn't tell us much. And in terms of influence and perceptions, even isolated incidents can punch above their weight.

If Democrats don't distance themselves from a perspective that—whatever you call it—maintains that race is paramount, hard work doesn't pay off, or individual merit is an illusion, they risk alienating voters and pushing them farther right than they might otherwise be.

Legal Coalition Forming to Stop Critical Race Theory Training Around the Country

Per the Sam Dorman Fox News January 2021 legal brief "Legal Coalition Forming to Stop Critical Race Theory Training Around the Country":

A network of private attorneys and the conservative organizations are launching a "war" against critical race theory trainings across the country as President Biden rolls back the Trump administration's efforts on the issue. Why? Because federal diversity trainers weaponize critical race theory to systemically attack the unifying ideals of America.

Led by Discovery Institute researcher Chris Rufo, the network's stated goal is to bring a complaint before the U.S. Supreme Court and "effectively abolish critical race theory programs from American life."

It comes just after Biden repealed Trump's executive order banning critical race theory training from the federal government, a move by Trump that Rufo appeared to precipitate by releasing documents leaked from federal employees.

"Critical race theory is a grave threat to the American way of life," read Rufo's press release, which echoed Trump's previous condemnation of the training.

"It divides Americans by race and traffics in the pernicious concepts of race essentialism, racial stereotyping, and race-based segregation—all under a false pursuit of 'social justice.' Critical race theory training programs have become commonplace in academia, government, and corporate life, where they have sought to advance the ideology through cult-like indoctrination, intimidation, and harassment."

The Discovery Institute's Center on Wealth and Poverty is leading the effort with help from the Southeastern Legal Foundation, Upper Midwest Law Center, Jonathan O'Brien with Schoolhouserights.org, The Pivtorak Law Firm, Wally Zimolong of Zimolong, LLC, and Eric Early and Peter Scott of Early, Sullivan, Wright, Gizer, & McCrae.

Fox News previously reported on O'Brien's lawsuit, which involved a multiracial high school student's complaint over a Nevada charter school course directing him and others to choose oppressive aspects of their identity.

That particular lawsuit alleged discrimination "on the basis of race and color, in addition to sex, gender, and religion, in violation of Title VI and Title IX of the Education Amendments of 1972."

Critical race theory, or diversity training, appeared to grow in the aftermath of George Floyd's death, which prompted a wave of calls to dismantle alleged institutional racism. Governments and schools from around the country have adopted so-called anti-racist initiatives with training for employees and students.

The Spirit of 1776

From the Editors *National Review* January 2021 post "The Spirit of 1776": Joe Biden went out of his way on his first day in office to cancel Donald Trump's 1776 Commission that was established to research and promote patriotic education, and the commission was a welcome initiative— while it lasted.

It sought to counterbalance the hostile view of American history advanced by the "1619 Project," which jumped almost directly from the pages of the *New York Times* to the curriculum in schools around the country. That project made basic historical errors that it corrected only grudgingly and under pressure from some of the foremost historians in the country, absurdly argued for 1619—the first year that African slaves were brought to these shores—as the "true" founding of the country (before subsequently editing out this claim without explanation), and distorted the American Revolution, Abraham Lincoln, and the history of slavery, among other things.

In the blink of an eye, the 1619 Project re-oriented the discussion about American history.

During its brief life, the 1776 commission tried to re-center it (and attempted to do so, it's worth noting, simply by providing information to the public, not by interfering in curricular decisions of states and localities).

The contents of the 1776 Commission's report, released earlier this week, should be uncontroversial. As the authors write in its introduction, its purpose is to "enable a rising generation to understand the history and principles of the founding of the United States in 1776 and to strive to form a more perfect Union."

It starts by outlining in fairly incontrovertible terms the political principles of both the Declaration of Independence and of the Constitution. The report then discusses the obstacles that stood in the way of the Founding vision's realization and how they were overcome. There is no whitewashing of slavery, nor any suggestion that the moral fabric of the early republic was without hideous stains. The authors merely insist along with Lincoln, whom they quote, that the purpose of the Constitution as ratified in 1787 was "to declare the right, so that the enforcement of it might follow as fast as circumstances should permit."

Much of the fire directed at the 1776 report has been directed at the decision to loosely group "Progressivism" and "Identity Politics" alongside "Fascism" and "Communism" in a section titled "Challenges to America's Principles." But the report's discussion correctly states early-20th-century Progressivism's disregard for the Founding and constitutional government, and regarding identity politics, obviously neither Louis Farrakhan nor David Duke thinks much of the notion that "all men are created equal."

That President Biden acted so swiftly against the commission is another sign of how desperately we need voices to combat what is rapidly becoming the new orthodoxy about American history.

Parents' Guide to Children's Rights Aims to Save America's Public Schools From CRT

Per the Jack Fitzhenry The Heritage Foundation June 2022 article "Parents' Guide to Children's Rights Aims to Save America's Public Schools From CRT":

he most important battleground in the fight to save our American republic is the public schools." So says Kimberly Hermann, general counsel at the Southeastern Legal Foundation, in the introduction to the foundation's guide for parents, "Your Child's Rights and What to Do About Them: A Parent's Guide to Saving America's Public Schools."

Hermann's outlook is increasingly common among anyone taking stock of the proliferation of lessons on critical race theory (a radical worldview that advocates for the primacy of racial identity) in public school curriculums. And her foundation, a national nonprofit law firm that has litigated numerous cases arising in public schools and universities, is ready to persuade anyone else who will listen.

Renewed interest in curricular content is not coming from conservative quarters alone—parents of various political stripes have been galvanized by their children's encounters with critical race theory-based lessons to oppose its dominance in classrooms. That's the audience the Southeastern Legal Foundation addresses in its guide—those who "have had enough."

Why should any parent feel they've had enough of critical race theory? To many parents, the theory's doctrines of "white supremacy" and black/brown victimhood are anathema to their civic or religious convictions on the nature of the person, his or her agency, and the sources of his or her goodness, guilt, and redemption.

To others, critical race theory is just a time- and resource-intensive distraction from their schools' persistent failure to bring students somewhere near a grade-level competence in reading and mathematics.

Fair-minded parents can and should be skeptical of the pedagogic value in a theory that dismisses "legal reasoning" and "rationalism" as mere instruments of white supremacy. After all, critical race theory-based impulses led the Smithsonian to opine that "objective, rational linear thinking" was only an "assumption of whiteness."

Yet for all the legitimate concern parents feel when they find this racialist thinking in their child's homework, there is often a gap between their desire to oppose critical race theory-based instruction and their ability to advocate effectively for that outcome. The foundation's guide is meant to bridge that gap with introductions to the core legal concepts in play when a public school introduces a critical race theory-based curriculum.

Latest Polls Show Education and Critical Race Theory Could Define the Midterms

From the Claire Brighn AMAC March 2022 update "Latest Polls Show Education and Critical Race Theory Could Define the Midterms":

Late last week, Beto O'Rourke made headlines by becoming the first prominent Democrat to explicitly come out against Critical Race Theory (CRT) in schools. While that announcement is unlikely to save O'Rourke's floundering gubernatorial campaign in Texas, it is an indication that at least some Democrats are coming to the realization that perceived support for CRT and politicized education is a major electoral liability—a fact made all the more apparent by recent public polling on the subject. But after first denying the very existence of CRT and then defending its inclusion in K-12 curriculum, Democrats may have already sealed their fate this fall.

According to a recent CNN poll, 46% of voters—including about half of parents with children under ages of 18—said education would be "extremely important" in how they vote in the Congressional midterm elections this November. A recently released Cyngal poll makes the importance of education even more clear and finds that, among swing-state voters on the question of which party is more trusted to protect parental control in education, Republicans hold a 10-point lead, 47 to 37.

These numbers clearly have Democratic leaders on high alert. According to polling of voters in swing districts in late January and paid for by the Democrat Congressional Campaign Committee, Democrats would lose to Republicans by 4 points on a generic ballot. One of the big reasons why? An astounding 61% of voters surveyed agreed with the statement that "Democrats are teaching kids as young as five Critical Race Theory, which teaches that America is a racist country, and that white people are racist."

While such numbers may be easy to gloss over as obvious or self-evident, it's worth noting just how significant those findings are. In today's highly polarized political climate, it's difficult to get a majority of voters to agree on anything— which means that a political party that can effectively appeal to those sentiments has a formidable advantage in any election.

What's more, there is at least some reason to believe that the power of the concerned parent is likely underestimated in a number of these polls. Robert Cahaly of Trafalgar, one of the most accurate pollsters throughout the last several election cycles, made an important distinction months ago in saying that what people think of critical race theory itself is "very different" from what parents "think should be done if critical race theory came to their school."

A recently released Manhattan Institute poll confirms this, showing that 54% of voters support removing "lessons based on critical race theory about concepts such as white privilege and systemic racism from public school curriculum." But when the same question was asked of parents, that number skyrocketed to 66%, with well over half of every demographic concurring, including black and white parents alike. That could very well indicate that normally Democratic voters will be pushed to vote Republican by Democrats' education extremism.

Republicans in Other Swing States Are Already Taking a Page Out of Youngkin's Playbook

Americans already saw the power of this phenomenon last year in Virginia, when Republican Glenn Youngkin turned a 10-point victory for Joe Biden in 2020 into a 3-point Republican win in 2021. The pivotal moment in the race was when Democrat Terry McAuliffe said that "I don't think parents should be telling schools what they should teach." Even Democrats found in their own post-election research that voters swung over to Youngkin because "education dominated," with CRT a top voter frustration.

A Scott Rasmussen national poll conducted after the election in mid-December showed voters nationwide doubling down, with a resounding 85 percent agreeing with the statement that parents "should be allowed to see all curriculum, books, and other materials in classes their children are taking."

Republicans in other swing states are already taking a page out of Youngkin's book for their elections this year. In Wisconsin, for example, the Republican-led Assembly and Senate have hammered Democrat Governor Tony Evers over education. The Wisconsin Senate passed a bill on a near party-line vote that would ban the teaching of CRT in classrooms, only for Evers to veto it. (Evers, for context, has the endorsement and tens of thousands of dollars' worth of campaign donations from the Wisconsin Education Association Council—a powerful group that actively promotes the 1619 Project.) A parental bill of rights was also recently shepherded by Wisconsin Republicans to Evers—which he also plans to veto.

Evers's stance in favor of CRT in schools and against parental rights in education will likely do him no favors with voters, as according to a recent Marquette poll, an overwhelming majority of Independents in Wisconsin side with Republicans in saying parents should play the biggest role in deciding school curriculum.

Republicans in other states have followed suit, and candidates for everything from school board seats to governorships have now made parents' rights central to their campaigns. Since the beginning of this year, lawmakers have introduced nearly 90 curriculum transparency and anti-CRT bills in 37 states.

Thanks to these efforts, the distinction between Republicans and Democrats on education is clearer than ever. As Democrats' odds of winning this fall continue to fade, conservatives may finally have a golden opportunity to roll back decades of liberal activism poisoning school curricula—but only if Republicans continue to prioritize parents and students over special interests and fulfill their promises to enact lasting changes once they win power.

13 – Foreign Policy Pros & Cons: China, Russia, Afghanistan, Ukraine, Iran, Israel, Syria & More

Credit: WSJ - Chaotic evacuation scene at Kabul airport as people try desperately to flee.

From the Daniel Kochis *The Hill* September 2021 report "Biden's Afghanistan debacle will cast a long shadow over transatlantic security":

President Biden declared that he would "repair our alliances and engage with the world once again." Seven months later, his bungled Afghanistan pullout has left our alliances bruised and battered and the president's credibility abroad about as believable as Taliban promises to respect women.

Repairing the damage will not be easy. The sudden withdrawal showed callous disregard for our allies. This was compounded by the administration's pollyannaish response to the international deluge of criticism that followed.

The administration fails to comprehend the ownership stake which many European allies retained in a secure and democratic Afghanistan. The Germans, for example, deployed 150,000 soldiers to Afghanistan from 2002- 2021, many for repeat tours. Berlin's decision to join the U.S.-led effort was not easy. For historical reasons, Germany is extremely cautious about overseas military deployments, and getting the mission extended year over year was tortuous and politically taxing.

Yet the Germans and other allies stood with the U.S. year over year. Last year, NATO's Resolute Support (RS) mission to train and equip the Afghan National Security Forces counted 16,000 troops from 38 allies and partner nations.

Yet Biden decided to pull all U.S. forces from Afghanistan unilaterally, leaving allies—many of whom had recently committed additional troops to RS at the behest of the U.S.—feeling as though the rug had been pulled out from under them.

Some allies, such as Italy, Turkey and the United Kingdom, reportedly sought to sustain a presence in the country but were unable without U.S. support, in particular American air support. UK Prime Minister Boris Johnson tried desperately to find out what the U.S. was doing, but the White House ignored his calls for 36 hours. If the administration can't be bothered to talk with the British, something deeply dysfunctional is happening.

Biden's precipitate action created a crush of desperation at Hamid Karzai International Airport, leaving Europeans stranded and allies like France and the UK resorting to dangerous, clandestine rescues of their own citizens from the streets of Kabul.

Now, the Taliban are back in charge and flush with billions in abandoned western equipment and weapons. Afghanistan will soon be a haven for transnational terrorists once more. Even Gen. Mark Milley, chairman of the Joint Chiefs of Staff, acknowledges, "you could see a resurgence of terrorism coming out of that general region within 12, 24, 36 months."

The allied reaction has been scathing. Armin Laschet, leader of Germany's Christian Democratic Union, called the Afghanistan withdrawal "the greatest debacle that NATO has seen since its foundation."

Calling it "the biggest foreign policy disaster since Suez," Tom Tugendhat, chairman of the UK's Foreign Affairs Committee added, "We need to think again about how we handle friends, who matters and how we defend our interests."

Said German Chancellor Angela Merkel: "For those who believed in democracy and freedom, especially for women, these are bitter events."

Europe's disillusionment and anger with Biden and the U.S. is understandable. They remember how President Obama's Iraq withdrawal led to a flood of refugees, the rise of ISIS and years of terror attacks. They are bracing for a repeat.

Biden Mostly Gets it Right in Ukraine

Per the Kyle Smith *National Review* March 2022 article "Maybe Biden Is Right on Ukraine?":

Biden's Ukraine policy so far is broadly correct, and his actions have been the appropriate ones: severe economic sanctions, military aid, weapons shipments, attempts at making diplomatic contact, aid to refugees, and proposals to welcome 100,000 of them to the U.S.

This is pretty much the slate of options short of war, and declaring a no-fly zone would mean entering the war, so it seems Biden is doing just about everything he can that makes sense.

When former president Trump was asked what he'd do differently on Fox News, and couldn't give a coherent answer.

Biden's Policy Towards War in Ukraine is Appropriate

Per the Luis Fleischman palmbeachdemocracy.org June 2022 post "Biden's Policy Towards War in Ukraine is Appropriate": The War in Ukraine has eliminated the post-cold war illusion that wars can be avoidable in the future and that the danger of another world war does not exist.

Vladimir Putin intends to restore Russia's ethos as a great world power or even empire. Thus, he dared attack Ukraine because he could. He saw in front of his eyes a divided NATO. Likewise, Germany, the most powerful country in Europe, found itself in a situation of high dependency on the Russian energy supply.

Above all, Putin saw a pacifist West that would do anything to avoid a confrontation. Along these lines, the Obama and Trump Administrations' inclination to withdraw from the world enabled Putin to annex Crimea and deepen its intervention in Syria. The road seemed to be clear for another Russian military adventure.

At the beginning of the war, President Biden made a mistake in voicing his fears over the possibility of a Third World War. This alarmist message further emboldened Putin, who did not seem too concerned about the crippling sanctions imposed on Russia.

Furthermore, Biden's and NATO initial cautious approach prevented setting military red lines on Russia. Hysterical rejections of No-Fly zones were irrelevant since the Russian air force operations were practically nonexistent, and attitudes of countries such as Germany that initially failed to provide weaponry to Ukraine also contributed to Putin's belligerency.

However, contrary to Putin's expectations, the USA is now leading the coalition of democratic nations against Putin, NATO is now united and expanding., sanctions on Russia's energy sector have intensified, and the United States and other NATO allies have exponentially increased their aid to Ukraine's war effort.

A great victory for the Biden Administration approach was the recent NATO meeting, where the alliance declared Russia a primary adversary and even refreshed its dormant post-cold war spirit by going further and declaring China, a Russian ally, to be a "strategic challenge."

Likewise, Sweden and Finland, which have historically abstained from joining NATO, are on the path to joining the organization. NATO also announced the deployment of thousands of additional new troops in eight countries that face the East. NATO seems to be heading In the direction of being a protector of the liberal-democratic world transcending the narrow cold-war definition of the group as being simply a north-Atlantic alliance.

The Biden Administration policy, for the time being, is appropriate, but options must be left open if circumstances change.

The United States Speaks Clearly on Russia's Ukraine War

Per the William B. Taylor United States Institute of Peace June 2022 article "The United States Speaks Clearly on Russia's Ukraine War":

President Biden's essay on the Ukraine war in the *New York Times* has vitally clarified America's interests and goals following weeks of public debate weighted with uncertainty and concern over U.S. intentions and methods in that conflict. It offers a straightforward, positive approach—one that the world's democracies should sustain—for confronting Russia's assault against not only Ukraine, but global peace, stability and the rule of law.

"America's goal is straightforward," Biden wrote in the essay. "We want to see a democratic, independent, sovereign and prosperous Ukraine with the means to deter and defend itself against further aggression."

That succinct, positive formulation of the U.S. objective contrasts with negative goals focused on Russia, such as weakening its geostrategic position or power. It forms a clear message, pro-Ukraine and pro-freedom rather than anti-Russia, that is vital to strengthen the necessary alliances against the Kremlin's brutal aggression. It helps strengthen the U.S. partnership with Europe. Also, as USIP experts have noted, it's an essential first step to building more support among nations in Africa, Asia and Latin America that have hesitated to fully oppose Russia's effort to turn back the 75-year struggle to build an international rules-based order.

"I want to be clear about the aims of the United States," Biden wrote, and he was. It is the positive goals he emphasized—a restoration of Ukraine's independence and ability to define its future, that will advance the vital U.S. and allied interests in the protection of democracy, sovereignty and rule of law.

Biden emphasized that he "will not pressure Ukraine—in private or in public—to make any territorial concessions" as part of any eventual peace process with Russia. Rather, he said, U.S. military aid is meant to help Ukrainians defend themselves well enough to "be in the strongest possible position at the negotiating table."

This approach is in contrast to suggestions, including by former Secretary of State Henry Kissinger last week, that Ukraine cede to Russia the Crimean Peninsula and portions of Donbas that Russia seized in 2014. Volodymyr Zelenskyy sharply rejected the notion as redolent of the 1938 Munich Agreement in which European governments forced Czechoslovakia to cede its Sudetenland region to Nazi Germany.

Russia's Ukraine Invasion May Have Been Preventable

Per the Zeeshan Aleem MSNBC March 2022 article "Russia's Ukraine Invasion May Have Been Preventable": The U.S. refused to reconsider Ukraine's NATO status as Putin threatened war. Experts say that was a huge mistake.

The prevailing wisdom in the West is that Russian President Vladimir Putin was never interested in President Joe Biden's diplomatic efforts to avert an invasion of Ukraine. Bent on restoring the might of the Soviet empire, this narrative goes, the Russian autocrat audaciously invaded Ukraine to fulfill a revanchist desire for some combination of land, power and glory.

In a typical account operating under this framing, Politico described Putin as "the steely-eyed strongman" who proved immune to "traditional tools of diplomacy and deterrence" and had been "playing Biden all along." This telling suggests that the United States exhausted its diplomatic arsenal and that Russia's horrifying and illegal invasion of Ukraine, which has involved targeting civilian areas and shelling nuclear plants, could never have been prevented.

But according to a line of widely overlooked scholarship, forgotten warnings from Western statesmen and interviews with several experts—including high-level former government officials who oversaw Russia strategy for decades—this narrative is wrong.

Many of these analysts argue that the U.S. erred in its efforts to prevent the breakout of war by refusing to offer to retract support for Ukraine to one day join NATO or substantially reconsider its terms of entry. And they argue that Russia's willingness to go to war over Ukraine's NATO status, which it perceived as an existential national security threat and listed as a fundamental part of its rationale for the invasion, was so clear for so long that dropping support for its eventual entry could have averted the invasion.

Recognizing this possibility does not excuse Moscow's actions, which are heinous. Nor does it mean Russia's insistence on regional hegemony is fair or ethical. And ultimately, it is no guarantee that Putin would not have invaded anyway. There are other factors—including, but not limited to, Putin's general anger over Kyiv drifting away from Russian influence and domination and his isolation as a decision-maker—that may have been sufficient to drive the invasion.

But the abundance of evidence that NATO was a sustained source of anxiety for Moscow raises the question of whether the United States' strategic posture was not just imprudent but negligent.

Russia Perceives NATO as an Existential Threat

Russia is no longer at the helm of a global superpower, but it is still, at the very least, a regional great power, and as such it devotes considerable resources to exerting its influence beyond its borders and using the states around it as buffers. Russia views Ukraine, a large country to which it has long-running cultural and historical ties, as a particularly critical buffer state for protecting its capital.

The issue that Russia saw in NATO was not just an expanding military alliance, but one that had shifted gears to transforming and proactively intervening in global affairs. After the end of the Cold War, NATO's raison d'être no longer existed, but instead of disbanding, its mission shifted to democracy promotion. The carrot of membership in NATO was used to encourage countries to adopt liberalization and good governance and align with U.S. political, economic and military interests.

As a way to reassert its dominance in the region, and counter NATO's influence and alignment with Western principles, Putin annexed the Ukrainian territory of Crimea in 2014 in the wake of the protest-spurred ouster of Ukraine's Russia-friendly president, who the West favored.

It is imperative that America develops a clearer understanding of its adversaries and behaves more judiciously in an increasingly multipolar world. It is not difficult to imagine the U.S. making a miscalculation over what China would be willing to do to secure its domination of the South China Sea. The U.S. may want to be the only great power in the world, free to expand its hegemony with impunity, but it is not. Refusing to see this is dangerous for us all.

Biden's Grand China Strategy: Eloquent But Inadequate

From the Ian Johnson Council on Foreign Relations (CFR) May 2022 report "Biden's Grand China Strategy: Eloquent But Inadequate": The Biden administration's freshly announced China strategy offers a welcome change in tone but few new policies.

U.S. Secretary of State Antony Blinken's speech in May 2022 outlining the Joe Biden administration's China strategy was eloquent, logical, and gave Biden's oft-criticized China policy some much-needed coherence. But it was also a year late and neglected many major issues facing the two countries.

Blinken's talk was billed as an explanation of the administration's grand strategy toward China. The Donald Trump administration essentially tore up decades of largely bipartisan consensus on China, seeing the need to confront China on a range of issues—and to do so largely alone.

After taking office, Biden was expected to unveil a new policy toward his chief foreign challenge. Instead, 2021 passed with the new administration pursuing many of the same policies as its predecessor. It kept in place tariffs meant to punish China for unfair trading practices, and it did not try to revive the person-to-person and academic programs that the Trump administration killed.

These choices mirrored a growing consensus in Washington to get tough on China. But they also reflected clear divisions in the administration over China policy and confusion over how to handle critical issues, such as Taiwan.

Blinken's speech went some way toward unifying the administration's policies. Called "invest, align, compete," the strategy is in some ways a restatement of Blinken's March 2021 speech, when he said U.S. policy toward China will be "competitive when it should be, collaborative when it can be, and adversarial when it must be."

What Biden's Big Shift on Taiwan Means

From the David Sacks Council on Foreign Relations (CFR) May 2022 article "What Biden's Big Shift on Taiwan Means": In moving away from strategic ambiguity, Biden made a long overdue adjustment to U.S. policy.

In May 2022, standing next to Japanese Prime Minister Fumio Kishida, President Biden dispensed with forty years of strategic ambiguity by making clear he would use military force to come to Taiwan's defense. This was not the first time President Biden has seemed to endorse what Richard Haass and I have termed "strategic clarity."

In all three instances, the Biden administration walked back the president's comments, undercutting deterrence and confusing U.S. allies and partners. But regardless of administration officials claiming that there is no change to U.S. policy, President Biden's comments are significant and represent a long overdue shift.

First, it is important to note that while President Biden asserted the United States has a commitment to come to Taiwan's defense, it does not. Under the 1979 Taiwan Relations Act (TRA), the United States pledged to provide Taiwan with arms of a defensive character and maintain the capacity to come to Taiwan's defense, while the president must inform Congress of any threat to Taiwan.

The TRA does not, however, obligate the United States to directly intervene on Taiwan's behalf. Instead, for four decades Washington has maintained a policy of "strategic ambiguity," leaving unanswered the question of whether it would defend Taiwan. The logic underpinning strategic ambiguity is that China could not be sure the United States would not come to Taiwan's defense, while Taiwan could not be sure the United States would defend it, thus simultaneously deterring China from attacking and Taiwan from provoking China.

Nonetheless, President Biden's decision to state that the United States would come to Taiwan's defense was the correct one, as failing to do so would severely undermine America's position in Asia. If China were to subjugate Taiwan, it would be the biggest step to date in Beijing's quest to establish hegemony in the world's most consequential region. As President Biden noted, a Chinese use of force against Taiwan would "dislocate the entire region."

If China were to place its military on the island, it could more easily threaten Japan and the Philippines, two U.S. treaty allies. Economically, China would gain control of an economy that is the global epicenter of semiconductor manufacturing and the United States' eighth-largest trading partner. While U.S. allies did not expect Washington to use military force to repel Russia's invasion of Ukraine, they assume the United States would defend Taiwan.

If the United States stood on the sidelines, this would likely lead its allies to lose confidence in U.S. security guarantees and either develop nuclear weapons of their own or accommodate China's strategic interests.

In addition to the stakes, Beijing's growing assertiveness calls for a change in U.S. policy. Over the past two decades, China has pursued a rapid military modernization, focusing above all on developing capabilities that would allow it to defeat Taiwan and prevent the United States from coming to Taiwan's aid.

China has also grown bolder and its tolerance for risk has increased, as it militarized the South China Sea, crushed democracy in Hong Kong, fought with India alongside their disputed border, and economically coerced countries in Asia and Europe. Beijing is also putting more pressure on Taipei, redoubling its efforts to isolate Taiwan internationally, punishing it economically, and increasing its military activities near the island.

However, to counter Beijing's policy objectives towards Taiwan, and moving to a position of strategic clarity, the United States should emphasize that it is doing so within the context of its one-China policy and offer reassurances that it does not support Taiwanese independence. In other words, the ends of U.S. policy would not change.

Making AUKUS Work

Per the Jennifer D. P. Moroney and Alan Tidwell Rand Corporation March 2022 article "Making AUKUS Work":

Russia's war in Ukraine brings into stark relief the true meaning of revisionist power. It could serve as a catalyst to urgent action in countering both Russian and Chinese revisionism. On September 15, 2021 President Biden announced the creation of AUKUS, a trilateral, experimental arrangement among the United States, Australia, and the United Kingdom focused on defense technology that would deliver nuclear powered submarines to Australia by 2039. The President also made clear that AUKUS would extend beyond cooperation on submarines, and these sentiments have been echoed in Canberra and London.

AUKUS is an example of mini-lateralism, which can be thought of as a complement to—or a substitute for—traditional intergovernmental cooperation. AUKUS isn't a new alliance. It's an additive, focused security partnership that is intended to deepen collaboration on advanced military capabilities and technologies including cyber, artificial intelligence, and quantum concepts. It builds on the Defense Trade Cooperation treaties negotiated by the Bush administration in 2007 and ratified in 2010.

AUKUS presents new opportunities, the first and most often mentioned is that it provides Australia with nuclear powered submarine capability. The U.S. has only ever shared nuclear propulsion technology once before, and that was with the United Kingdom. Second, AUKUS aims to promote greater sovereign capability for Australian and British defense industry by providing access to U.S. technology. Third, it is designed to push back against any potential weakening of the alliance bonds by selectively combining defense capability between Australia, United Kingdom, and United States in the face of strategic competition with China and Russia.

AUKUS could not only deliver new submarines for Australia, but it could become the springboard for revolutionizing how the U.S. works with a select group of its most capable allies.

The promise of AUKUS stems from the bringing together of three capable allies in a grand experiment, with a high-stakes mini-lateral relationship that depends first and foremost upon trust to deliver highly valued capabilities.

If effectively implemented, AUKUS would not only deliver new submarines for Australia, but perhaps more importantly, it could become the springboard for revolutionizing how the U.S. works with a select group of its most capable allies through the extraordinary depth of technological development, access to highly classified materials and expanded sharing of intellectual property.

Given its considerable current international challenges, the United States counts AUKUS as only one among many tasks it must undertake. An essential element of AUKUS's success would require Congressional action, including approval for the nuclear agreement under the Atomic Energy Act.

Beyond legislative compliance, the bureaucratic infrastructure to implement AUKUS would need to quickly be established. This includes funding and empowering the working groups with deep analytic expertise to hammer out the details of the security pact. The imbalance of interest between the three nations suggests that Australia has the most to lose, and so it will likely invest the greater effort to see that AUKUS succeeds.

What does AUKUS need to be effective?

AUKUS success depends upon the development of a new legislative framework in the U.S., the commitment of organizational resources, empowering the working groups tasked with governing AUKUS, ensuring access to the requisite expertise, the ability to identify and manage barriers to success, and the employment of measurable indicators of success. These are not easy tasks, and each carries some risk.

AUKUS is likely to shine a bright light on the barriers to collaboration—not only technical, but also bureaucratic, budgetary, cultural, regulatory, political, and strategic.

The Indo-Pacific Economic Framework for Prosperity

From the "Fact Sheet: In Asia, President Biden and a Dozen Indo-Pacific Partners Launch the Indo-Pacific Economic Framework for Prosperity" report from The White House in May 2022:

In Tokyo, Japan, in May 2022, President Biden launched the Indo-Pacific Economic Framework for Prosperity (IPEF) with a dozen initial partners: Australia, Brunei, India, Indonesia, Japan, Republic of Korea, Malaysia, New Zealand, the Philippines, Singapore, Thailand, and Vietnam. Together, we represent 40% of world GDP.

The United States is an Indo-Pacific economic power, and expanding U.S. economic leadership in the region is good for American workers and businesses—as well as for the people of the region. IPEF will enable the United States and our allies to decide on rules of the road that ensure American workers, small businesses, and ranchers can compete in the Indo-Pacific. As the President has said, tackling inflation is a top economic priority, and this framework will help lower costs by making our supply chains more resilient in the long term, protecting us against costly disruptions that lead to higher prices for consumers.

U.S. foreign direct investment in the region totaled more than $969 billion in 2020 and has nearly doubled in the last decade, and we are the leading exporter of services to the region, helping fuel regional growth. Trade with the Indo-Pacific supports more than three million American jobs and is the source of nearly $900 billion in foreign direct investment in the United States. With 60 percent of the world's population, the Indo-Pacific is projected to be the largest contributor to global growth over the next 30 years.

The United States and our partners in the region believe that much of our success in the coming decades will depend on how well governments harness innovation—especially the transformations afoot in the clean energy, digital, and technology sectors—while fortifying our economies against a range of threats, from fragile supply chains to corruption to tax havens.

The past models of economic engagement did not address these challenges, leaving our workers, businesses, and consumers vulnerable. The framework will focus on four key pillars to establish high-standard commitments that will deepen our economic engagement in the region:

Democrats Can't Hide Their Israel Problem

Credit: Erin Scott/Reuters - The Quad, from left: Rep. Ayanna Pressley, Rep. Alexandria Ocasio-Cortez, Rep. Ilhan Omar, and Rep. Rashida Tlaib hold a news conference on Capitol Hill, July 15, 2019.

Per the Philip Klein *National Review* September 2021 article "Democrats Can't Hide Their Israel Problem":

For the past decade or so, top Democrats have been desperately trying to downplay the increasing size and influence of the anti-Israel wing of the party. But it keeps getting harder to hide what's happening. This week provided yet another stark reminder when a group of progressives banded together to force House speaker Nancy Pelosi to rip $1 billion for Israel's Iron Dome missile-defense system out of a spending bill meant to avert a government shutdown. It's hard to overstate what a radical turn this is for the party.

Iron Dome has been an enormously successful shield that has allowed Israel to protect its people by shooting down rockets that Palestinian terrorist groups indiscriminately fire at civilians. By limiting Israeli casualties, the system also protects Palestinian civilians. That is, were the rocket attacks more deadly, Israel would have no choice but to launch a more aggressive military campaign—and likely a ground invasion in Gaza—which would mean the loss of more lives on both sides.

Polling bears out the dramatic shift in the partisan split on Israel in the past several decades. Take a basic question on whether people sympathize more with Israel or the Palestinians. In 1978, according to the Pew Research Center, Republicans were only marginally more supportive of Israel than were Democrats, 49 percent to 44 percent. But when the poll was taken in 2018,

79 percent of Republicans said they sympathized more with Israel, compared with 27 percent of Democrats—a staggering 52-point gap. Ideologically, the numbers are more dramatic, as liberal Democrats actually sympathize with the Palestinians over Israelis by a nearly two-to-one margin.

More recently, a Gallup poll taken this past March found that 53 percent of Democrats wanted the U.S. to put more pressure on Israelis, compared with just 17 percent of Republicans.

When Barack Obama came to the presidency, he pursued a "daylight" policy based on the mistaken notion that if the U.S. were seen as more distant from Israel, Americans would come to be viewed as a more honest broker by Arab countries, which would improve the prospects for peace. By the end of his administration, he abandoned Israel at the U.N., allowing the global body to pass a U.N. resolution condemning Jews for building homes in communities surrounding the Israeli capital city of Jerusalem.

He also negotiated a nuclear deal that allowed hundreds of billions of dollars to flow to Iran. The agreement made Iran a greater conventional threat, allowed it to expand its ballistic-missile program, and kept alive its path to nuclear weapons.

The Biden Administration's Syria Policy: A Forecast For War

From the Joel D. Rayburn Hoover Institution December 2021 report "The Biden Administration's Syria Policy: A Forecast For War":

Syria as a continuing danger and if the United States ignores it—we do so are our own peril. After almost eleven years, the Syrian conflict is as acutely dangerous an international security problem as ever.

What began in 2011 as a popular revolt against Bashar al-Assad's rule quickly expanded into a regional conflict that has no end in sight. With five external military forces jostling with each other in or over Syria (Russia, Iran, Turkey, the United States, and Israel), the potential for intrastate conflict in any given week is high.

Syria is the source of the world's largest refugee crisis, with about twelve million Syrians--half of the country's prewar population--either registered as refugees or internally displaced. The country is a cockpit of terrorism, with Al Qaeda, ISIS, and other such groups present in large numbers and sometimes controlling territory.

Bashar al-Assad's determination to maintain vast chemical weapons makes Syria the world's most glaring WMD problem as well. The Assad regime's mass killing and jailing of hundreds of thousands of Syrians makes it the worst human rights problem of the 21st century. Add to these horrors the recent development that the Assad regime has become a major narco-state.

The internal war among Syrian political factions shows no sign of resolving itself. After a decade of war, the country is de facto partitioned into three zones: the rump failed state ruled by Assad, containing perhaps 10 million Syrians; a de facto Turkish protectorate of opposition-held territories in the northwest with about five million Syrians; and a de facto U.S. protectorate in the northeast with about four million Syrians under the control of the Kurdish-led Syrian democratic forces.

Assad finds himself without the military or financial means of reconquering the other two zones, and the world finds Assad without any inclination to make peace with the other two. In short, Syria remains a tense battlefield with all the necessary ingredients to flare into broader warfare at any time.

The Biden team's newly articulated Syria policy is a welcome change from its ten months of silence and the regional anxiety that accompanied it. But it's likely the administration's stripped-down Syria priorities list will leave much of the surrounding region with the judgment that the United States, for the time being, is not interested in a more comprehensive approach that accounts for the priorities of Syria's neighbors.

While it is true the Trump administration's Syria policy was not perfect, most notably in its on-again, off-again treatment of the U.S. military presence in eastern Syria, the real difference between the Trump and Biden approaches is that the latter has chosen to focus on four symptoms of the Syrian conflict, rather than addressing its fundamental causes--the nature of the Assad regime and the Iranian regime's regional expansion--as the former attempted to do.

The Biden team proposes to focus on the terrorism and humanitarian crisis emanating from Syria without seeking a solution to the overall conflict from which those problems spring. They intend to reduce violence in Syria through cease fires that will not be connected to a broader process to resolve the political conflict that creates the violence in the first place.

They signal a green light for Israel to "mow the grass" by attacking Iranian bases and weapons in Syria without addressing the unprecedented (at least in modern times) Iranian military expansion into the Levant more broadly. And they omit mention of the Syrian regime's weapons of mass destruction that came close to leading the United States to war with Damascus in 2013, and did lead the United States to war with Damascus in 2017 and 2018.

In short, the Biden administration aspires to manage rather than to end the Syrian conflict, while deflecting calls for more comprehensive solutions as maximalist and unrealistic. By ignoring causes in favor of symptoms, Biden's approach will ensure that the conflict will not end anytime soon and that the potential for an explosive escalation will remain at all times.

Why Joe Biden's Nuclear Talks With Iran Look Like a Disaster

Per the James Phillips The Heritage Foundation February 2022 article "Why Joe Biden's Nuclear Talks With Iran Look Like a Disaster":

After months of indirect negotiations in Vienna, the Biden administration has lurched into a last-ditch effort to entice Iran into rejoining the flawed 2015 nuclear deal. The State Department announced it was waiving sanctions on Iran's "civilian" nuclear program so that foreign companies could resume work on key aspects of the project.

The Administration had promised to negotiate a "longer and stronger" nuclear deal, but clearly, that will not happen. Due to Iranian foot-dragging and maximalist demands, the negotiations will either yield a shorter, weaker deal or collapse without an agreement.

Either way, the Administration's complacent squandering of the leverage afforded by U.S. sanctions will be a contributing factor.

The sanctions waiver announced is only the most recent of a series of one-sided goodwill gestures and concessions made by the administration that has reduced the pressure on Tehran to accept an agreement that includes more effective and longer-lasting non-proliferation guarantees, which the administration admits are needed to correct flaws in the 2015 agreement.

Iran says waivers are "not sufficient"

The new waivers permit foreign countries and companies to work on projects at Iran's Arak heavy water plant, the Bushehr nuclear power station, and the Tehran Research Reactor. The Trump administration had revoked the waivers in May 2020, as part of its "maximum pressure" strategy to extract a more effective and durable nuclear agreement from Iran.

Secretary of State Mike Pompeo at the time accused Iran of committing "nuclear extortion" by expanding work at the facilities.

The State Department now maintains that the waivers should not be considered a concession to Iran. Rather, they are "designed to facilitate discussions that would help to close a deal." But the overture apparently carries little weight with Iran.

Concessions only encourage Iran's maximalist demands

Iran's unyielding stance at the Vienna talks reflects both confidence that it can withstand half-hearted U.S. economic sanctions and skepticism that it will face more serious consequences if it continues ignoring its nonproliferation commitments.

The Biden administration has encouraged this calculus by denouncing the Trump administration's maximum pressure strategy, relaxing enforcement of sanctions, and turning a blind eye to surging Chinese imports of Iranian oil.

Instead of the longer, stronger version of the 2015 deal promised by candidate Joe Biden, what is emerging from the Vienna talks is a shorter, weaker and riskier diplomatic gambit to appease Tehran. The inconvenient truth is that the 2015 nuclear agreement did not end Iran's nuclear weapons ambitions; it merely slowed Iran's nuclear progress with a diplomatic speed bump.

In 2031, after key restrictions on uranium enrichment and the size of Iran's uranium stockpile expire, Tehran will be well-positioned for a possible nuclear breakout or sneakout.

The bottom line

The 2015 nuclear agreement rewarded Iran with disproportionate economic benefits in return for weak, temporary, and easily reversible restrictions on important aspects of its nuclear program. Rather than returning to the defective old deal, Washington should have insisted on a stronger new deal. The Biden administration has made a bad situation worse by unwisely relaxing pressure on Iran and offering carrots while downplaying the role of sticks in its negotiating strategy.

Under these circumstances, the Vienna negotiations are likely to yield a half-baked deal that will only postpone a festering nuclear crisis, not resolve it. And it will kick the can down the road while flooding Iran with sanctions relief that will embolden the regime, aid its military buildup, and strengthen its proxy terrorist networks for future attacks.

14 – The Democratic 'Party's Over' for So Many Independent, Hispanic, Asian & Black Voters

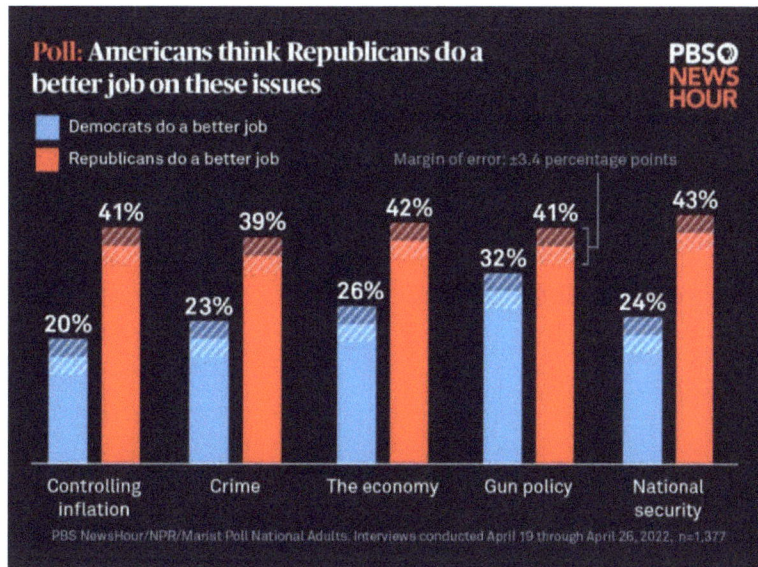

From the Morris P. Fiorina *Hoover Digest* Spring 2021 (Issue 2) article "The Majority-Minority Myth": Identity politics, which supposedly boost the Democrats' electoral chances, aren't the sure bet they might appear. Why? Because Americans' identities are steadily blending into each other.

In 2002, influential political observers John Judis and Ruy Teixeira published a book that helped craft an enduring narrative. *The Emerging Democratic Majority* postulated that ongoing sociodemographic trends worked to the advantage of the Democratic Party. These trends included a growing percentage of ethnic minorities, along with increasing percentages of younger voters, unmarried working women, and the college-educated. Individually and cumulatively these developments suggested a bright future for Democrats' electoral prospects.

The 2008 presidential election seemed to herald the arrival of this "new American electorate" or "coalition of the ascendant." Four years later, in the aftermath of President Obama's re-election, the Republican National Committee recognized the apparent new order when it issued an "autopsy" of Mitt Romney's loss. In it, the GOP declared that it needed to become more inclusive and increase its appeal to ethnic and racial minorities, women, and young voters.

A few years later, the United States Census Bureau put an official stamp on one of the important demographic trends when it reported that "non-Hispanic whites may no longer comprise over 50 percent of the US population by 2044." Most official government reports go unnoticed. Not this one. The idea of a majority-minority country quickly dominated the national political conversation. Other announcements reinforced the 2015 report: in every year since 2013, minority births have exceeded white births. Beginning in 2019, a majority of Americans under sixteen years old are nonwhite.

There is no downplaying the political impact of what has been called "the browning of America." The narrative of the majority-minority nation has become a staple of political commentary, especially on the left.

Contrary to expectations, however, in the short run--the 2016 elections--many Democrats believe the party suffered from acceptance of the thesis and its apparent support for an electoral emphasis on identities. Although the contributions of ethnocentrism and racism to Donald Trump's vote have arguably been exaggerated, social changes, particularly rapid and cumulative social changes, are certainly unnerving to some elements of the population, with political reaction a natural result.

Gallup Records 14-Point Shift in Party Identification During 2021

Per the Charles C.W. Cooke *National Review* January 2022 survey "Gallup Records 14-Point Shift in Party Identification During 2021":

Gallup reports that Joe Biden has presided over a remarkable resurgence in support for the Republican party: On average, Americans' political party preferences in 2021 looked similar to prior years, with slightly more U.S. adults identifying as Democrats or leaning Democratic (46%) than identified as Republicans or leaned Republican (43%).

However, the general stability for the full-year average obscures a dramatic shift over the course of 2021, from a nine-percentage-point Democratic advantage in the first quarter to a rare five-point Republican edge in the fourth quarter.

Both the nine-point Democratic advantage in the first quarter and the five-point Republican edge in the fourth quarter are among the largest Gallup has measured for each party in any quarter since it began regularly measuring party identification and leaning in 1991.

The bottom line:

The year 2021 was an eventful one in politics, after a similarly eventful 2020 that also saw major shifts in party preferences. In early 2021, Democratic strength reached levels not seen in nearly a decade. By the third quarter, those Democratic gains evaporated as Biden's job approval declined. The political winds continued to become more favorable to Republicans in the fourth quarter, giving the GOP an advantage over Democrats larger than any they had achieved in more than 25 years.

Minorities Are Finding a New Political Home With the Republican Party

From the Ronna McDaniel *The Hill* April 2022 update "Minorities Are Finding a New Political Home With the Republican Party":

Many polls consistently show Hispanics are moving away from the Democratic Party. A *Wall Street Journal* poll from December found that Hispanic voters were equally divided over who they would vote for in the next election. The momentum certainly seems to be with the GOP: A record 103 Republican Hispanic candidates are seeking congressional seats this year. It's an early sign that our efforts to take our message to new voters and investment in Hispanic community centers in states like Texas, Wisconsin and Florida are making an impact.

The GOP has been making inroads into the Asian American community for years. Under the Trump administration, Republicans saw a 7 percent gain with Asian Americans from 2016 to 2020. The shift was even greater among Vietnamese Americans, who experienced a 14 percent shift toward Republican candidates. And if that news wasn't bad enough for Democrats, 43 percent of the Asian American and Pacific Islander community see race relations "getting worse" under Joe Biden.

A similar pattern is playing out among Black voters, who have been particularly hard hit by Democrats' destructive agenda. Democratic support for the defund-the-police movement has led to a surge in violent crime that's disproportionately impacting Black Americans. Inflation is hitting Black Americans—especially women—hardest, with 44 percent saying rising prices pose a serious financial hardship. That's why Black support for Democrats is quickly eroding: Backing for Democratic Congressional candidates fell from 56 percent in November to only 35 percent in March.

Meanwhile, the RNC is building relationships with Asian Americans by opening Asian Pacific American community centers in California, Georgia, Texas and a brand new one in Nevada, with more to come. These grassroots, local offices are part of how we're building relationships with Asian Americans and taking our message of law and order, educational opportunity, and economic growth to new voters.

Asian Americans aren't the only community where the RNC is making inroads. While Democrats push socialism, radical abortion policies and refer to them as "Latinx," Hispanic Americans are concerned about preserving freedoms, raising strong families and putting food on the table. It's no wonder a recent Quinnipiac poll found that Biden's approval rating with Hispanic voters was lower than any other racial or ethnic group: just 12 percent say they "approve strongly" of his time in office.

Democrat-Leaning Voters Trend Toward GOP: Poll

From the Rita Li *Epoch Times* May 2022 article "Democrat-Leaning Voters Trend Toward GOP: Poll": Democrats further lost public approval among voters under 45, with 50 percent of those saying they would choose a Republican compared to 40 percent that plan to go for a Democrat. Young Americans tend to lean Democrat. In 2020, 55 percent of those aged 30–49 support Biden, while 59 percent of those aged 18–29 voted for him, according to the Pew Research Center.

Overall, the poll shows 47 percent of U.S. adults would support a Republican candidate, while 44 percent said they would vote for Democrats—the first time the GOP has led the poll since they won full control of Congress in 2014. The Republican Party, meanwhile, is holding an edge among independent voters, as 45 percent said to stand by a Republican, with 38 percent saying they prefer a Democrat.

More Likely to Choose Republicans Than Democrats in Midterms: Poll

From the Zachary Evans *National Review* April 2022 article "More Likely to Choose Republicans Than Democrats in Midterms: Poll": Voters are more likely to choose Republicans over Democrats in the 2022 midterms, according to a new NPR/PBS NewsHour/Marist poll.

Among registered voters surveyed, 47 percent said they are "more likely" to choose a Republican candidate in their congressional district during the midterms, while 44 percent said they would choose a Democratic candidate.

The poll has a margin of error of 3.7 points. It marks the first time since 2014 that Marist found more support for Republicans than Democrats prior to an election, NPR noted. Among surveyed voters, 40 percent thought the Republican Party could handle crime more effectively, while 23 percent said the Democratic Party would do a better job.

The poll showed similar results when respondents were asked about inflation. With inflation reaching its highest level in decades in March, 43 percent of surveyed voters said Republicans could better handle inflation, compared with 21 percent for Democrats.

Meanwhile, Democrats outperformed Republicans among pluralities of registered voters on issues including handling of the Covid pandemic (38 percent for Democrats versus 27 percent for Republicans) and LGBT issues (48 percent for Democrats versus 20 percent for Republicans). Additionally, 42 percent of surveyed voters preferred the Democratic Party's handling of abortion compared with 33 percent who preferred Republicans.

Parents of children under the age of 18 swung massively toward Republicans. Sixty percent said they would vote for a Republican, while 39 percent said they'd cast their ballot for a Democrat. Latinos also preferred Republicans, 52-39 percent.

The survey was conducted from April 19-26, 2022, and included 1,377 American adults over age 18, of which 1,162 were registered voters.

Biden's Job Approval Drops to Record-Low

Per the Arjun Singh *National Review* May 2022 update "Biden's Job Approval Drops to Record-Low": In May 2022, President Joe Biden's job approval rating dropped to the lowest level of his presidency, falling to 39 percent in a new poll.

Biden's approval rating declined by six percentage points, from 45 percent the previous month, according to a poll conducted by the Associated Press and National Opinion Research Center at the University of Chicago (AP-NORC). Biden's approval rating had been falling for the last 12 months of his presidency, per the poll, and dropped below 50 percent for the first time in September.

The May poll was conducted using a sample of 1,172 adults reflecting the U.S. population and has an error margin of 4.0 percentage points. Other polls taken in conjunction with AP-NORC also yielded poor findings for the Biden Administration. Asked whether the country is headed in the right direction, only 20 percent agreed—a figure also reported for confidence in the U.S. economy.

Among the sources of the decline, per analysis by the AP, was a loss of support for Biden among Democrats. Only 73 percent of Biden's party expressed approval for the president's performance, a sharp decline from an 82 percent average in earlier polls. Just 33 percent of Democrats believe the country is headed in the right direction, a 16-point drop from April.

The poll also showed how Biden's approval numbers have declined across the board among ethnic, gender, and age groups.

Among women, Biden's approval ratings fell seven points to 41 percent, while men rated him even worse at 37 percent. While among Black adults, Biden's approval rating is still 57 percent—the highest of any group measured—this is also a seven-point decline from last month. Both white and Hispanic voters gave Biden 36 percent approval each.

On age, the poll lumped voters into only two categories—those above and below 45—and reflected a slight gap in approval: older voters tended to approve of Biden at 42 percent while those under 45 rated him at 36 percent, a six point difference.

Juan Williams: Democratic Infighting Could Spell Doom

From the Juan Williams *The Hill* June 2022 news report "Juan Williams: Democratic infighting could spell doom":

You've heard loud right-wing talkers 'skinning' the Democrats as a bunch of commies and socialists. What if I told you that more than a third of Democrats, 37 percent, identify as moderates? Here's another eye-popper—12 percent of Democrats say they are conservatives.

Yes, that means that despite all the talk about Democrats as a radical political party, only 50 percent of Democrats even go far enough to the left to call themselves liberals. These poll numbers from Gallup reveal a fascinating fight inside the party over what it means to be a Democrat in 2022.

The biggest change among Democrats since the turn of the century is that the party includes more liberals. The so-called 'progressives' have sharply increased their numbers since 2000 when they were about 30 percent of the party, according to Gallup. The share of Democrats identifying as liberal, which had been steadily rising, only hit 50 percent after Donald Trump won the presidency.

Democrats have won the popular vote in seven of the last eight presidential elections. They are the dominant party in the nation's most economically productive cities and their senators collectively represent millions more voters than their Republican counterparts.

History will also note Republican success in diluting Democrats' power in Congress due to the GOP's dominance among conservative white voters. This has helped Republicans win elections in smaller states with more rural and small-town populations.

The result is divided, polarized, often paralyzed federal government. And that has led to a tremendous rise in the influence of swing voters. The percentage of voters who say they are independent of both parties, 42 percent, is now bigger than the percentage of voters who tell Gallup they are Democrats (28 percent) or Republicans (28 percent).

The power of swing voters is evident in that seven of the last eight midterm and presidential elections have seen a switch in party control in the House, Senate or White House.

Democratic Party Is Alienating Its Base, Heading for Trouble in November Midterms, Analysts Say

This section is from the Michael Washburn *Epoch Times* April 2022 article "Democratic Party Is Alienating Its Base, Heading for Trouble in November Midterms, Analysts Say":

Dismal poll numbers suggesting that a low number of Americans think highly of the job that President Joe Biden is doing—a mere 33 percent of respondents in a Quinnipiac poll in April 2022 said they approved—have helped prompt a pivot on Biden's part toward a greater focus on domestic issues, even as the Ukraine crisis continues to consume much of his attention.

Biden hopes to bolster his party's image in time for the midterm elections in November. But experts say that an enhanced focus on domestic issues—or the appearance of one—is unlikely to salvage the prospects of the Democratic Party. The party, they say, continues to allow its most radical left-wing elements to shape its policies and stances on the issues of concern to voters, particularly Hispanic voters and others who have long been crucial to the electoral prospects of a party that promotes itself as a champion for working people and diversity.

Alienating the Base

The same Quinnipiac poll found that within the category of Hispanic voters, Biden's approval rating is a mere 26 percent. The party depends to a great extent on the Latino vote, and at this juncture, no other demographic gives the current president a lower rating of approval.

Experts say that the Democratic Party's missteps on immigration, crime, and the economy have eroded its support among the working people that it depends on, and the disenchantment is particularly acute among Hispanic voters.

In the view of Jeronimo Cortina, a professor of political science at the University of Houston, the administration suffers from a perception among Hispanic voters that it hasn't kept promises and that, in general, it isn't very good at getting things done.

"Things are not going very well for President Biden, domestically speaking. One of the issues that we have to identify is the pandemic. A lot of people have been hurt, and Latinos and African Americans have had to look at how it has affected them. And then there are other issues that affect the Latino community, such as the economy, jobs, child care, and education," Cortina said.

Inflation, fueled by the pandemic and, according to experts, driven partly by the Federal Reserve's expansionary monetary policy, has had noticeable effects on gas costs and prices at the supermarket. The 8.5 percent jump in the Consumer Price Index over the past year—and particularly the rise in gas prices—hasn't been lost on Hispanic voters who don't work remotely and have to divert a certain amount of their income to get to work, Cortina noted.

Although a pivot toward domestic issues may be a wise move, the Democratic Party may continue to lose ground through a mistaken assumption that Hispanic voters are essentially a monolithic category whose interests are defined by one issue—immigration—and that the party that says the correct things on that issue has the Latino vote locked up.

"A lot of people make that mistake, and it is completely untrue. Immigration is an issue for Latino voters. However, it is not the most important issue. If you want to have a campaign based on immigration, it's only going to get you so far," Cortina said.

In his view, a party with a successful electoral strategy is one with a balanced approach and one that avoids signaling its virtue on immigration policy at the expense of other issues of concern to voters in their day-to-day lives.

Gallup polls tend to find that roughly a third of respondents favor more immigration, a third favor less, and a third are fine with maintaining current levels, Cortina said. He described Latinos as no different when it comes to the breakdown of opinion on the issue. He characterized Latinos as sophisticated voters unlikely to be swayed by a one-sided pro-immigration platform when they see that their economic situation isn't improving.

Failing to Keep the Public Safe

Americans' perceptions that they're less safe may also impact the incumbent party's prospects in the midterms, according to experts, pointing to the uptick in violent crime across big cities since the start of the COVID-19 pandemic.

While some researchers attribute the rise in crime to factors caused by the pandemic, others believe that the rise in violent crime was directly linked to the Black Lives Matter protests of 2020, progressive policies under the banner of "defund the police," and the resulting pullback by law enforcement.

"For Biden to be underwater with Hispanics, a traditionally Democratic constituency, is disastrous. If Hispanics vote just 40 percent for the GOP or stay at home, Democrats don't stand a chance in Florida, Texas, Arizona, or Georgia races," said Keith Naughton, principal of Silent Majority Strategies, a Maryland-based consulting firm.

Naughton faults Democratic leadership for making bold pronouncements in public, but lacking the resolve and ideological unity to back them up with effective policies. He identified the internal tensions alluded to by Cortina above as a persistent problem for the party.

"The Democratic Party has become a collection of squabbling interest groups, each of whom has a laundry list of uncrossable red lines. The only thing holding the Democrats together is hating Donald Trump. Biden did not run on an affirmative policy, he just ran as 'not Trump,'" Naughton said.

This lack of coherence and negative campaigning have benefited Republicans, he said.

"Trump and the Republicans became much more appealing to working-class voters and discovered that the issue of securing the border was not toxic for Hispanics. Like most working-class voters, they see mass, uncontrolled immigration as a threat to their livelihoods," Naughton said.

He said he doubts that the Democrats can pull out of their tailspin and get their numbers up in advance of the midterms. The issues of top concern to voters may be beyond Biden's power to resolve.

Hispanics Are Abandoning Biden in Droves. Here's Why

From the Joe Concha *The Hill* April 2022 report "Hispanics Are Abandoning Biden in Droves. Here's Why":

Poll after poll shows President Biden losing support from every demographic in the book. The April 2022 Quinnipiac University has the 46th president at 33 percent approval overall, or just 9 points higher than President Nixon had on the day he resigned from office.

But perhaps the most disturbing number for Team Biden comes when looking at his stunning fall among Hispanics, a hugely important voting bloc that went to him to the tune of 61 percent.

In the Quinnipiac poll released this week, Biden receives just 26 percent approval. Upon entering office, FiveThirtyEight.com had Biden at 69 percent approval, so we're talking a 43-percentage point drop in the span of 15 months. And just 12 percent of Hispanics "approve strongly" of Biden's performance as president, while 54 percent "disapprove strongly" or "disapprove somewhat."

For Democrats, these are keep-you-up-at-night numbers. Because Latinos are the country's largest minority voting bloc. Pandering to Latinos in the most obvious and phony ways possible ain't helping, either.

By the way, "Latinx," the term preferred by most progressives, is an attempt to refer to the group in a gender-neutral manner. But according to Bendixen & Amandi International, 40 percent of Latino voters are offended by the use of "Latinx," while just 2 percent identified as Latinx. Two percent!

Latinos' two greatest concerns are skyrocketing inflation and crime. A recent Axios poll found that 37 percent of Latino voters say inflation is their top concern, while 35 percent listed crime.

Biden's handling of the border may yield the most surprising data coming out of border states such as Texas. More than 50 percent of registered Latino voters there disapprove of the administration's handling of the border. And as you may recall, Biden tapped Vice President Kamala Harris to handle the border crisis, but she has been almost entirely apathetic on this front.

Joe Biden, the presidential candidate who captured more votes than any other person in U.S. history, currently has the support of just one-third of the country. The Latino community is leading the exodus—a prospect the Democratic Party could not have imagined 15 months ago after taking complete power in D.C.

The Democrats' Hispanic Voter Problem

Per the Ruy Teixeira "The Democrats' Hispanic Voter Problem" The Liberal Patriot December 2021 post "The Democrats' Hispanic Voter Problem" and ss noted numerous times in this chapter:

The Democrats are steadily losing ground with Hispanic voters. The seriousness of this problem tends to be underestimated in Democratic circles for a couple of reasons: (1) they don't realize how big the shift is; and (2) they don't realize how thoroughly it undermines the most influential Democratic theory of the case for building their coalition.

On the latter, consider that most Democrats like to believe that, since a relatively conservative white population is in sharp decline while a presumably liberal nonwhite population keeps growing, the course of social and demographic change should deliver an ever-growing Democratic coalition. It is simply a matter of getting this burgeoning nonwhite population to the polls.

But consider further that, as the Census documents, the biggest single driver of the increased nonwhite population is the growth of the Hispanic population. They are by far the largest group within the Census-designated nonwhite population (19 percent vs. 12 percent for blacks). While their representation among voters considerably lags their representation in the overall population, it is fair to say that voting trends among this group will decisively shape voting trends among nonwhites in the future since their share of voters will continue to increase while black voter share is expected to remain roughly constant.

It therefore follows that, if Hispanic voting trends continue to move steadily against the Democrats, the pro-Democratic effect of nonwhite population growth will be blunted, if not cancelled out entirely, and that very influential Democratic theory of the case falls apart. That could—or should—provoke quite a sea change in Democratic thinking.

Hispanic Voters Are Losing Faith in the Democratic Party: Poll

This section is from the J.M. Phelps *Epoch Times* May 2022 article "Hispanic Voters Are Losing Faith in the Democratic Party: Poll":

The support of Hispanic voters at the midterms later this year could prove to be "extremely instrumental" in turning the tide of liberal policies of the current administration, a conservative Hispanic group says.

According to a Quinnipiac University poll published in April 2022, only 26 percent of Hispanic survey participants approved of President Joe Biden's job performance. This marks the lowest approval rating of any demographic group.

The *Epoch Times* spoke to Santiago Avila, national vice chairman of the Republican National Hispanic Assembly (RNHA), who offered a number of reasons why support among Hispanic voters is plummeting.

While Hispanics have historically registered as Democrats, Avila said their values are generally conservative. "[Many Hispanics] grow up being told that Republicans are for the rich and

Democrats are for the poor." What they should understand, he said, is that "Democrats are more liberal, and Republicans are more conservative."

Having spoken to many different left-leaning Hispanics, Avila said, "they are really beginning to feel like the Democratic party has become too extreme to the point where it's starting to scare some of them." Many are beginning to turn away from the Democratic party because "they're getting vibes of a communist Cuba and socialist Venezuela here in America. "

As a result, Avila said Hispanics are going to be "extremely instrumental" in the upcoming midterm elections. "They are starting to come to the realization that their conservative values are in opposition to what the media has been trying to feed them in favor of Biden and the Democrats."

RNHA's National Chairman Ronnie Lucero agreed, pointing to the liberal policies of the current administration as a problem. More often than not, "a lot of changes in policies are reflected against the values of the Hispanic community," he said.

Lucero said progressive leaders push for abortion and the abolishment of the Second Amendment, for example. "The Hispanic community is very pro-life and does not want a power grab [that restricts the lawful possession of firearms]," he said. "These are issues Hispanics want to speak up, stand up, and be vocal about when it comes time to vote."

Legal, Not Illegal, Immigration

The topic of immigration is often a prevailing narrative when talking to Hispanics about the policies of any administration, Avila noted. As the son of two immigrants, he wants to see immigration but said it has to be accomplished by the rule of law.

"Illegal immigration puts a burden on the country and both parties are to blame," Avila said, pointing out that Democrats play with "emotions, sentiments, and pull at the heartstrings" when speaking about the topic. And all the while, he said, too many conservatives are assuming they're not going to get the Hispanic vote. Yet, he said, former President Donald Trump and his administration were "very effective" at reaching the Hispanic community.

Lucero agreed that illegal immigration is harmful to the country, adding that "a country with open borders is not a country." Rule of law must be "cherished" and "respected," he said. "The people who take the wrong process and beat the system must be rejected."

Values and the America Dream

While immigration is a hot topic, Avila said, "it's not the number one topic for the Hispanic community." He said Hispanics care more about their families and their independence. "We didn't come into this country to live off of welfare; we're running away from that."

Most Hispanics are "chasing the American dream," according to Avila. Hispanics want the opportunities found in the United States and that's why many have immigrated to the country.

"We come here, because when you become an American, you get endowed with inherent, unalienable rights that aren't enjoyed in other countries," he said. "We want to prosper and live out our values in this great country."

When it comes time to vote in the midterm election, "one thing about the Hispanic voter is that we stick to our values," Avila said. "We see ourselves as Americans and our voices will be heard at the voting booth later this year," he said.

A Word of Caution on the Hispanic 'Realignment'

Per the Nate Hochman *National Review* March 2022 article "A Word of Caution on the Hispanic 'Realignment'":

Nowhere has this Hispanic realignment been more dramatic than South Texas. As I wrote in January, "the last year or so has seen a rightward turn in the Tejano border communities in South Texas, mirroring or outpacing the shift toward the GOP in Hispanic voters nationwide. (Five of America's six biggest county-level shifts to Trump from 2016 to 2020 occurred in South Texas:

In Texas's 99 percent Hispanic Starr County, for example, Trump's numbers improved by a remarkable 55 points)." Chuck DeVore of the Texas Public Policy Center told me at the time that South Texas' heavily Hispanic Rio Grande Valley was a "litmus test" for the Texas Hispanic population's partisan loyalties. "If that's true, things look bleak indeed," I wrote. "Not only did the heavily Hispanic border region move rapidly toward Trump from 2016 to 2020, but a Hispanic Democrat from Rio Grande City went so far as to switch parties and register as a Republican in November."

The GOP has good reason to be optimistic about the potential for inroads with Hispanics—and perhaps even nonwhites more broadly—both in Texas and across the country. But they can't take it for granted. The so-called "realignment" of working-class nonwhites moving into the Republican coalition isn't inevitable. If it happens, it will be the result of years of hard work.

Poll: Biden Approval Rating Drops among Young Americans

From the Alexandra DeSanctis *National Review* April 25, 2022 report "Poll: Biden Approval Rating Drops among Young Americans":

A new youth poll from the Harvard Kennedy School's Institute of Politics suggests that President Biden is plummeting in popularity among young Americans, a category where he previously was doing fairly well.

The poll surveyed more than 2,000 U.S. residents between the ages of 18 and 29, was conducted from March 15 to March 30 of 2022, and has a margin of error of +/- 2.89 percent.

Among these Americans, only a plurality (41 percent) approve of the job Biden is doing as president, a notable drop from last fall, when 46 percent said they approved. But most interesting is the fact that Biden has dropped 18 points among young voters since this time last year, a significant decline.

Seventy percent of Democratic respondents said they approve of Biden's job performance, a decline of five points since last fall. Meanwhile, just one-third of Independents say they approve of Biden's job performance, a six-point drop from Fall 2021, and only about one in ten Republicans approves.

The chief reason respondents gave for their disapproval of Biden's job performance was is "ineffectiveness" (36 percent). A slight majority (52 percent) said Biden has handled the Covid-19 pandemic well, and 46 percent say they approve of his handling of the crisis in Ukraine. But his biggest pitfall: Just one-third of respondents said Biden has done a good job handling the economy.

Why Asian Americans Are Leaving the Democratic Party

Per the Helen Raleigh *Newsweek* January 2022 article "Why Asian Americans Are Leaving the Democratic Party":

We recognize that the U.S. still has a lot of work to do to improve outcomes across different racial groups. The Democrats have not helped matters by openly endorsing a racial hierarchy system that values some races more than others, excluding our children from receiving a good education and punishing them for their hard work and success.

This is not progress but the very definition of bigotry.

Asian American and Pacific Islander (AAPI) voters have been solid supporters of Democrats and their policies for decades. But these days, the AAPI community feels abandoned by the Democrats. We are not only disappointed about Democrats' education policies, but concerned about how soft-on-crime policies have affected our safety.

Feeling abandoned by the Democratic Party, some Asian Americans have taken their votes and loyalty elsewhere. Last November 2021, in New York City's mayoral race, Republican candidate Curtis Sliwa beat Democratic opponent Eric Adams in 10 assembly districts where working-class Asian Americans are the majority. In Virginia's gubernatorial race, many Asian Americans switched sides and helped elect Republican Glenn Youngkin to the governor's office and Winsome Sears as the state's first black female lieutenant governor.

But it's this November's election that the Democratic Party should worry about most. This may be the year when it finally loses the support of the majority of AAPI voters. However, the Republican Party should not assume it will automatically benefit from Asian Americans' political shift. The Republican Party has done little to reach out to Asian American voters over the years.

Although they currently represent less than 6 percent of voters, Asian Americans are projected to become the largest immigrant group in the U.S., surpassing Hispanics in 2055. This population trend means AAPI voters will play a critical role in shaping America's future. No party should either overlook Asian American voters or take their votes and loyalty for granted.

Blackout: How Black America Can Make Its Second Escape from the Democrat Plantation

Political activist and social media star Candace Owens addresses the many ways that Democrat Party policies hurt, rather than help, the African American community, and why she and many others are turning right. "It's time for a black exit," she says from her bestseller *Blackout: How Black America Can Make Its Second Escape from the Democrat Plantation.*

Black Americans have long been shackled to the Democrats. Seeing no viable alternative, they have watched liberal politicians take the black vote for granted without pledging anything in return. In *Blackout*, Owens argues that this automatic allegiance is both illogical and unearned.

She contends that the Democrat Party has a long history of racism and exposes the ideals that hinder the black community's ability to rise above poverty, live independent and successful lives, and be an active part of the American Dream. Instead, Owens offers up a different ideology by issuing a challenge: It's time for a major black exodus.

From dependency, from victimhood, from miseducation—and the Democrat Party, which perpetuates all three.

Owens explains that government assistance is a double-edged sword, that the Left dismisses the faith so important to the black community, that Democrat permissiveness toward abortion disproportionately affects black babies, that the #MeToo movement hurts black men, and much more.

Weaving in her personal story, which ushered her from a roach-infested low-income apartment to1600 Pennsylvania Avenue, she demonstrates how she overcame her setbacks and challenges despite the cultural expectation that she should embrace a victim mentality.

Well-researched and intelligently argued, Blackout lays bare the myth that all black people should vote Democrat—and shows why turning to the right will leave them happier, more successful, and more self-sufficient.

15 – California's 'Progressive' Democratic Supermajority Nightmare: A Dire Warning to America

Credit: California's most famous Democrat Kamal Harris - Los Angeles Times.

From *California Madness* comes many reports for this chapter regarding the ideological failure of California falling squarely on the shoulders of progressive politicians and activists, social justice reformers, civil rights workers, cultural appropriation enforcers, diversity, and inclusion warriors and the like who have spread into the media, government, college campuses, neighborhood organizations and workplaces.

This July 2020 *City Journal* article and section "California's Woke Hypocrisy" is from Joel Kotkin and explains how California's woke leaders offer platitudes and counterproductive policies rather than opportunities and better living standards for the state's minorities. Vice-President Kamal Harris is a perfect example of this wokeness.

No state wears its multicultural veneer more ostentatiously than California. The Golden State's leaders believe that they lead a progressive paradise, ushering in what theorists Laura Tyson and Lenny Mendonca call "a new progressive era." Others see California as deserving of nationhood; it reflects, as a *New York Times* columnist put it, "the shared values of our increasingly tolerant and pluralistic society."

Despite these progressive intentions, Hispanics and African-Americans—some 45 percent of California's total population—fare worse in the state than almost anywhere nationwide. Based on cost-of-living estimates from the U.S. Census Bureau, 28 percent of California's African-Americans live in poverty, compared with 22 percent nationally. Fully one-third of Latinos, now the state's largest ethnic group, live in poverty, compared with 21 percent outside the state.

"For Latinos," notes longtime political consultant Mike Madrid, "the California Dream is becoming an unattainable fantasy."

More than 30 years ago, the Population Reference Bureau predicted that California was creating a two-tier economy, with a more affluent white and Asian population and a largely poor Latino and African-American class. Rather than find ways to increase opportunity for blue-collar workers, the state imposed strict business regulations that drove an exodus of the industries—notably, manufacturing, and middle-management service jobs—that historically provided gateways to the middle class for minorities.

California: Wave of the Future? Wake of the Past? Or Something in Between?

This section's content comes from the 2020 research brief by Joel Kotkin and Marshall Toplansky "Beyond Feudalism: A Strategy to Restore California's Middle Class" at the Chapman University Center for Demographics & Policy:

The notion of the Golden State as a "nation-state" is a valid descriptor given that California has a population (nearly 40 million residents) that's larger than all but 35 countries (California would fall between Sudan and Iraq), the fifth largest economy in the world (ahead of India's and behind Germany's), plus remarkable diversity (92 languages other than English are spoken in the Los Angeles public school system).

California has always been a state where excess flourished, conscious of its trend-setting role as a world-leading innovator in technology, economics, and the arts. For much of the past century, it also helped create a new model for middle and working-class upward mobility while addressing racial, gender and environmental issues well in advance of the rest of the country.

The End of the California Dream?

Furthermore, if California fails to offer young people and newcomers the opportunity to improve their lot, the consequences will be catastrophic—and not only for California. The end of the California Dream would deal a devastating blow to the proposition that such a widely diverse polity can thrive.

California-based *Atlantic* writer Conor Friedersdorf offers a broad and harsh critique of the state in an article entitled "The California Dream is Dying."

Despite the state's many attributes, he writes, "I fear for California's future." The generations that benefited from California's dizzying ascent into global prominence, he says, "should be striving to ensure that future generations can pursue happiness as they did. Instead, they are poised to take the California Dream to their graves by betraying a promise the state has offered from the start.

While California publicly celebrates diversity and inclusion, Friedersdorf continues, "the state's leaders and residents shut the door on economic opportunity," citing a chronic shortage of housing, high poverty, poor educational services, homelessness, and other factors that limit upward mobility.

Friedersdorf warns that "blue America's model faces its most consequential stress test in one of its safest states, where a spectacular run of almost unbroken prosperity could be killed by a miserly approach to opportunity."

Thus, while Governor Newsom still sees California as "America's coming attraction," it's jarring that writers who share his ideological orientation are joining those on the right to warn the nation against emulating the state.

The Middle Class Squeeze

More from the 2020 research brief by Joel Kotkin and Marshall Toplansky *Beyond Feudalism: A Strategy to Restore California's Middle Class* at the Chapman University Center for Demographics & Policy:

California policies, often steeped in good intentions, have had deeply deleterious consequences, especially on its middle and working-class families. The state's rich have enjoyed an unprecedented bounty. But California also suffers the widest gap between middle and upper-middle income earners of any state. California's signatures of upward mobility, homeownership, and the availability of economically sustainable jobs, have fallen well below the national average.

High real estate prices have fostered high rents, and prevented many Californians, notably the young and minorities, from purchasing houses. This is occurring at a time when the vast majority of jobs being produced in the state pay under the median wage, and 40% pay under $40,000 a year. Since 2008 the state has created five times as many low wage jobs as high wage jobs. Yes, the state's employment growth in the past decade has outperformed the rest of the country, but most of the new jobs pay poorly, and now seem to be permanent for many.

California is the single worst state in the nation when it comes to creating jobs that pay above average, while it is at the top of the nation in creating below average and low-paying jobs. High wage jobs have increased marginally in the state during the past decade, but our competitors—Utah, Texas, Arizona, Nevada, and Washington have seen much higher growth. At the same time, middle-skill job growth in California is well below competitive states. California lost 1.6 million above-average-paying jobs in the past decade, more than twice as many as any other state.

Given the sophistication of its economy and its enormous natural advantages, California should lead, not lag, in creating high wage jobs.

California Feudalism: The Squeeze on the Middle Class

This section is also from the 2018 article "California Feudalism: The Squeeze on the Middle Class" also comes from Chapman University researchers Joel Kotkin and Marshall Toplansky:

However, California's economy is dominated by a handful of Bay Area tech firms that have expanded at one of the most dynamic paces in economic history. Most of these companies are in a relatively constrained geography along the San Francisco Peninsula.

Together, these tech firms—Apple, Netflix, Facebook, Google—along with Microsoft and Amazon, have achieved a combined net worth equal to one-quarter of the NASDAQ and equal to the GDP of France. The S&P 500, the broad index of stocks, has a total market capitalization of approximately $24.2 trillion slightly more than the GDP of the country. They represent 15% of the entire S&P 500 companies' market capitalization.

This has been a heady period for the Bay Area, with San Jose and San Francisco boasting the first and third highest average per capita income in the country. Between 2007 and 2016, according to an analysis of Bureau of Labor Statistics data, the Bay Area created 200,000 jobs that paid better than $70,000 annually. Yet during that same period, high wage jobs dropped in Southern California and statewide; simply put, the Bay Area replaced the high wage jobs lost in the recession while the rest of the state did not.

For Latinos, the 'California Dream' Is Becoming Unattainable

From *California Madness,* our collective badge of shame is the prevalence of poverty amidst enormous affluence. This correlates with a state that, amidst high living costs, produces a disproportionate number of low wage jobs. Nearly one in five Californians—many working— lives in poverty (using a cost-of-living adjusted poverty rate); the Public Policy Institute of California estimates another fifth live in near-poverty—roughly 15 million people in total.

Most tragic, roughly 17% of California's children live in or near poverty. Poverty rates for California's Latinos and African Americans, most of them working, are well above the national average, and considerably higher than in Texas, our primary competitor, and a state with a similarly diverse population. Over half of all California Latino households, now a plurality in the state, can barely pay their bills, according to a United Way study. "For Latinos," notes long-time political consultant Mike Madrid, "the California Dream is becoming an unattainable fantasy."

The loss of jobs, particularly in hospitality and retail, from the coronavirus could exacerbate this situation further. California's cost adjusted poverty are among the highest in the country, and, even during the recovery, remained higher in 2019 than in 2007.

On the most extreme end, the most obvious expression of pervasive inequality and economic dysfunction lies evident on our streets. Even as homelessness has been reduced in much of the country, it has continued to swell in California. Roughly half the nation's homeless population lives in the Golden State, many concentrated in disease and crime-ridden tent cities in either its largest city, Los Angeles, or San Francisco. This surge, notes the Council of Economic Advisors, is largely attributable to the state's "excessive regulatory barriers."

The High Cost of Housing In the 'Can't Afford' State

According to the most recent data available from the California Department of Finance, the median price for a home in the Golden State was $611,420 in June 2019, a new record price.

Housing prices hit record highs despite a "weak" California housing market—home sales statewide were down nearly 6 percent in the first half of 2019 compared to the year earlier. Transactions monitored by online real estate database Zillow show that, over the past 10 years, median home sale prices in California have increased by 72 percent, from $291,000, adjusted for inflation, to about $501,000. They estimate that the median home listing price is currently $549,000. And the median monthly rent has increased, too.

The median monthly rent paid for a one-bedroom apartment was $1,679, adjusted for inflation, in November 2010. Currently, median rent paid for a one-bedroom unit is $1,906. But rent is much higher in certain locations. According to apartment rental platform Zumper, the median monthly rent for a one-bedroom apartment in San Francisco is $3,720, a record high and the highest rent in the nation.

Meanwhile, the average household income in California has not kept pace. In 2009, the median California household income was $70,300 per year in 2019 dollars. By 2017, the most recent year for which data are available, median household annual income only increased about 6.5 percent, to $75,000 (adjusted), while home prices increased 72 percent. A third of California renters and 16 percent of homeowners spend more than half their income on housing.

Only 30 percent of households in the state can afford a median-priced home in the county in which they live, according to the California Association of Realtors. The national average is 54 percent. Elliot Eisenberg, partner economist at MLS Listings, sums up California's housing market, "This is truly a housing market that's a complete wreck."

California's High Housing Costs are Especially Burdensome for Low-Income Households

Many people have responded to the high housing costs by leaving California as noted in *California Madness*. The US Census Bureau's American Community Survey has shown a consistently negative net domestic migration for California during the past several years: more people left California for other states than came to California from other states.

On net, from 2007 to 2018, California lost nearly 1.3 million residents to domestic migration (see here and here). And since 2016, overall net migration (including international migration) has been negative in California.

The outward-migration has been concentrated among lower-income and middle-class residents and the less educated, who are increasingly stretched thin in California. Testimonials and patterns of movement reveal a lack of affordable housing to be a driving factor among people increasingly looking elsewhere to achieve the American dream. The exodus is likely to continue.

A July 2019 Quinnipiac University poll found that 45 percent of Californians believe they cannot afford to live in the Golden State, and nearly 80 percent of Californians think the state has a housing crisis. In August 2019, California Gov. Gavin Newsom (D) bluntly acknowledged, "The California dream is in real peril if we don't address the housing crisis."

California to Business: Get Out!

This December 2017 article "California Ranks Second Worst in U.S. on Economic Freedom Index: High Taxes, Overregulation Causing Exodus of Workers and Employers to Other States" comes from the Independent Institute's David J. Theroux:

California's policymakers have enacted policies more harmful to economic freedom and opportunity than those of almost any other state, according to the 2017 Economic Freedom of North America report by the Independent Institute in conjunction with Canada's Fraser Institute.

Not only does California rank 49th out of all 50 U.S. states, but its burdensome combination of high taxes and regulatory overreach is so toxic for economic opportunity that it is causing a major out-migration of both workers and enterprises to other states.

"California's lack of economic freedom helped motivate more than 10,000 businesses to leave the Golden State, reduce operations, or expand elsewhere during the past seven years," said Dr. Lawrence J. McQuillan, Senior Fellow and Director of the Independent Institute's Center on Entrepreneurial Innovation. Census data show that 3.5 million people left California for greener pastures from 2010 to 2015.

"The freest economies operate with comparatively less government interference, relying more on personal choice and markets to decide what's produced, how it's produced, and how much is produced," said Fred McMahon, who co-authored the report with economists Dean Stansel of Southern Methodist University and José Torra of the Mexico City–based Caminos de la Liberta.

A Failing Education System

From the 2020 research brief by Joel Kotkin and Marshall Toplansky *Beyond Feudalism: A Strategy to Restore California's Middle Class at the* Chapman University Center for Demographics & Policy:

The demand for middle-skill jobs is high and meeting it could prove a crucial challenge. I In 2015 we identified over 50% of all jobs in California as middle-skill, but only 39% of the state's workers were trained at that level. Demand for these skills is expected to continue for years, and will provide benefits for the students who obtain them, as well as for the California business community. The California Employment Development Department (EDD) estimates that by 2026, the state will need 9.5 million mid-skill workers, an increase of 858,000 over 2016 levels.

Sadly, our educational system seems ill-prepared to train either mid-skilled or college educated people. Since 1998 California has ranked, on average, 46th in 8th-grade reading and mathematics subject-area performance on the National Assessment for Educational Progress (NAEP), the only comparable assessment between states nation-wide.

It includes comparisons with demographically similar states such as Texas, which spends less money per student, as well as New York. Almost three of five California high schoolers are not prepared for either college or a career; the percentages are far higher for Latinos, African Americans, and the economically disadvantaged. Among the 50 states, California ranked 49th in the performance of poor, largely minority, students. San Francisco, the epicenter of California's woke culture, suffers the worst scores for African-Americans of any county in the state.

California's Public-Sector Unions Rake in $921 Million in Annual Revenue

This section's content from the August 2020 article "California's Public-Sector Unions Rake in $921 Million in Annual Revenue" by the California Policy Center's Edward Ring.

There is no special interest in California that wields more influence over state and local politics than public sector unions. At every level of government, from the office of the governor to a school board managing a district with only a few hundred students, public sector unions are omnipresent. With rare exceptions, to defy their agenda is certain political suicide.

The reason for this power is money. Lots of money. Every two-year election cycle, not millions, but hundreds of millions of dollars are spent by California's public-sector unions to support or oppose candidates, campaign for ballot measures, lobby the legislature, and pay for public relations campaigns.

While wealthy individuals or powerful corporations may at times challenge these unions, their concerns are narrow in focus. Nothing matches the perennial torrent of public sector union money; the opposition may stir up a flash flood, but these unions are the Amazon.

This time, using the same methods as 2018, but going into somewhat more detail, the new estimate is $921 million. It should be noted that available information online is usually about 18-24 months behind. For example, our 2018 report referenced Form 990s that were filed for 2015. This 2020 report used Form 990 data for the year 2018, the most recent currently available.

Billions and Billions Spent of Political Donations

California's public-sector unions collect and spend well over $900 million per year, or $1.8 billion per two-year election cycle.

While only about one-third of this money is spent on explicitly political purposes such as campaign contributions and lobbying, this is still a staggering amount of money. What other special interest in California is willing and able to spend $600 million every two years on political advocacy, year after year, for decades on end?

California's public-sector unions are not only the most powerful political special interest in the state, but most of them are nakedly partisan.

With only a few exceptions–primarily among the law enforcement unions–the websites of these public sector unions read like a pamphlet describing the agenda of the Democratic party. Is this appropriate? Does this represent the membership? And even if so, shouldn't public sector unions, with all the power they wield, be politically neutral?

A long-overdue reckoning with public sector unions faces California's electorate. It might start with the public schools, which labor under a public-sector union monopoly that has nearly destroyed accountability.

California's Budget "Surplus" Ignores Crushing Debt Burden

This January 2019 article "California's Budget 'Surplus' Ignores Crushing Debt Burden" comes from the California Policy Center's Edward Ring:

When new governor, Gavin Newsom, delivered an inaugural address in January 2019, it accurately reflected the mentality of his supporters. Triumphalist, defiant, and filled with grand plans. But are these plans grand, or grandiose?

While California's 2021-22 budget outlook currently offers a unique surplus in excess of $76 billion, that is an order of magnitude less than what it will cost to do what Newsom is planning to do in the long run. And this surplus, while genuine, is the result of an extraordinary, unsustainable surge in income tax payments by wealthy people from Silicon Valley.

As people sell their overpriced homes to move inland or out-of-state, and as tech workers cash out their burgeoning stock options, hundreds of billions of capital gains generate tens of billions in state tax revenue.

But can homes continue to double in value every six or seven years? Can tech stocks continue to quadruple in value every six or seven years? Apparently Gavin Newsom thinks they can. Reality may beg to differ.

Just a Slowdown in Capital Gains Will Cause Tax Revenue to Crash

The problem with Gavin Newsom's grand plans is that it won't take a downturn in asset values to sink them. All that has to happen to throw California's state budget into the red again is for these asset values to stop going up. Just a plateauing of their value–will wreak havoc on state and local government budgets in California.

The reasons for this are clear enough. Wealthy people, making a lot of money, pay the lion's share of state income taxes, and state income taxes constitute the lion's share of state revenues.

Returning to the 2017 fiscal year, of the $86 billion collected in state income taxes, $28 billion was from only 70,437 filers, all of them making over $1.0 million in that year. Another $7.3 billion came from 131,120 filers who made between a half-million and one million in that year. And since making over $200,000 in income in one year is still considered doing very, very well, it's noteworthy that another 807,000 of those filers ponied up another $15.1 billion in FYE June 30, 2017.

There is an obvious conclusion here: if people are no longer making killings in capital gains on their sales of stock and real estate, California's tax revenues will instantly decline by $20 billion, if not much more. And it won't even take a slump in asset prices to cause this, just a leveling off.

Debt, Unfunded Pension Liabilities, Neglected Infrastructure

When considering how weakening tax revenues in California will impact the ability of the state and local governments to cope with existing debt, it's hard to know where to begin.

To get an idea of the scope of this problem, the California Policy Center released an analysis of California's total state and local government debt. California's total state and local government debt as of June 30, 2017 is over $1.5 trillion. More than half of it, $846 billion, is in the form of unfunded pension liabilities.

The controversy over what is an accurate estimate of a pension liability arises due to the extreme sensitivity that number has to how much the fund managers think they can earn. Using the official projection, which is typically around 7.0 percent per year, the official pension liability for all of California's government pension funds is "only" $316 billion.

But Moody's, the credit rating agency, discounts pension liabilities with the Citigroup Pension Liability Index (CPLI), which is based on high grade corporate bond yields. In June 2017, it was 3.87 percent, and using that rate, CPC analysts estimated the unfunded liability for California's state and local employee pension systems at $846 billion. Using the methodology offered by the prestigious Stanford Institute for Economic Policy Research, California's unfunded pension debt is even higher, at $1.26 trillion!

Where pension liabilities move from controversial theories to decidedly non-academic real world consequences, however, is in the budget busting realm of how much California's government agencies have to pay these funds each year.

California's State Budget is Extraordinarily Vulnerable to Economic Downturns

California's public sector employers contributed an estimated $31 billion to the pension systems in 2018. Extrapolating from officially announced pension rate hikes from CalPERS, California's largest pension system, by 2024 those payments are projected to increase to $59 billion. And these aggressive increases the pension systems are requiring are a reflection more of their crackdown on the terms of the "catch up" payments employers must make to reduce the unfunded liability than on a reduction to their expected real rate of return.

Huge unfunded pension liabilities are another reason, equally significant, as to why California's state budget is extraordinarily vulnerable to economic downturns. If assets stop appreciating, not only will income tax revenue plummet—at the same time, expenses will go up, because pension funds will demand far higher annual contributions to make up the shortfall in investment earnings.

A cautionary overview of the economic challenges facing California's state government would not be complete without mentioning the neglected infrastructure in the state. For decades, this vast state, with nearly 40 million residents, has been falling behind in infrastructure maintenance. The American Society of Civil Engineers assigns poor grades to California's infrastructure. They rate over 1,300 bridges in California as "structurally deficient," and 678 of California's dams are "high hazard."

They estimate $44 billion needs to be spent to bring drinking water infrastructure up to modern standards, and $26 billion on wastewater infrastructure. They estimate over 50 percent of California's roads are in "poor condition." In every category–aviation, bridges, dams, drinking water, wastewater, hazardous waste, the energy grid, inland waterways, levees, ports, public parks, roads, rail, transit, and schools, California is behind. The fix? Literally hundreds of additional billions.

What Governor Newsom might consider is refocusing California's state budget priorities on areas where the state already faces daunting financial challenges, rather than acquiescing to the utopian fever dreams of his constituency and his colleagues.

If Latino's Upward Mobility Doesn't Improve—California Will Suffer

From the Winter 2012 *City Journal* article "California's Demographic Revolution: If the upward mobility of the impending Hispanic majority doesn't improve, the state's economic future is in peril" is by Heather Mac Donald:

Unless Hispanics' upward mobility improves, the state risks becoming more polarized economically and more reliant on a large government safety net. And as California goes, so goes the nation, whose own Hispanic population shift is just a generation or two behind.

The scale and speed of the Golden State's ethnic transformation are unprecedented. In the 1960s, Los Angeles was the most Anglo-Saxon of the nation's ten largest cities; today, Latinos make up nearly half of the county's residents and one-third of its voting-age population.

A full 55 percent of Los Angeles County's child population has immigrant parents. California's schools have the nation's largest concentration of "English learners," students from homes where a language other than English is regularly spoken. From 2000 to 2010, the state's Hispanic population grew 28 percent, to reach 37.6 percent of all residents, almost equal to the shrinking white population's 40 percent.

Nearly half of all California births today are Hispanic. The signs of the change are everywhere—from the commercial strips throughout the state catering to Spanish-speaking customers, to the flea markets and illegal vendors in such areas as MacArthur Park in Los Angeles, to the growing reach of the Spanish-language media.

Many of California's Hispanic students who have been schooled in the U.S. for all their lives and are orally fluent in English remain classified as English learners in high school because they have made so little academic progress. In the Long Beach Unified School District, for example, nearly nine-tenths of English learners entering high school have been in a U.S. school at least since first grade.

But the gap between Hispanics' performance and that of whites and Asians narrowed only modestly, since white and Asian scores rose as well. Latino students' rate of B.A. completion from the University of California and California State University is the lowest of all student groups, reports the Institute for Higher Education Leadership and Policy at California State University, Sacramento.

The state spends vast sums each year trying to get more Hispanics into college and to keep them there—$100 million in 2009, for instance, on the education of full-time community-college students who dropped out after their first year, according to the American Institutes for Research. (Facilitating transfers from community college is a favored strategy for increasing Hispanic enrollment in four-year colleges.)

The Battle for California is the Battle for America

These sections below are from the October 2020 article "The Battle for California is the Battle for America" and comes from the California Policy Center's Edward Ring:

By now, this is a familiar story that California is a failed state.

Thanks to years of progressive Democratic Party mismanagement and neglect, the cities are lawless, and the forests are burning. Residents pay the highest prices in America for unreliable electricity. Water is rationed. Homes are unaffordable. The public schools are a joke. Freeways are congested and crumbling. And if they're not still on lockdown or otherwise already destroyed by it, business owners contend with the most hostile regulatory climate in American history.

It is understandable that conservatives in the rest of the United States would be happy to write off California. But California is not writing off the rest of the United States, and therein lies grave danger to American prosperity and freedom.

What if California doesn't implode, a victim of its own political mismanagement? What if California instead completes its transformation into a successful plutocracy, run by a clique of big-techmulti-billionaires in a partnership of convenience with environmentalist extremists and backed by the power of a unionized state bureaucracy?

What if the people who would resist this tyranny leave, and the remaining population peacefully accepts universal basic income and subsidized housing? What if all it takes to be a feudal overlord in progressive California is to proffer to the proletarians a pittance of alms, while reliably spouting incessant, blistering social justice and climate change rhetoric?

California is by Far the Wealthiest, Most Influential State in America

What happens in California matters to the rest of the United States because California's internal market is huge, its political and financial influence is powerful, and it rallies political allies throughout the U.S. If what California does to transform its own culture and economy isn't stopped, the rest of the U.S. will fall into line. The result will be a comprehensive reinvention of society in all areas, political, economic, and cultural.

The difficult reality that conservative Americans must accept is that while California may be a failed state by the standards Middle America has come to take for granted, California may not fail by its own standards. The society California is building may prove viable, even if it is hideous to contemplate and morally wrong. It may prove viable even though the alternatives that it displaces offer more prosperity and freedom to more people. It amounts to an all-powerful tech plutocracy ruling over a micro-managed, dependent population, with rationing and redistribution in the name of social justice and saving the planet.

This model, which is a modern form of feudalism, may work not merely because it is politically and economically sustainable despite its many shortcomings, nor merely because it offers more power and profit to its handful of resident billionaires who already possess obscene levels of power and wealth. These reasons don't fully explain the popularity of progressive feudalism. There is one more piece in the puzzle.

The progressive model also becomes viable because of a moral narrative that is flawed but nonetheless compelling: We live in an inherently oppressive society, so we must reduce the privileged middle class in the interests of social justice. We live in an era of limited resources and a stressed planet, so we must reduce everyone's standard of living.

Countering that narrative is the mission that must be sent into California. The misery that Californians have condemned themselves to live is not a moral choice. They are victims of a con job, and it could be coming to the rest of America.

Left and Lefter in California

From the Joel Kotkin *City Journal* article "Left and Lefter in California" in March 2018:

To its many admirers back east, California has emerged as the role model for a brave new Democratic future. The high-tech, culturally progressive Golden State seems to be an ideal incubator of whatever politics will follow the Trump era.

Certainly, California is an ideal place to observe this shift, as radicalism faces no restraints here. The Republican Party has little to no influence in politics and culture and not much even among business leaders.

For the Democrats, this vacuum allows for a kind of internecine struggle resembling that of the Bolsheviks after the death of Lenin. And just as happened then, a new Stalinism of sorts seems to be emerging—in this case, to the consternation not only of conservatives but also of traditional liberals and moderates of the Feinstein stamp.

Yet as California Democrats exult in what they see as a glowing future, they are turning away from the models that once drove their party's (and the state's) success—a commitment to growth, upward mobility, and dispersed property ownership. California's current prosperity is largely due to the legacy of Governor Democrat Pat Brown, who, a half-century ago, built arguably the world's best transportation, water, and power systems, and created an incubator for middle-class prosperity.

Ironically, the politician most responsible for undermining this achievement has been Pat's son, Democrat Governor Jerry Brown. Long skeptical of his father's growth-oriented, pro-suburban policies, Brown the Younger put strong constraints on growth, especially when these efforts concerned the fight against global warming—a quasi-religious crusade. Battling climate change has awakened Brown's inner authoritarian; he has lauded the "coercive power of the state" and embraced "brainwashing" on climate issues.

The key issues for the glitterati are not income inequality, upward mobility, or the preservation of middle-class neighborhoods but the feverish pastimes of the already rich: gender and racial issues, climate change, guns, and anything that offends the governesses and schoolmarms of intersectionality.

To the ranks of these over-exposed but influential voices, you can also add California's media and most of its intelligentsia, who seem to get their talking points from progressive sources and work assiduously to limit the influence of moderate (much less conservative) views. With Silicon Valley increasingly able to control content and ever more willing to curb debate, the policy agenda of the state's new elite may well become reality—a nightmarish one for millions of ordinary Californians—and the rest of America if other states try to emulate California.

Stopping California's Downward Spiral Into Progressivism Madness

This section's content is from both the Summer 2010 *City Journal* article "The Golden State's War on Itself" by Joel Kotkin and the December 2020 article "Fixing California–Part One: The Themes That Make Anything Possible" is from the California Policy Center's Edward Ring:

In the 19th and 20th centuries, California was the destination for those seeking a better place to live. For most of its history, the state enacted sensible policies that created one of the wealthiest and most innovative economies in human history. California realized the American dream—but better—fostering a huge middle class that, for the most part, owned their homes, sent their kids to public schools, and found meaningful work connected to the state's amazingly diverse, innovative economy.

In the middle of the 20th century, the leadership of Governor Pat Brown and his practical Democrats made California, the Golden State, the envy of all others. These were the sapient leaders with old school Democrats values, ideas and policies that helped create the California dream.

However, since the dawn of the 21st century, the dream has been evaporating. Between 2003 and 2007, California state and local government spending grew 31 percent, even as the state's population grew just 5 percent. The overall tax burden as a percentage of state income, once middling among the states, has risen to the sixth-highest in the nation, says the Tax Foundation.

Today's California represents most everything wrong with today's Progressivism movement. In retrospect, California's progressive mistakes provide an incubator and testing ground to show America and prove to the world, why it's not in the best interest of the overwhelming number of Californians and Americans.

Since 1990, according to an analysis by California Lutheran University, the state's share of overall U.S. employment has dropped a remarkable 10 percent. When the state economy has done well, it has usually been the result of asset inflation—first during the dot-com bubble of the late 1990s, and then during the housing boom, which was responsible for nearly half of all jobs created earlier in this decade, and big tech most recently.

Guiding the agenda of California's Democrats are a ruling elite, small in number, but wielding incredible power. Among these elites are government union leaders, liberal billionaires from Hollywood to Silicon Valley, extreme environmentalists, and the social justice vanguard. The money and influence these elites bring to California politics cannot possibly be matched by the opposition. But all the money in the world cannot make up for the fact that their policies have made life miserable for millions of ordinary Californians.

We've heard all this before. Much of what Californians face are challenges confronting everyone in America. But California, the biggest state, and the bluest state, is a powerful trendsetter. California is broken, hijacked by opportunists wielding overwhelming financial and political power. How does this change?

For conservatives across America, California has become the cautionary tale for the rest of the country. Anyone who actually lives in the Golden State, and enjoys the best weather and the most beautiful, diverse scenery on earth, knows there are two sides to the story of this captivating place. Nevertheless, the story keeps getting worse.

For every essential—homes, rent, tuition, gasoline, electricity, and water—Californians pay the among the highest prices in the continental United States. Californians endure the most hostile business climate in America, and pay the highest taxes. The public schools are failing, crime is soaring, electricity is unreliable, water is rationed, and the mismanaged forests are burning like hell.

California's Frightening Rankings

This section's content is from the January 2020 report "A Perverse Way To 'Solve' California's Housing Crisis: People Are Leaving The Golden State" by the Hoover Institution's Lee Ohanian.

To be sure, California has enjoyed faster income and job growth than the rest of the country over the past decade. But over the past few years, even before Covid-19, it has fallen behind other states, such as Texas, Utah, Washington, Nevada, and Arizona.

The state is often praised for its elaborate environmental and labor protections, but its record on economic mobility, middle-class disposable income, and even on greenhouse gas reductions, is not encouraging. The gap between middle-class Californians and the more affluent is becoming greater.

Ironically, California's elected officials claim that they support low earners and historically disadvantaged groups, including African Americans and Latinos. But nothing could be further from the truth. The California of today reflects a very specific failure of governance and policy choices that are enormously biased towards very wealthy political elites who strongly support incumbent politicians and who can easily afford the rising cost of living that comes with their political preferences.

Just how bad are things in California? Here is a partial breakdown:

- Poverty rate: 50th

- Housing affordability: 49th

- Cost of living: 49th

- Inflation-adjusted household income: 27th

- Tax rate for top earners: 50th

- Sales tax rate: 50th

- Business taxes: 49th

- Overall tax burden: 40th

- Business climate: 47th, 48th, 50th

- Infrastructure quality: average grade of D+

- Traffic congestion: 47th

- K–12 learning outcomes: 42nd

- Homelessness rate: 50th

For the first time since 2010, when the state's unemployment rate was over 12 percent and exceeded the national average, California is losing population. Over the last year, nearly 200,000 people have left California, primarily for states with much lower housing costs and with better growth opportunities for middle-income earners. Under the current conditions, it's easy to understand why.

Yet all of this can be fixed. The solutions aren't mysteries and consist of the following:

- Deregulate housing permits.

- End the disastrous "housing-first" policies and instead give the homeless safe housing in inexpensive barracks where sobriety is a condition of entry.

- Repeal Proposition 47, which downgraded property and drug crimes.

- Build reservoirs, desalination, and wastewater recycling plants.

- Build nuclear power plants and develop California's abundant natural gas reserves.

- Recognize that the common road is the future of transportation, not the past, and widen California's freeways and highways.

- Let the timber companies harvest more lumber in exchange for maintaining the fire roads and power line corridors.

- Implement school choice and make public schools compete with private schools on the basis of excellence.

Done!

This isn't just about ideology. The politicians who governed California during what arguably were its greatest yesteryears were Democrats. Old-timers refer to them as the Pat Brown Democrats (not to be confused with his son Jerry Brown and his progressive Democrat constituents), leaders whose approach to politics was pragmatic and focused on serving the people.

During that heyday, homes were affordable, and freeways weren't crowded. Public schools were good, and the University of California campuses offered the best public higher education in the country. The California Water Project, taking barely more than a decade to construct, remains the most successful feat of interbasin water transfers in the world.

The Coalition That Will Realign California and Help Save America

Across several areas of policy, the Democratic party, led by Gavin Newsom, has not merely alienated, but enraged millions of Californians.

The key to political realignment in California is not only to offer these groups a political agenda that incorporates solutions to all their grievances, but does so in a manner so coherent, so practical, and so promising, that a common solidarity is generated which transcends all the ways California's ruling class has thus far divided them.

Hardcore populist support for Democrats in California comes primarily from millions of white liberals, living in inherited homes, who pay minimal property taxes and are hence immune from the consequences of an out-of-control public sector bureaucracy, along with the government employees that work in that bureaucracy.

The critical swing constituency, currently solidly in the Democratic camp, are black, Latino, and Asian voters—and the battle to turn back California's progressive downward spiral is in the hands of these critical groups.

Appendix

2000 Mules -- IMDb Review and Trailer: https://www.imdb.com/title/tt18924506/?ref_=tt_mv_desc

40 *MADNESS* Textbook Titles: https://www.fratirepublishing.com/madnessbooks

- *Fake News Madness*

- *Crime Rate Madness*

- *Voting Madness*

- *California Madness*

- *Free Speech Madness*

AllSides: "Form the Left" and "From the Center" and "From the Right" News Comparison: https://www.allsides.com/unbiased-balanced-news

Annual Media Fibbys – Top Mainstream Media Fails of 2021: https://www.youtube.com/watch?v=3T5De2S2luw

Betraying the American people: Leaked video reveals Joe Biden's 'hush hush' migrant invasion: https://nypost.com/633280bf-449e-465a-a4c6-32ed45daacf8

Election Fraud Database from The Heritage Foundation: https://www.heritage.org/article/about-the-election-fraud-database

George Soros Donations to Democratic Candidates and Super PACS list from Open Secrets: https://www.opensecrets.org/donor-lookup/results?name=george+soros&order=desc&page=2&sort=D

Introducing Real Clear Investigations' Jan. 6-BLM Riots Dataset: https://www.realclearinvestigations.com/articles/2021/09/09/realclearinvestigations_jan_6-blm_comparison_database_791370.html

Judicial Watch: https://www.judicialwatch.org/jwtv/

Map of Sanctuary Cities, Counties, and States–Center for Immigration Studies: https://cis.org/Map-Sanctuary-Cities-Counties-and-States

Neighborhood Scout Ranking of the Most Crime-Ridden Cities and Their Mayors: https://www.neighborhoodscout.com/blog/top100dangerous

Pew Research Center: https://www.pewresearch.org/about/

SAPIENT BEING PROGRAMS:

- **Sapient Conservative Textbooks (SCT) Program:** https://www.sapientbeing.org/programs

- **Conservative Campus Advisor (CCA) Program:** https://www.sapientbeing.org/programs

- **Make Free Speech Again On Campus (MFSAOC) Program:** https://www.sapientbeing.org/programs

- **SAPIENT Being program handbooks:** https://www.sapientbeing.org/resources

The Facts About H.R. 1 - The "For the People Act of 2021": https://www.heritage.org/election-integrity/report/the-facts-about-hr-1-the-the-people-act-2021

The Joy of Being Wrong – Video by the John Templeton Foundation: https://youtu.be/mRXNUx4cua0 The S.A.P.I.E.N.T. Being: https://www.fratirepublishing.com/books

Vote Integrity – Data Analytics For Election Integrity by Vote P. Analysis: https://votepatternanalysis.substack.com/people/20957397-vote-integrity

Glossary

Civil Rights Act of 1964 – Outlawed discrimination on the basis of race, color, religion, sex, or national origin, required equal access to public places and employment, and enforced desegregation of schools and the right to vote.

Filibusters and Cloture – The Senate tradition of unlimited debate has allowed for the use of the filibuster, a loosely defined term for action designed to prolong debate and delay or prevent a vote on a bill, resolution, amendment, or other debatable question. In 1917 the Senate adopted a rule to allow a two-thirds majority to end a filibuster, a procedure known as "cloture." In 1975 the Senate reduced the number of votes required for cloture from two-thirds of senators voting to three-fifths of all senators duly chosen and sworn, or 60 of the 100-member Senate.

Fake News – A broad term that collectively includes media bias manifested in many different ways in mainstream journalism, social media, and illiberal establishments that in principle and practice are antithetical to an intellectually vibrant and viewpoint diverse sapient being mindset. Per Andrew Klavan's edited definition at: https://www.youtube.com/watch?v=FOZ0irgLwxU.

Fox News Fallacy – The idea that if Fox News and the like are criticizing the Democrats on such issues there must be absolutely nothing to the criticisms and the criticized policies should be defended at all costs.

Idiocracy – An idiocracy is a disparaging term for a society run by or made up of idiots (or people perceived as such). Idiocracy is also the title of 2006 satirical film that depicts a future in which humanity has become dumb.

Illiberalism – The 21st century term is used to describe an attitude that is close-minded, intolerant, and bigoted.

Insurrection -- The term broadly means a revolt against an established government, usually employing violence.

Intersectionality – A theoretical framework for understanding how aspects of one's social and political identities might combine to create unique modes of discrimination.

Jim Crow – Racial segregation laws up to 1965, that were enacted and enforced in the South in the late 19th and early 20th centuries by white Southern Democrat-dominated state legislatures to disenfranchise and remove political and economic gains made by blacks during the Reconstruction period.

Libertarian - An advocate of the doctrine of free will; a person who upholds the principles of individual liberty especially of thought and action; a member of a political party advocating libertarian principles.

Mainstream Media (MSM) – Traditional forms of mass media, as television, radio, magazines, and newspapers, as opposed to online means of mass communication.

Mediacrats – Is an often used term throughout the MADNESS textbooks to mean that the liberal media and Democrats are closely aligned in their philosophical views and association with each other.

Marxism – The political, economic, and social principles and policies advocated by Marx and a theory and practice of socialism including the labor theory of value, dialectical materialism, the class struggle, and dictatorship of the proletariat until the establishment of a classless society.

Open Inquiry – Is the ability to ask questions and share ideas without risk of censure.

Political Correctness – A term used to describe language, policies, or measures that are intended to avoid offense or disadvantage to members of particular groups in society.

Projection-- The compulsion to accuse others of the very sins and crimes of which they themselves are guilty. It's in their nature, they can't help it, it's reflexive and automatic.

Progressivism – A political philosophy in support of social reform based on the idea of progress in which advancements in science, technology, economic development, and social organization are vital to improve the human condition.

Sapience – Also known as wisdom, is the ability to think and act using knowledge, experience, understanding, common sense and insight. Sapience is associated with attributes such as intelligence, enlightenment, unbiased judgment, compassion, experiential self-knowledge, self-actualization, and virtues such as ethics and benevolence.

Shorist Principles -- David Shor is a data analyst and socialist who has become something of a cult figure on the center left for his critique of the Democratic Party's leftward lurch, which he believes is out of step with the values of most of its voters.

Social Justice – A political and philosophical theory which asserts that there are dimensions to the concept of justice beyond those embodied in the principles of civil or criminal law, economic supply and demand, or traditional moral frameworks.

Socialism – Any various economic and political theories advocating collective or governmental ownership and administration of the means of production and distribution of goods. A system of society or group living in which there is no private property. A system or condition of society in which the means of production are owned and controlled by the state. A stage of society in Marxist theory transitional between capitalism and communism and distinguished by unequal distribution of goods and pay according to work done.

Useful Idiot – Is attributed to Vladimir Lenin. It describes naïve people who can be manipulated to advance a political cause.

Voter Suppression – An artificially created term that unfairly condemns any perfectly legal election reform with which liberal critics disagree. It is a linguistic trick designed to taint reasonable and commonsense safeguards that protect voters by lumping these policies together with illegal activities like poll taxes and literacy tests that did occur in the Democratic South prior to the Civil Rights Act of 1964 and Voting Rights Act of 1965.

Voting Rights Act of 1965 – The Voting Rights Act of 1965 expanded the 14th and 15th amendments by banning racial discrimination in voting practices. The act was a response to the barriers that prevented African Americans from voting for nearly a century.

Woke – Having or marked by an active awareness of systemic injustices and prejudices, especially those related to civil and human rights.

References

Aleem, Zeeshan. "Russia's Ukraine Invasion May Have Been Preventable." MSNBC. March 4, 2022. https://www.msnbc.com/opinion/msnbc-opinion/russia-s-ukraine-invasion-may-have-been-preventable-n1290831.

Alexander, Inigo. "Joe Biden's 6 Biggest Failures During His First Year as President." *Newsweek*. January 1, 2022. https://www.newsweek.com/joe-biden-biggest-failures-first-year-president-1671036.

Alexander, Larry. "Joe Biden's Growing List of Failures." *Newsweek*. Nov. 30, 2021. https://www.newsweek.com/joe-bidens-growing-list-failures-opinion-1654002.

Berger, Judson. "The 'Fox News Fallacy' Explains a Lot." *National Review*. April 1, 2022. https://www.nationalreview.com/corner/the-fox-news-fallacy-explains-a-lot/.

Berger, Judson. "The Hunter Biden Story Goes Mainstream." *National Review*. April 8, 2022. https://www.nationalreview.com/the-weekend-jolt/the-hunter-biden-story-goes-mainstream/?utm_source=recirc-desktop&utm_medium=blog-post&utm_campaign=river&utm_content=top-bar-latest&utm_term=first.

Beto O'Rourke confronts Texas governor at school shooting news conference. KCRA. May 27, 2022. https://www.kcra.com/article/texas-school-shooting-beto-o-rourke-greg-abbott/40106935#.

Biden's Immigration Insanity is Breaking the Nation. Editorial Board. *New York Post*. July 2, 2022. https://nypost.com/2022/07/02/bidens-immigration-insanity-is-breaking-the-nation/.

Blumberg, Peter. "Insurrection? Sedition? Incitement? A Legal Guide to the Capitol Riot." Bloomberg. June 10, 2022. https://www.washingtonpost.com/business/insurrection-sedition-incitement-a-legal-guide-to-the-capitol-riot/2022/06/09/4fd1c176-e839-11ec-a422-11bbb91db30b_story.html.

Brighn, Claire. "Latest Polls Show Education and Critical Race Theory Could Define the Midterms." AMAC. March 16, 2022. https://amac.us/latest-polls-show-education-and-critical-race-theory-could-define-the-midterms/.

Burns, Tobias. "Democratic Discontent Brews With Federal Reserve." *The Hill*. May 26, 2022. https://thehill.com/policy/finance/3501737-democratic-discontent-brews-with-federal-reserve/.

Burns, Tobias. "Five Takeaways From the Stunning Inflation Numbers." *The Hill*. July 13, 2022. https://news.yahoo.com/five-takeaways-stunning-inflation-numbers-154632790.html?guccounter=1.

Capretta, James C. "Tracking the Trillions." The Dispatch. April 8, 2021. https://thedispatch.com/p/tracking-the-trillions.

Chait, Jonathan. "Joe Biden's Big Squeeze." New York Intelligencer. Nov. 22,2021. https://nymag.com/intelligencer/2021/11/joe-biden-agenda.html.

Chang, Daniel. "Young Democrats Are Less Politically Tolerant Than Republicans, Poll Shows." El American. Dec. 9, 2021. https://elamerican.com/young-democrats-are-less-politically-tolerant-than-republicans-poll-shows/.

Cheney, Kyle and Nicholas Wu. "'Sprint Through the Finish': Why the Jan. 6 Committee Isn't Nearly Done." Politico. July 19, 2022. https://www.politico.com/news/2022/07/19/sprint-through-the-finish-why-the-jan-6-committee-isnt-nearly-done-00046453.

Cole, Tom. "Biden's Busted Budget." Weekly Column. April 4, 2022. https://cole.house.gov/media-center/weekly-columns/bidens-busted-budget.

Concha, Joe. "Georgia Voting Explosion Marks Beginning of the End for Stacey Abrams." *The Hill.* May 25, 2022. https://thehill.com/opinion/campaign/3500904-georgia-voting-explosion-marks-beginning-of-the-end-for-stacey-abrams/.

Concha, Joe. "Hispanics Are Abandoning Biden in Droves. Here's Why." *The Hill.* April 17, 2022. https://thehill.com/opinion/campaign/3270602-hispanics-are-abandoning-biden-in-droves-heres-why/.

Continetti, Matthew. "Biden's Blunders." *National Review.* August 26, 2021. https://www.nationalreview.com/magazine/2021/09/13/bidens-blunders/.

Cooke, Charles C.W. "Gallup Records 14-Point Shift in Party Identification During 2021." *National Review.* January 17, 2022. https://www.nationalreview.com/corner/gallup-records-14-point-shift-in-party-identification-during-2021/.

Cooke, Charles C.W. "The Democrats Have a Kamala Harris Problem." *National Review.* May 19, 2021. https://www.nationalreview.com/2021/05/the-democrats-have-a-kamala-harris-problem/.

D'Souza, Dinesh. "2000 Mules." D'Souza Media LLC. May 2022. https://node-3.2000mules.com/

Daws, Jim. "These Are Not Your Grandfather's Democrats." American Thinker. January 9, 2019. https://www.americanthinker.com/blog/2019/01/these_are_not_your_grandfathers_democrats.html.

DeAngelis, Ph.D., Corey and Jason Bedrick. "Parents Wanted School Choice—and They Voted." The Heritage Foundation. June 3, 2022. https://www.heritage.org/education/commentary/parents-wanted-school-choice-and-they-voted.

Dennard, Paris. "Democrats Embracing Socialism is Dangerous for America." *The Hill.* August 12, 2018. https://thehill.com/opinion/campaign/401427-democrats-embracing-socialism-is-dangerous-for-america/.

DeSanctis, Alexandra. "Nearly Three-Quarters of Americans Support School Choice." *National Review.* March 1, 2022. https://www.nationalreview.com/corner/nearly-three-quarters-of-americans-support-school-choice/.

DeSanctis, Alexandra. "Poll: Biden Approval Rating Drops among Young Americans." *National Review.* April 25, 2022. https://www.nationalreview.com/corner/poll-biden-approval-rating-drops-among-young-americans/.

Ditch, David. "New Charts Reveal Harms of Biden's Budget-Busting Binge." The Heritage Foundation. June 8, 2022. https://www.heritage.org/budget-and-spending/commentary/new-charts-reveal-harms-bidens-budget-busting-binge.

Dorman, Sam. "Legal Coalition Forming to Stop Critical Race Theory Training Around the Country." Fox News. January 20, 2021. https://www.foxnews.com/politics/legal-coalition-critical-race-theory.

Earle, Geoff. "AOC slams Clinton strategist James Carville for blaming 'stupid wokeness' on the Democrats' crushing election defeats because it is 'a term almost exclusively used by older people'." DailyMail.com.

November 2021. https://www.dailymail.co.uk/news/article-10170955/AOC-slams-James-Carville-saying-stupid-wokeness-caused-Democrats-defeat.html.

Edwards, Chris. "Downsides to the Democratic Spending Plan." Cato Institute. October 29, 2021. https://www.cato.org/blog/10-downsides-democratic-spending-plan.

Ellefson, Lindsey. "AOC Roasted for 'Sexual Frustrations' Tweet About GOP Critics: Taking Up the 'Plight of the Super-Hot'." The Wrap. January 2022. https://www.thewrap.com/aoc-cnn-mary-katherine-ham/.

Evans, Zachary. "More Likely to Choose Republicans Than Democrats in Midterms: Poll." *National Review*. April 29, 2022. https://www.nationalreview.com/news/voters-including-parents-and-latinos-more-likely-to-choose-republicans-than-democrats-in-midterms-poll/.

Fact Sheet: In Asia, President Biden and a Dozen Indo-Pacific Partners Launch the Indo-Pacific Economic Framework for Prosperity. The White House. May 23, 2022. https://www.whitehouse.gov/briefing-room/statements-releases/2022/05/23/fact-sheet-in-asia-president-biden-and-a-dozen-indo-pacific-partners-launch-the-indo-pacific-economic-framework-for-prosperity/.

Farrell, Gwen. "What Is Going On? 57 People From Bill And Hillary Clinton's Inner Circle Have Died In Strange Circumstances In The Last 30 Years." Evie. May 20, 2022. https://www.eviemagazine.com/post/57-people-from-bill-and-hillary-clintons-inner-circle-died-strange-circumstances.

Fiorina, Morris P. "The Majority-Minority Myth." *Hoover Digest*. Spring 2021 (Issue 2). https://go.gale.com/ps/i.do?p=AONE&u=anon~58685278&id=GALE|A661724989&v=2.1&it=r&sid=googleScholar&asid=c8f44629.%20Accessed%2011%20July%202022.

Fitzhenry, Jack. "Parents' Guide to Children's Rights Aims to Save America's Public Schools From CRT." The Heritage Foundation. June 14, 2022. https://www.heritage.org/education/commentary/parents-guide-childrens-rights-aims-save-americas-public-schools-crt.

Fleischman, Luis. "Biden's Policy Towards War in Ukraine is Appropriate." PalmBeachDemocracy.org. June 29, 2022. https://intdemocratic.org/bidens-policy-towards-war-in-ukraine-is-appropriate/.

Foxx, Virginia. "Student Loan Forgiveness Scam is Already Biden Policy." Fox News. June 24, 2022. https://www.foxnews.com/opinion/student-loan-forgiveness-scam-biden-policy.

Galston, William A. "Democrats Move Left, But the Center Holds." *The Wall Street Journal*. August 14, 2020 https://accf.org/2020/08/14/democrats-move-left-but-the-center-holds/.

Geraghty, Jim. "Biden's Plan to Punish the Responsible." *National Review*. April 27, 2022. https://www.nationalreview.com/the-morning-jolt/bidens-plan-to-punish-the-responsible/

Giaritelli, Anna. "Illegal Immigration Soars Under Biden to Third-Highest in 97 Years." *Washington Examiner*. October 22, 2021. https://news.yahoo.com/illegal-immigration-soars-under-biden-200400500.html.

Graham, David A. "How Far Have the Democrats Moved to the Left?" *The Atlantic*. Nov. 5, 2018. https://medium.com/the-atlantic/how-far-have-the-democrats-moved-to-the-left-f393b8f98618.

Greenblatt, Alan. "You Don't Need to Be a Fortune Teller: Signs Point to GOP Sweep This Year" *Governing* May 27, 2022 https://www.governing.com/now/you-dont-need-to-be-a-fortune-teller-signs-point-to-gop-sweep-this-year.

Hammer, Josh. "Democrats Would Be Shortsighted to Nuke the Senate Filibuster." *Newsweek.* March 19, 2021. https://www.newsweek.com/democrats-would-shortsighted-nuke-senate-filibuster-opinion-1577248.

Hammer, Josh. "Democrats' Recent Rejection of COVID Insanity Will Not Save Them This Fall." *Epoch Times.* February 11, 2022. https://www.theepochtimes.com/democrats-recent-rejection-of-covid-insanity-will-not-save-them-this-fall_4272213.html?utm_source=ai&utm_medium=search.

Hankinson, Simon. "6 Pillars" Border Security Plan Is Delusional." The Heritage Foundation. May 24th, 2022. https://www.heritage.org/immigration/commentary/mayorkas-6-pillars-border-security-plan-delusional.

Hanson, Victor Davis. "A Cabinency of Dunces." *Epoch Times.* May 30, 2022. https://www.theepochtimes.com/a-cabinency-of-dunces_4492973.html.

Haq, Masooma and Paul Greaney. "Democrats' Opposition to Fossil Fuels is Political: Grover Norquist." *Epoch Times.* April 25, 2022. https://www.theepochtimes.com/democrats-opposition-to-fossil-fuels-is-political-grover-norquist_4426198.html?utm_source=ai&utm_medium=search.

Haq, Masooma. "Key Things You Need to Know About HR 1, the For the People Act of 2021." *Epoch Times.* March 10, 2021. https://www.theepochtimes.com/key-things-you-need-to-know-about-hr-1-the-for-the-people-act-of-2021_3722659.html?utm_source=ai&utm_medium=search.

Harsanyi, David. "The 'Putin's Price Hike' Canard." *National Review.* April 12, 2022. https://www.nationalreview.com/2022/04/the-putins-price-hike-canard/.

Haskins, Justin. "Joe Manchin Just Killed Build Back Better—and Saved the US Economy in the Process." *The Hill.* Dec. 22, 2021. https://thehill.com/opinion/finance/586867-joe-manchin-just-killed-build-back-better-and-saved-the-us-economy-in-the/.

Head, Timothy. "Biden is Handing the Midterms to the GOP." *The Hill.* March 25, 2022. https://thehill.com/opinion/campaign/599501-biden-is-handing-the-midterms-to-the-gop/.

Hickey, Christopher, Curt Merrill, Richard J. Chang, Kate Sullivan, Janie Boschma and Sean O'Key. "Here Are the Executive Actions Biden Signed in His First 100 Days." CNN. April 30, 2021 https://www.cnn.com/interactive/2021/politics/biden-executive-orders/.

Hochman, Nate. "A Word of Caution on the Hispanic 'Realignment'" *National Review.* March 12, 2022. https://www.nationalreview.com/corner/a-word-of-caution-on-the-hispanic-realignment/.

Homan, Tom. "Effective Immigration Enforcement Can't Rely on Honor System." The Heritage Foundation. March 8, 2022. https://www.heritage.org/immigration/commentary/effective-immigration-enforcement-cant-rely-honor-system.

Huennekens, Preston. "Mayorkas' New Policies Effectively Abolish ICE." ImmigratoinReform.com. October 13, 2021. https://www.immigrationreform.com/2021/10/13/mayorkas-moves-abolish-ice-immigrationreform-com/.

Introducing Real Clear Investigations' Jan. 6-BLM Riots Dataset. Editors. Real Clear Investigations. September 09, 2021. https://www.realclearinvestigations.com/articles/2021/09/09/study_in_contrasts_rcis_new_dataset_on_jan_6_and_the_black_lives_matter_riots_791200.html.

Jennifer D. P. Moroney and Alan Tidwell "Making AUKUS Work" Rand Corporation March 22, 2022 https://www.rand.org/blog/2022/03/making-aukus-work.html.

Johnson, Ian. "Biden's Grand China Strategy: Eloquent But Inadequate." Council on Foreign Relations (CFR). May 27, 2022. https://www.cfr.org/in-brief/biden-china-blinken-speech-policy-grand-strategy.

Kan, Janita. "House Committee Approves Another Attempt to Grant DC Statehood in Party-Line Vote." *Epoch Times.* April 15, 2021. https://www.theepochtimes.com/house-committee-approves-another-attempt-to-grant-dc-statehood-in-party-line-vote_3775363.html?utm_source=ai&utm_medium=search.

Klein, Philip. "Democrats Can't Hide Their Israel Problem." *National Review.* September 23, 2021. https://www.nationalreview.com/2021/09/democrats-cant-hide-their-israel-problem/.

Kochis, Daniel. "Biden's Afghanistan debacle will cast a long shadow over transatlantic security." *The Hill.* Sept. 9, 2021. https://thehill.com/opinion/national-security/571404-bidens-afghanistan-debacle-will-cast-a-long-shadow-over/.

Kupelian, David. "The Party of Insurrection." WND. January 30, 2022. https://www.wnd.com/2022/01/party-insurrection/.

Li, Rita. "Democrat-Leaning Voters Trend Toward GOP: Poll." *Epoch Times.* May 2, 2022. https://www.theepochtimes.com/democrat-leaning-voters-trend-toward-gop-poll_4440173.html.

Lowry, Rich. "Big Lie About Georgia Voting Has Been Shredded." *National Review.* May 23, 2022. https://www.nationalreview.com/2022/05/the-big-lie-about-georgia-voting-has-been-shredded/.

Lowry, Rich. "BLM Is a Moral, Political, and Policy Disaster." *National Review.* February 22, 2022. https://www.nationalreview.com/2022/02/blm-is-a-moral-political-and-policy-disaster/.

Lowry, Rich. "Elizabeth Warren: The Bonfire of the Democrats." Politico. February 06, 2019. https://www.politico.com/magazine/story/2019/02/06/virginia-governor-attorney-general-224820/.

Lowry, Rich. "The Kamala Harris Problem." *National Review.* June 14, 2022. https://www.nationalreview.com/2022/06/the-kamala-harris-problem/?utm_source=Sailthru&utm_medium=email&utm_campaign=NR%20Daily%20Monday%20through%20Friday%202022-06-14&utm_term=NRDaily-Smart.

MacKinnon, Douglas. "When Trump is Right, He's Right—But Many Refuse to Admit It." *The Hill.* June 4, 2022. https://thehill.com/opinion/white-house/3510113-when-trump-is-right-hes-right-but-many-refuse-to-admit-it/

Manchester, Julia. "58 Percent Say Jan. 6 House Committee is Biased: Poll." *The Hill.* August 2, 2021. https://thehill.com/homenews/house/565981-58-percent-say-jan-6-commission-is-biased-poll/.

Mangual, Rafael A. "Soft on Crime." *City Journal.* Winter 2021. https://www.city-journal.org/biden-soft-on-crime.

McCarthy, Andrew C. "The January 6 Committee's Futile Prime-Time Political Ad." *National Review.* June 9, 2022. https://www.nationalreview.com/2022/06/the-january-6-committees-futile-prime-time-political-ad/?utm_source=Sailthru&utm_medium=email&utm_campaign=NR%20Daily%20Monday%20through%20Friday%202022-06-09&utm_term=NRDaily-Smart.

McDaniel, Ronna. "Minorities Are Finding a New Political Home With the Republican Party." *The Hill.* April 29, 2022. https://thehill.com/opinion/campaign/3471496-minorities-are-finding-a-new-political-home-with-the-republican-party/.

McDonald, Kerry. "Teachers Unions Are More Powerful Than You Realize—but That May Be Changing." Cato Institute. August 31, 2020. https://www.cato.org/commentary/teachers-unions-are-more-powerful-you-realize-may-be-changing.

McLaughlin, Dan. "More Pills the Democrats Will Find Hard to Swallow." *National Review.* November 24, 2021. https://www.nationalreview.com/corner/more-pills-the-democrats-will-find-hard-to-swallow/.

Mehlman, Ira. "Alejandro Mayorkas, Architect of DACA, Tapped to be DHS Secretary." FAIR. December 2020. https://www.fairus.org/issue/publications-resources/alejandro-mayorkas-architect-daca-tapped-be-dhs-secretary.

Miranda Devine "Petulant Nancy Pelosi is Everything Wrong With Democratic Party: Devine" *New York Post* February 9, 2020 https://nypost.com/2020/02/09/petulant-nancy-pelosi-is-everything-wrong-with-democratic-party-devine/.

Nerozzi, Timothy H.J. "Texas Seized Enough Fentanyl to Kill 200 Million People This Year Alone, Officials Say." Fox News. December 9, 2021. https://www.foxnews.com/us/texas-seized-enough-fentanyl-kill-200-million-people-year.

Newport, Frank. "Identity Politics in Context." Gallup. December 3, 2021. https://news.gallup.com/opinion/polling-matters/357812/identity-politics-context.aspx.

Owens, Candace (Author)and Larry Elder (Introduction). *Blackout: How Black America Can Make Its Second Escape from the Democrat Plantation.* Threshold Editions. 2020 https://www.amazon.com/Blackout-America-Second-Democrat-Plantation/dp/1982133279.

Patrick, Jim. "Thousands of Cops Were Injured, Over $2 billion in Damage During Floyd Riots. Where are the "Congressional Hearings"?" Law Enforcement Today. July 28, 2021. https://www.lawenforcementtoday.com/thousands-of-cops-were-injured-over-2-billion-in-damage-during-floyd-riots-where-are-the-congressional-hearings/.

Phelps, J.M. "Hispanic Voters Are Losing Faith in the Democratic Party: Poll," *Epoch Times,* May 9, 2022, https://www.theepochtimes.com/hispanic-voters-are-losing-faith-in-the-democratic-party_4453450.html?utm_source=ai&utm_medium=search.

Phillips, James. "Why Joe Biden's Nuclear Talks With Iran Look Like a Disaster." The Heritage Foundation. Feb. 15, 2022. https://www.heritage.org/middle-east/commentary/why-joe-bidens-nuclear-talks-iran-look-disaster.

Raleigh, Helen. "Why Asian Americans Are Leaving the Democratic Party." *Newsweek.* January 25, 2022. https://www.newsweek.com/why-asian-americans-are-leaving-democratic-party-opinion-1672308.

Rayburn, Joel D. "The Biden Administration's Syria Policy: A Forecast For War." Hoover Institution. December 7, 2021. https://www.hoover.org/research/biden-administrations-syria-policy-forecast-war.

Ries, Lora and Mark Morgan. "Biden Encourages Massive Illegal Immigration and Tries to Hide It With Secret Flights." *New York Post.* January 27, 2022. https://nypost.com/2022/01/27/biden-is-hiding-illegal-immigration-with-secret-flights/?msclkid=152a082ebaa511ec81593c82aaef9915.

Rove, Karl. "AOC Is the Gift That Keeps Giving." *Wall Street Journal*. July 17, 2019. https://www.wsj.com/articles/aoc-is-the-gift-that-keeps-giving-11563404196.

Sacks, David, "What Biden's Big Shift on Taiwan Means," Council on Foreign Relations (CFR), May 24, 2022, https://www.cfr.org/blog/what-bidens-big-shift-taiwan-means.

Samuels, Brett and Amie Parnes. "Harris's Office Undergoes Difficult Reset." *The Hill*. Dec. 30, 2021. https://thehill.com/homenews/administration/584120-harriss-office-undergoes-difficult-reset/.

Sandberg, Erica. "Change in the Air in San Francisco." *City Journal*. February 17, 2022. https://www.city-journal.org/recall-election-brings-change-to-san-francisco-school-board.

Schoof, John. "Parents Are Going on Offensive to Fight Indoctrination in Education." The Heritage Foundation. Apr. 27, 2022. https://www.heritage.org/education/commentary/parents-are-going-offensive-fight-indoctrination-education.

Shaw, Adam. "House Republicans Call on Senate Leaders to Reject Biden DHS Picks, Warn They Won't End Border Crisis." Fox News. June 3, 2021. https://www.foxnews.com/politics/house-republicans-senate-leaders-biden-dhs-picks-border-crisis.

Sheffield, Carrie. "How Biden's Tunnel Vision on Oil and Gas Encouraged Putin's Invasion of Ukraine." NBC News. March 30, 2022. https://www.nbcnews.com/think/opinion/biden-isnt-blameless-russias-invasion-ukraine-rcna22111.

Singh, Arjun. "Biden's Job Approval Drops to Record-Low." *National Review*. May 20, 2022. https://www.nationalreview.com/news/bidens-job-approval-drops-to-record-low/.

Smith, Kyle. "Biden Made His Own Mess" *National Review* June 13, 2022 https://www.nationalreview.com/2022/06/biden-made-his-own-mess/.

Smith, Kyle. "Cackling Kamala" *National Review* October 28, 2021 https://www.nationalreview.com/magazine/2021/11/15/cackling-kamala/.

Smith, Kyle. "Maybe Biden Is Right on Ukraine?" *National Review* March 24, 2022 https://www.nationalreview.com/corner/maybe-biden-is-right-on-ukraine/.

Stieber, Zachary. "Democrats Introduce Bill to Expand Supreme Court, but Reception Is Tepid." *Epoch Times*. April 16, 2021. https://www.theepochtimes.com/democrats-introduce-bill-to-expand-supreme-court-but-reception-is-tepid_3777945.html?utm_source=ai&utm_medium=search

Stoddard, A.B. "Biden's Got Problems. Is Chuck Schumer One of Them?" Real Clear Politics. March 22, 2021. https://www.realclearpolitics.com/articles/2021/03/22/bidens_got_problems_is_chuck_schumer_one_of_them_.html#!.

Taylor, William B. "The United States Speaks Clearly on Russia's Ukraine War." United States Institute of Peace. June 3, 2022. https://www.usip.org/publications/2022/06/united-states-speaks-clearly-russias-ukraine-war.

Teixeira, Ruy. "How to Fix the Democratic Brand." The Liberal Patriot. Apr. 21, 2022. https://theliberalpatriot.substack.com/p/how-to-fix-the-democratic-brand.

Teixeira, Ruy. "The Democrats' Hispanic Voter Problem." The Liberal Patriot. Dec. 9, 2021. https://theliberalpatriot.substack.com/p/the-democrats-hispanic-voter-problem-dfc.

Thayer, Parker. "Living Room Pundit's Guide to Soros District Attorneys." Capital Research Center. January 18, 2022. https://capitalresearch.org/article/living-room-pundits-guide-to-soros-district-attorneys/.

The Economist. "Bernie Sanders' Permanent Revolution." Aug. 20, 2019. https://medium.com/@the_economist/bernie-sanderss-permanent-revolution-4f4399631ea0.

The Spirit of 1776. Editors. *National Review.* January 22, 2021. https://www.nationalreview.com/2021/01/the-spirit-of-1776/.

Thiessen, Marc A. "Biden's Budget Is a Lie." *The Washington Post.* June 1, 2021. https://www.aei.org/op-eds/bidens-budget-is-a-lie/.

Thomas, Cal. *Epoch Times.* "Democrats Need a Day of Atonement." June 22, 2021. https://www.theepochtimes.com/democrats-need-a-day-of-atonement_3867951.html?utm_source=ai&utm_medium=search.

Vazquez, Joseph. "STUDY: NewsGuard Ratings System Heavily Skews in Favor of Left-Wing Outlets." Free Speech America. December 13, 2021. https://www.newsbusters.org/blogs/free-speech/joseph-vazquez/2021/12/13/study-newsguard-ratings-system-heavily-skews-favor-left.

Ward, Myah and Jonathan Lemire. "Judge Blocks Biden Administration From Lifting Title 42 Border Policy." Politico. May 20, 2022. https://www.politico.com/news/2022/05/20/judge-blocks-biden-administration-from-lifting-title-42-border-policy-00034195.

Washburn, Michael. "Democratic Party Is Alienating Its Base, Heading for Trouble in November Midterms, Analysts Say." *Epoch Times.* April 28, 2022. https://www.theepochtimes.com/democratic-party-is-alienating-its-base-heading-for-trouble-in-november-midterms-analysts-say_4421206.html?utm_source=ai&utm_medium=search.

Weaver, Corinne. "SPECIAL REPORT: Big Tech Stole 2020 Election by Weaponizing Platforms." Free Speech America. December 17th, 2020. https://www.newsbusters.org/blogs/free-speech/corinne-weaver/2020/12/17/special-report-big-tech-stole-2020-election-weaponizing.

Wehner, Peter. "The Democratic Party Has Become Radicalized And Their Socialist, Pro-Death And Anti-Israel Agenda Should Be Truly Terrifying To All Americans." Before It's News. April 4, 2019. https://beforeitsnews.com/global-unrest/2019/04/the-democratic-party-has-become-radicalized-and-their-socialist-pro-death-and-anti-israel-agenda-should-be-truly-terrifying-to-all-americans-2515891.html.

Wexler, Natalie. "Democrats Can't Keep Dismissing Complaints About 'Critical Race Theory'." *Forbes.* Nov. 4, 2021. https://www.forbes.com/sites/nataliewexler/2021/11/04/democrats-cant-keep-dismissing-complaints-about-critical-race-theory/?sh=7a0574a24e9f.

Williams, Armstrong. "As Biden's America Becomes Less Safe, the Violence and Crime Could Cost Democrats." *The Hill.* July 23, 2021. https://thehill.com/opinion/criminal-justice/564448-as-bidens-america-becomes-less-safe-the-violence-and-crime-could/.

Williams, Juan. "Juan Williams: Democratic infighting could spell doom." *The Hill.* June 6, 2022. https://thehill.com/opinion/3512685-juan-williams-democratic-infighting-could-spell-doom/.

Zenn, Jacob. "What's Next for Antifa?" *City Journal.* November 16, 2020. https://www.city-journal.org/whats-next-for-antifa.

Index

J

K

L

Author Bio

Author: Corey Lee Wilson.

Corey Lee Wilson was raised an atheist by his liberal *Playboy* Bunny mother, has three Anglo-Hispanic siblings, a bi-racial daughter, a brother who died of AIDS, baptized a Protestant by his conservative grandparents, attended temple with his Jewish foster parents, baptized again as a Catholic for his first Filipina wife, attends Buddhist ceremonies with his second Thai wife, became an agnostic on his own free will for most of his life, and is a lifetime independent voter.

Corey felt the sting of intellectual humility by repeating the 4th grade and attended eighteen different schools before putting himself through college (without parents) at Mt. San Antonio College and Cal Poly Pomona University (while on triple secret probation). Named Who's Who of American College Students in 1984, he received a BS in Economics and won his fraternity's most prestigious undergraduate honor, the Phi Kappa Tau Fraternity's Shideler Award, both in 1985. In 2020, he became a member of the Heterodox Academy and in 2021 a member of the National Association of Scholars and 1776 Unites.

As a satirist and fraternity man, Corey started Fratire Publishing in 2012 and transformed the fiction "fratire" genre to a respectable and viewpoint diverse non-fiction genre promoting practical knowledge and wisdom to help everyday people navigate safely through the many hazards of life. In 2018, he founded the SAPIENT Being to help promote freedom of speech, viewpoint diversity, intellectual humility and most importantly advance sapience in America's students and campuses.

The SAPIENT Being has three programs: Make Free Speech Again On Campus (MFSAOC) Program, Conservative Campus Advisor (CCA) Program, and the Sapient Conservative Textbooks (SCT) Program—all working together to promote its mission and vision of sapience.

If you're interested in the MFSAOC Program and starting a S.A.P.I.E.N.T. Being club, chapter, or alliance on or off campus, please go to https://www.SapientBeing.org/start-a-chapter, e-mail SapientBeing@att.net, or call (951) 638-5562 for more information.

If you're interested in becoming a conservative campus advisor for right-leaning campus organizations as part of the CCA Program from the S.A.P.I.E.N.T. Being, please e-mail at SapientBeing@att.net, or call (951) 638-5562 for more information.

If you're interested as an educator, administrator, or student in the SCT Program and their 40 MADNESS series of textbooks from the S.A.P.I.E.N.T. Being, please check them out at the Fratire Publishing website at https://www.FratirePublishing.com/madnessbooks, for more information.

Hopefully, this book was enlightening and your journey through it—along with mine—made you aware of the issues and challenges ahead of us. If it has, your quest and mine towards becoming a sapient being has begun. If it hasn't, there's no better time to start than now. Come join us in creating a society advancing personal intelligence and enlightenment now together (S.A.P.I.E.N.T.) and become a sapient being.

www.ingramcontent.com/pod-product-compliance
Lightning Source LLC
Chambersburg PA
CBHW040833040426
42336CB00034B/3459